GRAPHIC GUIDE TO
Frame Construction

GRAPHIC GUIDE TO
Frame Construction

ROB THALLON

THIRD EDITION, REVISED AND UPDATED

The Taunton Press

The Taunton Press, Inc., 63 South Main Street, PO Box 5506, Newtown, CT 06470-5506
e-mail: tp@taunton.com

Editor: Peter Chapman
Copy editor: Karen Fraley
Indexer: James Curtis
Jacket/Cover design: Susan Fazekas
Interior design and layout: Susan Fazekas
Illustrators: Illustrations 6B (right), 23C, 25C, 33D, 44A–D, 45B, 61 (top left), 62B-D, 74, 75A & B, 76A, C & D, 82, 83, 84, 85A & B, 86A–D, 87A–D, 94B (top and center), 106B, 119, 120 (top right), 122–125, 152A & D, 153C, 157B (right), 160, 161A–D, 198, 199A–D, 204A & B, 205C, 215B & C rendered by Anthony Baron. Illustrations 6B (bottom, second and fourth from left), 23C (bottom left), 27A & B (right), 28A, 30 (left column, second, third, and fourth), 31, 37 (left center), 44C, 53B & C, 54B & C, 55B, 69A, 70A, 71B & D, 72C, 81A & B, 89B (bottom), 96 (bottom right), 100C, 110A & B, 118, 128A, 142B–D, 153B & C, 154A–C, 155A, 159C & D, 161B, 162, 198A, 201A rendered by Vinicent Babak. All other illustrations rendered by Scott Wolf.

Library of Congress Cataloging-in-Publication Data
Thallon, Rob.
  Graphic guide to frame construction / Rob Thallon. -- 3rd ed., rev. and updated.
    p. cm.
  Includes index.
  ISBN 978-1-60085-023-3
  1. Wooden-frame buildings--Design and construction. 2. Wooden-frame buildings--Drawings. 3. Framing (Building) 4. House framing.
I. Title.
  TH1101.T48 2009
  694'.2--dc22
                      2008026178

Printed in the United States of America
10 9 8 7 6 5 4 3 2

Homebuilding is inherently dangerous. Using hand or power tools improperly or ignoring safety practices can lead to permanent injury or even death. Don't try to perform operations you learn about here (or elsewhere) unless you're certain they are safe for you. If something about an operation doesn't feel right, don't do it. Look for another way. We want you to enjoy building, so please keep safety foremost in your mind whenever you're working.

To Dee

acknowledgments

This book has been enriched immeasurably by the contributions of professional architects, contractors, and engineers throughout the country. The first edition was reviewed in its entirety by the following architects and builders: Edward Allen, South Natick, MA; Judith Capen, Washington, DC; Steve Kearns, Ketchum, ID; Scott McBride, Sperryville, VA; Jud Peake, Oakland, CA; Dan Rockhill, LeCompton, KS; Joel Schwartz, Princeton, NJ; Stephen Suddarth, Miami Beach, FL; Blaine Young, Santa Fe, NM.

In addition, portions of the second edition were reviewed by: Edward Allen, South Natick, MA; John Carmody, Minneapolis, MN; Walter Grondzik, Tallahassee, FL; Christine Theodoropolous, Eugene, OR.

This third edition was reviewed in part by the following: Edward Allen, FAIA, South Natick, MA; Chris Anderson, Contractor, Eugene, OR; Chris Brandt, P.E., Weyerhauser/iLevel; Donald Corner, Professor, University of Oregon; Tom McClain, P.E., Simpson Strong-Tie; James McDonald, Contractor, Eugene, OR; Hal Pfeifer, P.E., Eugene, OR; Joe Johnson, Architect, Portland, OR.

The participation of all these reviewers has made the book significantly more comprehensive and the process of writing it more enjoyable.

It has been almost 20 years since the first edition was originally conceived. My gratitude to those who helped to formulate and develop that first effort persists because the importance of their contribution has only increased with the passing of time:

Paul Bertorelli, for helping to define the scope of the book and the method of producing it; Joanne Bouknight, for patient and skillful editing with just the right touch of humor; David Edrington, my architectural partner, for his patience and understanding; Dee Etwiler, my wife, for her research assistance, her loving support, and her patience; Lloyd Kahn, for inspiration and support for this project long before it was realized; Chuck Miller, for listening to my ideas and suggesting the project to the publishers in the first place; Don Peting, for valuable assistance in articulating my thoughts about structural relationships in early chapters; Scott Wolf, for insightful assistance with the format and for putting as much energy into rendering the original drawings as humanly possible.

And for the second edition, I remain grateful to: Steve Culpepper, for his unwavering belief in the importance of the Graphic Guide series and his deft facilitation of the second edition; Jennifer Renjilian Morris, my editor, for gracious management and astute tuning of the writing; David McClean, my assistant, for helpful suggestions about and multiple drafts of most of the new drawings; Anthony Baron, for skillful rendering of the new drawings in the style of the originals.

The production of this third edition has benefited greatly from the existence of the first two editions as well as from the digital revolution. Whereas for previous editions I have thanked long lists of people who contributed in numerous invaluable ways, this time around the work that did not fall to me directly was very graciously and efficiently managed at the publishers. For this I thank Peter Chapman, Senior Editor, and assistant editor, Courtney Jordan. Peter, of course, was also responsible for working with me to define the scope and focus of this edition, a task for which I am very grateful. Lastly, I need to thank my colleagues and especially my family for enduring unpredictable behavior and schedules on my part during the development of this volume.

contents

introduction

Light wood-frame construction originated in this country over 150 years ago and quickly evolved into the predominant construction system for houses and other small-scale buildings. Today, over 90% of all new buildings in North America are made using some version of this method. Remodeling projects follow the same track.

There are many reasons why this system has been the choice of professional and amateur builders alike over the years. A principal reason is its flexibility. Because the modules are small, virtually any shape or style of building can be built easily with the studs, joists, and rafters that are the primary components of wood-frame construction. In addition, the pieces are easily handled, the material is readily available, and the skills and tools required for assembly are easily acquired.

Given the popularity of the system, it was surprising to find that, before the publication of the first edition of this book, there existed no detailed and comprehensive reference focusing on light wood framing. Now, seventeen years and two editions later, over 275,000 copies of *Graphic Guide to Frame Construction* have found their way into the libraries of architects, contractors, owner-builders, and students.

The acceptance of the Graphic Guide as a standard reference has corresponded with great strides in building technology. Wood frame buildings today are built faster, stronger, and with more efficient use of materials. Engineered lumber products, relatively rare just 20 years ago, are now more common than

sawn lumber for many parts of a building. Wooden buildings are now greatly more resistant to the forces of hurricanes and earthquakes. Vinyl windows, which were just being introduced, are now the standard. Advanced framing that both conserves material and allows for upgraded insulation is rapidly gaining acceptance. These and many other advances were incorporated into the second edition, but the building culture is not static. Best practices are evolving rapidly because of improved communication and building science, and innovative materials are proliferating to meet increased demand.

This third edition expands on those issues covered in the first two editions with the addition of the most recently developed practices and materials. In particular, this edition updates the details for engineered lumber products and takes a closer look at the important issue of moisture in wood frame building assemblies. These two subjects have dominated the research in recent years and significantly impact each chapter of the book. The topic of environmental responsibility, which has gained serious traction in recent years, has been covered extensively in previous editions but receives further discussion here.

With all the attention given to advanced practices and materials, it is also important not to forget traditional principles and materials. These form the backbone of the system of wood frame construction and are the starting point for the important and considerable work of remodeling and renovation.

THE SCOPE OF THE BOOK

To provide a detailed reference, the scope of the book had to be limited. I decided to focus on the parts of a building that contribute most significantly to its longevity. Virtually all the drawings, therefore, describe details relating to the structural shell or to the outer protective layers of the building. Plumbing, electrical, and mechanical systems are described only as they affect the foundation and framing of the building. Interior finishes and details are not covered because they are the subject of a companion volume, *Graphic Guide to Interior Details* (The Taunton Press, 1996). The process of construction, covered adequately in many references, has here been stripped away so as to expose the details themselves as much as possible. Design, although integral with the concerns of this book, is dealt with only at the level of the detail.

The details shown here employ simple, standard materials. With this type of information, it should be possible to build a wood frame building in any shape, at any size, and in any style. Many local variations are included.

A FOCUS ON DURABILITY

Although the details in this book have been selected partly on the basis of their widespread use, the primary focus is on durability. I believe that wood-frame buildings can and should be built to last for 200 years or more. To accomplish this, a building must be built on a solid foundation; it must be designed and built to resist moisture; it must be protected from termites, ants, and other insect pests; it must be structurally stable; and it must be reasonably protected from the ravages of fire. All these criteria may be met with standard construction details if care is taken in both the design and the building process.

There are some accepted construction practices, however, that I do not think meet the test of durability. For example, the practice in some regions of building foundations without rebar is not prudent. The small investment of placing rebar in the foundation to minimize the possibility of differential settlement is one that should be made whether or not it is required by code. The stability of a foundation affects not only the level of the floors but also the integrity of the structure above and the ability of the building to resist moisture. Another common practice that I discourage is the recent overreliance on caulks and sealants for waterproofing. This practice seems counterproductive in the long run because the most sophisticated and scientifically tested sealants are warranted for only 20 to 25 years. Should we be investing time, money, and materials in buildings that could be seriously damaged if someone forgets to recaulk? It is far better, I believe, to design buildings with adequate overhangs or with flashing and drip edges that direct water away from the structural core by means of the natural forces of gravity and surface tension.

Durability, however, does not depend entirely upon material quality and construction detailing. Durability also depends heavily upon the overall design of the building and whether its usefulness over time is sufficient to resist the wrecking ball. The more intangible design factors such as the quality of the space and the flexibility of the plan are extremely important but are not a part of this book.

ON CODES

Every effort has been made to ensure that the details included in this book conform to building codes. Codes vary, however, so local codes and building departments should always be consulted to verify compliance.

HOW THE BOOK WORKS

The book's five chapters follow the approximate order of construction, starting with the foundation and working up to the roof (however, the last chapter on stairs is intentionally out of sequence). Each chapter begins with an introduction that describes general principles. The chapters are divided into subsections, also roughly ordered according to the sequence of construction. Subsections, usually with another more specific introduction and an isometric reference drawing, lead to individual drawings or notes.

Subsections are called out at the top of each page for easy reference. Each drawing has a reference letter, a title, and often a subtitle. Sometimes a reference and title is assigned to an entire topic. With this system, all the drawings (and topics) may be cross-referenced. The callout "see 42A", for example, refers to drawing A on page 42.

As many details as possible are drawn in the simple section format found on architectural working drawings. Most are drawn at the scale of 1 in. equals 1 ft. or 1½ in. equals 1 ft., although the scale is not noted on the drawings. This format should allow the details to be transferred to architectural drawings with minor adjustments. (Details will usually have to be adjusted to allow for different size or thickness of material, for roof pitch, or for positional relationships.) Those details that are not easily depicted in a simple section drawing are usually drawn isometrically in order to convey the third dimension.

Any notes included in a detail are intended to describe its most important features. By describing the relationship of one element to another, the notes sometimes go a little further than merely naming an element. Materials symbols are described on page 226. Abbreviations are spelled out on page 227.

A FINAL NOTE

My intention in writing and now in twice revising this book has been to assist designers and builders who are attempting to make beautiful buildings that endure. With the drawings, I have tried to describe the relationship among the parts of every common connection. Alternative approaches to popular details have been included as well. I have relied primarily on my own experiences but have also drawn significantly on the accounts of others. In order to build upon this endeavor, I encourage you, the reader, to let me know of your own observations and critical comments. Please send them to me care of The Taunton Press, P.O. Box 5506, Newtown, CT 06470-5506 or via email to thallonarch@continet.com.

chapter 1

FOUNDATIONS

A foundation system has two functions. First, it supports the building structurally by keeping it level, minimizing settling, preventing uplift from the forces of frost or expansive soils and resisting horizontal forces such as winds and earthquakes. Second, a foundation system keeps the wooden parts of the building above the ground and away from the organisms and moisture in the soil that both eat wood and cause it to decay.

The foundation is the part of a building that is most likely to determine its longevity. If the foundation does not support the building adequately, cracks and openings will occur over time, even in the most finely crafted structure. No amount of repair on the structure above the foundation will compensate for an inadequate foundation; once a foundation starts to move significantly, it will continue to move. We now have developed the knowledge to design and construct durable foundations, so there is no reason to invest in a modern building that is not fully supported on a foundation that will endure for the life of the structure.

In the United States, there are three common foundation types. Each performs in different ways, but all rely on a perimeter foundation, i.e., a continuous support around the outside edge of the building.

SLAB-ON-GRADE FOUNDATIONS

Slab-on-grade systems are used mostly in warm climates, where living is close to the ground and the frost line is close to the surface. The footing is usually shallow, and the ground floor is a concrete slab. Many slab-on-grade systems allow the concrete footing, foundation, and subfloor to be poured at the same time.

CRAWL SPACES

Crawl spaces are found in all climates but predominate in temperate regions. In this system, the insulated wooden ground floor is supported above grade on a foundation wall made of concrete or concrete block. The resulting crawl space introduces an accessible zone for ductwork, plumbing, and other utilities, and allows for simple remodeling.

BASEMENTS

Basements are the dominant foundation system in the coldest parts of the country, where frost lines mandate deep footings in any case. Like crawl spaces, basements are accessible, and in addition they provide a large habitable space. Basement foundation systems are usually constructed of concrete or concrete-block foundation walls. Drainage and waterproofing are particularly critical with basement systems.

Slab-on-Grade Foundation

Crawl Spaces

Basements

CHOOSING A FOUNDATION

Each foundation system has many variations, and it is important to select the one best suited to the climate, the soil type, the site, and the building program. With all foundations, you should investigate the local soil type. Soil types, along with their bearing capacities, are often described in local soil profiles based on information from the U.S. Geological Survey (USGS). If there is any question about matching a foundation system to the soil or to the topography of the site, consult a soil or structural engineer before construction begins. This small investment may save thousands of dollars in future repair bills.

DESIGN CHECKLIST

Because the foundation is so important to the longevity of the building and because it is so difficult to repair, it is wise to be conservative in its design and construction. Make the foundation a little stronger than you think you need to. As a minimum, even if not required by code, it is recommended that you follow this rule-of-thumb checklist:

1. Place the bottom of the footing below the frost line on solid, undisturbed soil that is free of organic material. (Local codes will prescribe frost-line depth.)

2. Use continuous horizontal rebar in the footing and at the top of foundation walls (joint reinforcing may be allowable in concrete-block walls). Tie the footing and wall together with vertical rebar.

3. Tie wood members to the foundation with bolts or straps embedded in the foundation. Anchoring requirements in hurricane and severe earthquake zones are shown in the following chapters, but specific requirements should be verified with local codes.

4. Provide adequate drainage around the foundation. Slope backfill away from the building and keep soil 6 in. below all wood.

Many codes and many site conditions require measures beyond these minimum specifications. In addition, there are several other considerations important

to a permanent foundation system, and these are discussed in this chapter. They include support of loads that do not fall at the perimeter wall, such as footings for point loads within the structure and at porches and decks; insulation and moisture barriers; waterproofing and drainage; protection against termites, other insects and wood-decaying organisms; and precautions against radon gas.

5. Get the details right. Use pressure-treated or other decay-resistant wood in contact with concrete. Straps, hangers, and fasteners in contact with pressure-treated lumber should be hot-dip galvanized to protect against degradation from the preservative chemicals. Use a moisture barrier between all concrete and untreated wood.

OTHER FOUNDATION SYSTEMS

The permanent wood foundation (PWF), developed in the 1970s, now accounts for about 5% of foundations in the United States and 20% in Canada. Made of pressure-treated framing, the crawl-space or basement walls sit on a bed of compacted gravel rather than a concrete footing. The same framing crew that constructs the structure above can build the foundation walls; and when insulation, wiring, and other utilities are required, they can be located in wall cavities between studs as they are in the rest of the building.

Insulating concrete formwork (ICF) may be used in place of wooden formwork for the walls of a basement or heated crawl space. The insulation stays in place after the concrete walls have been poured and provides thermal separation for the space within. ICF walls must be protected on the exterior, and wiring and other utilities must be either integrated or carved into the interior insulation surface.

ABOUT THE DRAWINGS

The sizes of building elements indicated in the drawings in this section are for the purposes of illustrating principles and reminding the designer and the builder to consider their use carefully. These drawings should therefore be used only for reference.

STEPPED
FOOTING
SEE 4D

PIER & GRADE-BEAM
SYSTEM
SEE 13

FIREPLACE FOOTING
SEE 5A

COLUMN FOOTING
SEE 6A

FORMED FOOTING
WITH KEYWAY SEE 4C

SLAB
FOOTING
SEE 22-24

FORMED
FOOTING
SEE 4B

TRENCH
FOOTING
SEE 4A

Footings are the part of a foundation that transfers the building's loads—its weight in materials, contents, occupants, and snow, and possibly wind and earthquake loads—directly to the ground. Consequently, the size and type of footing should be matched carefully to the ground upon which it bears.

Soil type—Concrete footings should be placed on firm, undisturbed soil that is free from organic material. Soil types are tested and rated as to their ability to support loads (bearing capacity).

Compaction of soil may be required before footings are placed. Consult a soil engineer if the stability of the soil at a building site is unknown.

Reinforcing—Most codes require steel reinforcing rods (called rebar) in footings. Rebar is a sound investment even if it is not required, because it gives tensile strength to the footing, thereby minimizing cracking and differential settling. Rebar is also the most common way to connect the footing to the foundation wall. For rebar rules of thumb, see 5B.

Size—Footing size depends mainly on soil type and the building's weight. The chart below shows footing sizes for soils with bearing capacities of 2,000 pounds per square foot (psf).

NO. OF STORIES	H	W
1	6 in.	12 in.
2	7 in.	15 in.
3	8 in.	18 in.

A rule of thumb for estimating the size of standard footings is that a footing should be 8 in. wider than the foundation wall and twice as wide as high.

Frost line—The base of the footing must be below the frost line to prevent the building from heaving as the ground swells during freezing. Frost lines range from 0 ft. to 6 ft. in the continental United States. Check local building departments for frost-line requirements.

SOIL TYPE	BEARING CAPACITY (PSF)
Soft clay or silt	do not build
Medium clay or silt	1,500–2,200
Stiff clay or silt	2,200–2,500
Loose sand	1,800–2,000
Dense sand	2,000–3,000
Gravel	2,500–3,000
Bedrock	4,000 and up

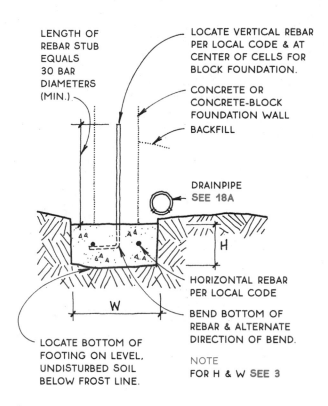

LENGTH OF REBAR STUB EQUALS 30 BAR DIAMETERS (MIN.)

LOCATE VERTICAL REBAR PER LOCAL CODE & AT CENTER OF CELLS FOR BLOCK FOUNDATION.

CONCRETE OR CONCRETE-BLOCK FOUNDATION WALL

BACKFILL

DRAINPIPE SEE 18A

H

HORIZONTAL REBAR PER LOCAL CODE

BEND BOTTOM OF REBAR & ALTERNATE DIRECTION OF BEND.

W

LOCATE BOTTOM OF FOOTING ON LEVEL, UNDISTURBED SOIL BELOW FROST LINE.

NOTE
FOR H & W SEE 3

(A) TRENCH FOOTING

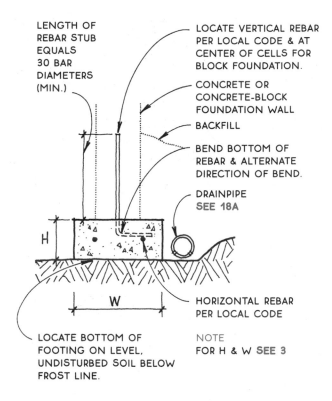

LENGTH OF REBAR STUB EQUALS 30 BAR DIAMETERS (MIN.)

LOCATE VERTICAL REBAR PER LOCAL CODE & AT CENTER OF CELLS FOR BLOCK FOUNDATION.

CONCRETE OR CONCRETE-BLOCK FOUNDATION WALL

BACKFILL

BEND BOTTOM OF REBAR & ALTERNATE DIRECTION OF BEND.

DRAINPIPE SEE 18A

H

W

HORIZONTAL REBAR PER LOCAL CODE

LOCATE BOTTOM OF FOOTING ON LEVEL, UNDISTURBED SOIL BELOW FROST LINE.

NOTE
FOR H & W SEE 3

(B) TYPICAL FORMED FOOTING

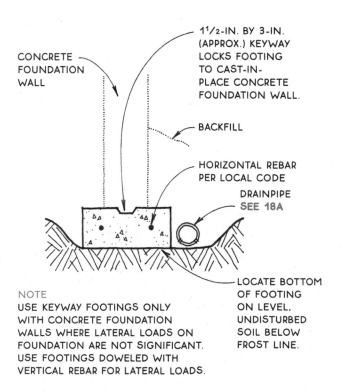

CONCRETE FOUNDATION WALL

1¹/₂-IN. BY 3-IN. (APPROX.) KEYWAY LOCKS FOOTING TO CAST-IN-PLACE CONCRETE FOUNDATION WALL.

BACKFILL

HORIZONTAL REBAR PER LOCAL CODE

DRAINPIPE SEE 18A

LOCATE BOTTOM OF FOOTING ON LEVEL, UNDISTURBED SOIL BELOW FROST LINE.

NOTE
USE KEYWAY FOOTINGS ONLY WITH CONCRETE FOUNDATION WALLS WHERE LATERAL LOADS ON FOUNDATION ARE NOT SIGNIFICANT. USE FOOTINGS DOWELED WITH VERTICAL REBAR FOR LATERAL LOADS.

(C) FOOTING WITH KEYWAY

REBAR CONTINUOUS THROUGH STEP

MULTIPLES OF 8 IN. FOR CONCRETE-BLOCK FOUNDATION WALL (MAX. DEPTH 24 IN.)

NOTE
KEEP CUT IN SOIL AS VERTICAL AS POSSIBLE AT STEP IN FOOTING.

MIN. WIDTH EQUALS DEPTH OF FOOTING.

LOCATE BOTTOM OF FOOTING ON LEVEL, UNDISTURBED SOIL BELOW FROST LINE.

(D) STEPPED FOOTING

EDGE OF
MASONRY
FIREBOX

6-IN. (MIN.)
PROJECTION
BEYOND FIREBOX
OR CHIMNEY
MASONRY

TIE FIREBOX TO
FOOTING AT
CORNERS WITH
REBAR DOWELS.
VERIFY WITH LOCAL
CODES.

12-IN (MIN.) DEPTH
WITHOUT REBAR

LOCATE BOTTOM OF
FOOTING BELOW
FROST LINE.

TIE FIREPLACE
& FOUNDATION
FOOTING WITH
REBAR.

Ⓐ FIREPLACE FOOTING

Code requirements for rebar use may vary, but a few rules of thumb can be helpful guidelines. Verify with local codes first.

Sizes—Rebar is sized by diameter in $\frac{1}{8}$-in. increments: #3 rebar is $\frac{3}{8}$-in. dia., #4 is $\frac{1}{2}$-in. dia., #5 is $\frac{5}{8}$-in. dia., etc. The most common sizes for wood-frame construction foundations are #3, #4, and #5.

Overlapping—Rebar is manufactured in 20-ft. lengths. When rebar must be spliced to make it continuous or joined at corners, the length of the lap should equal 30 bar diameters, as shown below.

30 BAR DIAMETERS

Clearance—The minimum clearance between rebar and the surface of the concrete is 3 in. for footings, 2 in. for formed concrete exposed to backfill or weather, and $\frac{3}{4}$ in. for formed concrete protected from the weather.

Ⓑ REBAR RULES OF THUMB

NOTE
X SHOULD NOT EXCEED H
WITHOUT REBAR IN FOOTING.

Cast-in-Place Round

Cast-in-Place Square

#4 REBAR AT 12 IN.
O.C. TYPICAL; VERIFY
WITH ENGINEER.

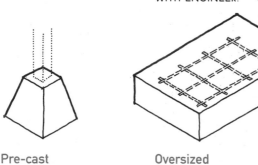

Pre-cast

Oversized

Column footings (also called pier pads) support columns in crawl spaces and under porches and decks. Place all footings on unfrozen, undisturbed soil free of organic material. The bottom of the footing must be located below the frost line unless it is within a crawl space. Columns may need to be anchored to column footings to prevent uplift caused by wind or earthquake forces (see 6B).

Typical sizes are 12 in. to 14 in. for square footings or 16-in. to 18-in. diameter for round footings.

Extreme loads may require oversize footings. The vertical load divided by the soil bearing capacity equals the area of footing, e.g.,

6,000 lb. ÷ 2,000 psf = 3 sq. ft.

To prevent moisture in the footing from damaging the column, use a pressure-treated wood column or place a 30-lb. felt moisture barrier between an untreated wood column and a concrete footing, or use steel connectors where required (see 6B).

Ⓐ COLUMN FOOTINGS

BOLT STRAP
TO WOOD
COLUMN.

BOLT OR
SCREW
BASE TO
WOOD
COLUMN.

NAIL OR
SCREW BASE
TO WOOD
COLUMN.

SCREW OR
BOLT BASE
TO WOOD
COLUMN.

BEARING
GROUT

EXPANSION
BOLTS

Single Strap
GALVANIZED STEEL STRAP IS OFTEN USED IN CRAWL SPACES OR UNDER PORCHES.

NOTE
USE P.T. WOOD COLUMN OR PLACE 30-LB. FELT MOISTURE BARRIER BETWEEN UNTREATED POST & CONCRETE.

Wet Base
THIS GALVANIZED STEEL BASE MUST BE PRECISELY LOCATED IN WET CONCRETE. AVAILABLE WITH STANDOFF TO RAISE THE WOOD COLUMN ABOVE THE CONCRETE.

Adjustable Base
MULTIPLE-PIECE GALVANIZED STEEL ASSEMBLY ALLOWS FOR SOME LATERAL ADJUSTMENT BEFORE NUT IS TIGHTENED. BASE ELEVATES WOOD COLUMN ABOVE CONCRETE FOOTING.

Drilled Base
EXPANSION BOLTS ARE DRILLED INTO FOOTING OR SLAB AFTER CONCRETE IS FINISHED, ALLOWING FOR PRECISE LOCATION OF COLUMN.

NOTE
EXPANSION BOLTS REQUIRE SPECIAL INSPECTION IN MOST JURISDICTIONS

Ⓑ COLUMN BASE CONNECTORS

CONCRETE CRAWL-SPACE
FOUNDATION WALL SEE 11A

CONCRETE-BLOCK CRAWL-SPACE
FOUNDATION WALL
SEE 9 & 10

BASEMENT
WALL
SEE 14 &
15A & B

RETAINING
WALL SEE 14

WINDOWS, DOORS & OTHER
OPENINGS
SEE 10C & D

BEAM SUPPORT SEE 16

CRIB & PONY WALLS SEE 12C & D

PEST CONTROL, TEMPERATURE, MOISTURE
& VENTILATION IN CRAWL SPACE
SEE 8

VENT
SEE 9C & 11B

MUDSILL
SEE 12A & B

BRICK-VENEER
FOUNDATION
SEE 11C & D

PIER & GRADE-BEAM SYSTEM
SEE 13

Foundation walls act integrally with the footings to support the building. They also raise the building above the ground. The primary decision to make about foundation walls is what material to make them of. There are several choices:

Concrete block—Also known as concrete masonry unit or CMU construction, concrete block is the most common system for foundation walls. Its primary advantage is that it needs no formwork, making it appropriate in any situation, but especially where the foundation is complex. Concrete masonry will be used most efficiently if the foundation is planned in 8-in. increments, based on the dimensions of standard concrete blocks (8 in. by 8 in. by 16 in.).

Cast concrete—Concrete can be formed into almost any shape, but formwork is expensive. The most economical use of cast concrete, therefore, is where the formwork is simple or where the formwork can be used several times. Cast-in-place concrete is used for forming pier and grade-beam systems, which are especially appropriate for steep sites or expansive soils (see 13).

Reinforcing—Some local codes do not require reinforcing of foundation walls. Codes in severe earthquake zones are at the other extreme. As a prudent minimum, all foundation walls should be tied to the footing with vertical rebar placed at the corners, adjacent to all major openings, and at regular intervals along the wall. There should be at least one continuous horizontal bar at the top of the wall. Joint reinforcing may be an adequate substitute (see 10B).

Width—The width of the foundation wall depends on the number of stories it supports and on the depth of the backfill, which exerts a lateral force on the wall. With minimum backfill (2 ft. or less), the width of the wall can be determined from the chart below.

The design of basement walls and foundation walls retaining more than 2 ft. of backfill should be verified by an engineer or an architect.

The minimum height of a foundation wall should allow for the adequate clearance of beams and joists from the crawl-space floor. A code-required 18-in. clearance usually requires 12-in. to 24-in. foundation walls, depending on the type of floor system.

NO. OF STORIES	FOUNDATION WIDTH
1	6 in.
2	8 in.
2	10 in.

(A) **FOUNDATION WALLS**
Concrete & Concrete Block

Moisture—Even with the best drainage, the soil under crawl spaces always carries some ground moisture, which will tend to migrate up to the crawl space in the form of vapor. This vapor can be substantially controlled with a vapor retarder laid directly on the ground, which must first be cleared of all organic debris. Crawl-space vapor retarders should be 6-mil (min.) black polyethylene. The dark plastic retards plant growth by preventing daylight from reaching the soil. Adding a concrete rat slab over the vapor retarder will enhance its effectiveness and durability.

Moisture cannot be allowed to build up in a crawl space where it can create catastrophic damage caused by mildew, fungus, and other organisms dependent on moisture. There are two basic strategies to remove the moisture – ventilation to the outside, and conditioning the air as part of the air volume inside the building. In both cases, air is moved through the crawl space to replace moisture-laden crawl-space air.

Ventilation—Crawl-space cross ventilation minimizes the buildup of excess moisture under a structure. In some regions, crawl-space ventilation is also required to remove radon gas.

The net area of venting is related to the under-floor area and to the climatic and groundwater conditions. Most codes require that net vent area equals $\frac{1}{150}$ of the under-floor area with a reduction to $\frac{1}{1500}$ if a vapor barrier covers the ground in the crawl space. Screened vents should be rated for net venting area.

Vents should supply cross ventilation to all areas of the crawl space. Locating vents near corners and on opposite sides of the crawl space is most effective.

Access doors can provide a large area of ventilation. Wells allow vents to be placed below finished grade.

As shown in the drawing above right, screened vents are available for installing in masonry, cast concrete, and wood. They are available in metal or plastic, and some have operable doors for closing off the crawl space during winter to conserve heat. Operable vents should be closed only during extreme weather conditions. Closing the vents for an entire season will increase moisture in the crawl space and can significantly increase the concentration of radon gas.

AN 8-IN. OR 10-IN.-DEEP SCREENED VENT MADE TO BE CAST IN PLACE IN CONCRETE BLOCK OR CONCRETE FOUNDATION WALL

AN 8-IN. X 16-IN. SCREENED VENT THAT FITS IN PLACE OF ONE CONCRETE BLOCK

ONE OF VARIOUS PLASTIC OR METAL VENTS MADE TO VENT THROUGH THE RIM JOIST AND FASTEN TO WOOD SIDING. CARE MUST BE TAKEN TO INSTALL PROPER FLASHING

Unvented crawl space—In climates with humid summer weather, ventilation actually brings moisture into a crawl space, where hot, humid air contacts cooler surfaces in the crawl space and condenses there. The best solution in this case is to insulate the crawl space, close it up tight, and heat and cool it as if it were another room. It doesn't add much to the heating or cooling load, being a small volume with little exterior wall area. This strategy is also appropriate in other climates.

Unvented crawl spaces must be insulated at the foundation wall. The insulation can be installed using the same details as for a basement wall (see 15C). Care must be taken to seal the space well against air infiltration. This includes sealing the joint between foundation wall and mudsill (see 12A) and sealing the joints of the floor assembly that bears on the mudsill (see 33-34).

Pests—Rodents and other large burrowing pests can be kept out of crawl spaces by means of a "rat slab," which is a 1-in. to 2-in.-thick layer of concrete poured over the ground in a crawl space. A concrete-rated moisture barrier should be placed below this slab (see 20). Termites and other insect pests are most effectively controlled by chemical treatment of the soil before construction begins.

Radon—Radon is an odorless radioactive gas that emerges from the ground and is present at very low concentrations in the air we breathe. This gas can build up to dangerous levels when trapped in a crawl space (or basement). Although present everywhere, radon concentration levels in the earth are higher in some regions, and all of North America has been mapped and evaluated for radon danger. The best protection against radon buildup is to ventilate the crawl space well and/or effectively seal the ground below the building. Radon test kits are readily available.

Ⓐ **CRAWL-SPACE CONTROLS**

KNOCK OUT WEBS
OF BOND BLOCKS
TO FORM CHANNEL
FOR REBAR.

Corner

Half Jam

$7^5/_8$ IN.

$15^5/_8$ IN.

VARIES

Jamb

JAMB BLOCKS ARE
AVAILABLE IN HALF
(SHOWN) AND
STRETCHER SIZES.
IN ONE SIDE A SLOT
LOCKS BASEMENT
WINDOWS IN PLACE.

Bond or Lintel

CUT HALF, CORNER, AND
OTHER BLOCKS ON SITE
TO CONTINUE BOND
BEAMS TO THE END OF
WALLS AND AROUND
CORNERS.

Stretcher or Regular

STANDARD WIDTHS ARE $3^5/_8$ IN.,
$5^5/_8$ IN., $7^5/_8$ IN., $9^5/_8$ IN., AND
$11^5/_8$ IN. ALL DIMENSIONS ARE ACTUAL.

NOTE
ALMOST ANY SIZE OR SHAPE OF
MASONRY WALL CAN BE BUILT WITH
BASIC BLOCK TYPES. CONSULT NCMA
FOR CONSTRUCTION TECHNIQUES AND
FOR SPECIAL BLOCKS WITH SPECIAL
EDGE CONDITIONS, TEXTURES, COLORS,
AND SIZES.

Ⓐ CONCRETE-BLOCK TYPES

FLOOR SYSTEM

P.T. MUDSILL SEE 12A

BOND BEAM WITH #4 REBAR
AT TOP COURSE OR BELOW
VENT OPENING. FOR JOINT-
REINFORCING ALTERNATIVE
SEE 10B

BACKFILL

VERTICAL REBAR

FULL MORTAR BASE
WHERE LATERAL LOADS
APPLY

SLOPE TOP OF
FOOTING WITH
MORTAR.

DRAINAGE
SEE 18A

FOOTING

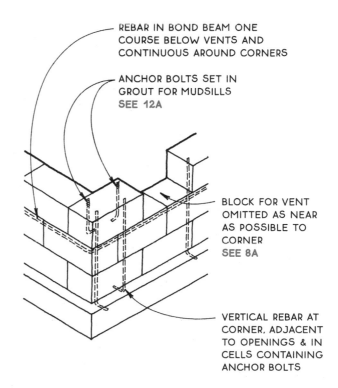

REBAR IN BOND BEAM ONE
COURSE BELOW VENTS AND
CONTINUOUS AROUND CORNERS

ANCHOR BOLTS SET IN
GROUT FOR MUDSILLS
SEE 12A

BLOCK FOR VENT
OMITTED AS NEAR
AS POSSIBLE TO
CORNER
SEE 8A

VERTICAL REBAR AT
CORNER, ADJACENT
TO OPENINGS & IN
CELLS CONTAINING
ANCHOR BOLTS

Ⓑ CRAWL-SPACE FOUNDATION WALL
Concrete Block

Ⓒ CORNER & VENT OPENING
Concrete-Block Foundation Wall

NOTE
HORIZONTAL REBAR SHOULD BE CONTINUOUS IN A BOND BEAM AT THE TOP COURSE, OR AT THE SECOND COURSE IF FOUNDATION VENTS ARE LOCATED IN THE TOP COURSE. HORIZONTAL REBAR MAY ALSO BE LOCATED IN INTERMEDIATE BOND BEAMS IF THE HEIGHT, WIDTH & FUNCTION OF THE WALL REQUIRE IT.

VERTICAL REBAR FROM TOP CELL TO FOOTING. FILL CELLS WITH GROUT.

HORIZONTAL REBAR CONTINUOUS IN TOP-COURSE BOND BEAM. FILL CELLS WITH GROUT.

SCREEN PREVENTS GROUT FROM ENTERING CELLS NOT FILLED WITH REBAR.

Ⓐ CONCRETE-BLOCK FOUNDATION
Rebar Placement

NOTE
TO REINFORCE A JOINT, A WELDED HEAVY-WIRE TRUSS MAY BE SUBSTITUTED FOR HORIZONTAL REBAR IN MANY CASES. IT IS EMBEDDED IN THE MORTAR JOINTS BETWEEN COURSES OF MASONRY.

VERTICAL REBAR FROM TOP CELL TO FOOTING. FILL CELLS WITH GROUT.

JOINT REINFORCING BETWEEN TOP TWO COURSES & AT ALTERNATE COURSES BELOW

Ⓑ CONCRETE-BLOCK FOUNDATION
Joint-Reinforcing Alternative

ANCHOR BOLTS SET IN ROUT FOR MUDSILL

BOND-BEAM TOP COURSE WITH REINFORCING
SEE 10A

BOND OR LINTEL BLOCKS WITH GROUT AND REBAR OR REINFORCED CAST-CONCRETE LINTEL

VERTICAL REBAR AT BOTH SIDES OF OPENING AND EXTENDED INTO FOOTING

CORNER AND HALF BLOCKS AT SIDE JAMBS

CAST OR FORMED CONCRETE OR MORTAR SILL

STRETCHER BLOCKS

BOND BLOCK

Ⓒ CONCRETE-BLOCK BASEMENT
Opening within Wall

DOUBLE RIM JOIST

JAMB BLOCKS WITH GROOVE TO LOCK SASH JAMBS

CAST OR FORMED CONCRETE OR MORTAR SILL

VERTICAL REBAR AT BOTH SIDES OF OPENING AND EXTENDED INTO FOOTING

STRETCHER BLOCKS

NOTE
ANCHOR BOLTS ARE NOT SHOWN FOR CLARITY.

Ⓓ CONCRETE-BLOCK BASEMENT
Opening at Top of Wall

FLOOR SYSTEM

P.T. MUDSILL
SEE 12A

#4 REBAR AT TOP OF WALL

VERTICAL REBAR AS REQUIRED
BY LOCAL CONDITIONS

BACKFILL

2500-PSI (1-STORY STRUCTURE)
OR 3000-PSI (2-STORY
STRUCTURE) CONCRETE

FOUNDATION KEYED TO
FOOTING WHERE VERTICAL
REBAR IS MINIMAL

FOOTING

DRAINAGE IF REQUIRED
SEE 18A

A **CRAWL-SPACE FOUNDATION WALL**
Concrete

HORIZONTAL REBAR CONTINUOUS
AROUND CORNERS AT TOP OF WALL

ANCHOR BOLTS SET IN
CONCRETE FOR MUDSILLS
SEE 12A

FORM VENT AS
NEAR AS POSSIBLE
TO CORNER
SEE 8

VERTICAL REBAR TIED TO
FOOTING AT ALL CORNERS,
ADJACENT TO OPENINGS
AND AT ANCHOR BOLTS

B **CORNER & VENT OPENING**
Concrete Foundation Wall

FRAMING WITH
SHEATING & MOISTURE
BARRIER

1-IN. AIR SPACE

BRICK VENEER

BRICK TIES
SEE 117B

P.T. MUDSILL
SEE 12A

WEEP HOLES, FLASHING
SEE 117B & C

BACKFILL
SEE 18

WIDTH OF FOUNDATION
WALL EQUALS WIDTH OF
VENEER
PLUS 1 IN.
PLUS WIDTH REQUIRED
BY NO. OF STORIES
SEE 3

CONCRETE-BLOCK
OR CONCRETE
FOUNDATION WALL

C **BRICK-VENEER FOUNDATION**
Brick below Mudsill

FRAMING WITH
SHEATHING &
MOISTURE BARRIER

1 IN. AIR SPACE

BRICK VENEER

BRICK TIES SEE 117B

P.T. MUDSILL SEE 12A

WEEP HOLES, FLASHING
SEE 117B & C

BACKFILL
SEE 18

WIDTH OF FOUNDATION
WALL EQUALS WIDTH OF
VENEER
PLUS 1 IN.
PLUS 3-IN. (MIN.)
BEARING FOR WOOD
STRUCTURE. MINIMUM
FOUNDATION WIDTH =
REQUIREMENT FOR NO.
OR STORIES.
SEE 3

CONCRETE-BLOCK
OR CONCRETE
FOUNDATION WALL

D **BRICK-VENEER FOUNDATION**
Brick Level with Mudsill

1/2-IN. STEEL ANCHOR BOLT AT 4 FT. OR 6 FT. O.C. (MAX.) & 12 IN. (MAX.) FROM END OF EACH PIECE OF MUDSILL. VERIFY WITH LOCAL CODES.

1/2-IN. STEEL NUT WITH STEEL WASHER

2X4 OR 2X6 P.T. WOOD MUDSILL

SILL GASKET OF CAULK OR FIBERGLASS AT BASEMENTS OR OTHER LIVING SPACE

CONTINUOUS TERMITE SHIELD IN TERMITE REGIONS

CONCRETE OR CONCRETE-BLOCK FOUNDATION WALL

REBAR

7-IN. MIN. DEPTH OF ANCHOR BOLT INTO FOUNDATION WALL

NOTE
SOME CODES REQUIRE LONGER BOLTS FOR MASONRY WALLS.

(A) MUDSILL WITH ANCHOR BOLT

BEND DOUBLE-STRAP ANCHOR AROUND MUDSILL & NAIL AT SIDE & TOP, OR NAIL ONE STRAP TO MUDSILL & OTHER TO FACE OF STUD.

2X4 OR 2X6 P.T. WOOD MUDSILL

SILL GASKET OF CAULK OR FIBERGLASS AT HEATED SPACE

PLACE MUDSILL ANCHORS INTO FRESH CONCRETE OR NAIL TO FORM BEFORE PLACING CONCRETE.

SLAB WITH TURNED-DOWN FOOTING
SEE 22

NOTE
VERIFY ACCEPTABILITY OF MUDSILL ANCHOR WITH LOCAL BUILDING CODE. THE MUDSILL ANCHOR ALLOWS THE ABILITY TO FINISH SLAB TO THE EDGE BUT IT IS DIFFICULT TO USE WITH TERMITE SHIELD.

(B) MUDSILL WITH MUDSILL ANCHOR

A CRIB WALL IS AN ALTERNATIVE TO COLUMNS & A BEAM SUPPORT FOR JOISTS IN A CRAWL SPACE. IT ALLOWS MORE CLEARANCE FOR DUCTS AND EQUIPMENT & AVOIDS THE POTENTIAL PROBLEM OF CROSS-GRAIN SHRINKAGE IN BEAMS.

JOISTS

SINGLE TOP PLATE

NOTE
CRIB WALL IS BRACED BY PERIMETER FOUNDATION WALL.

CRIB STUDS PLACED DIRECTLY BELOW EACH JOIST

P.T. 2X4 MUDSILL BOLTED TO CONTINUOUS FOOTING

(C) CRIB WALL

A PONY WALL IS USEFUL IN A STEPPED FOUNDATION WALL OR IN A SLOPING PIER & GRADE-BEAM FOUNDATION. THE PONY WALL PROVIDES A LEVEL SURFACE FOR CONSTRUCTION OF THE FIRST FLOOR.

RIM JOIST OR BLOCKING

FLOOR JOISTS

DOUBLE TOP PLATE CONTINUOUS WITH MUDSILL

PONY WALL RECEIVES THE SAME EXTERIOR FINISH AS THE FRAMED WALL ABOVE.

P.T. STUD ADJACENT TO FOUNDATION WALL

P.T. MUDSILL

FOUNDATION WALL OR GRADE BEAM

(D) PONY WALL

GRADE BEAM CAN SLOPE TO CONFORM TO CONTOUR.

PONY WALL ON TOP OF GRADE BEAM MAKES A LEVEL SURFACE FOR FLOOR CONSTRUCTION SEE 12D

GRADE BEAM SEE 13C

PIER SEE 13B

NOTE
PIER & GRADE-BEAM FOUNDATION SYSTEMS ARE PARTICULARLY SUITED TO EXPANSIVE SOILS OR STEEP HILLSIDES. THEY ARE ALSO USEFUL TO AVOID DAMAGING NEARBY TREE ROOTS. PIER & GRADE-BEAM SYSTEMS MUST BE ENGINEERED.

(A) PIER & GRADE-BEAM SYSTEMS

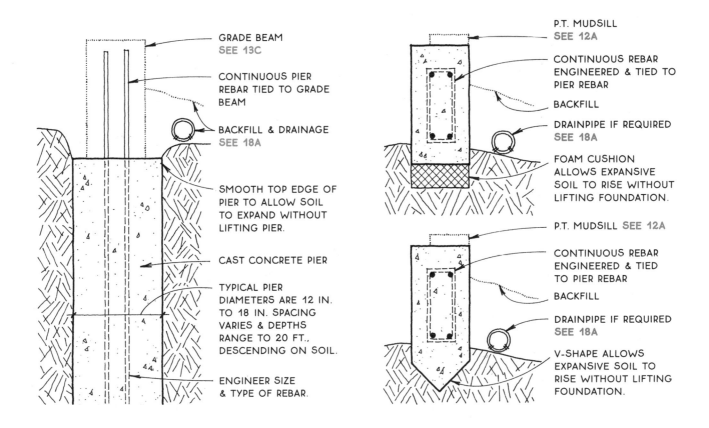

GRADE BEAM SEE 13C

CONTINUOUS PIER REBAR TIED TO GRADE BEAM

BACKFILL & DRAINAGE SEE 18A

SMOOTH TOP EDGE OF PIER TO ALLOW SOIL TO EXPAND WITHOUT LIFTING PIER.

CAST CONCRETE PIER

TYPICAL PIER DIAMETERS ARE 12 IN. TO 18 IN. SPACING VARIES & DEPTHS RANGE TO 20 FT., DESCENDING ON SOIL.

ENGINEER SIZE & TYPE OF REBAR.

P.T. MUDSILL SEE 12A

CONTINUOUS REBAR ENGINEERED & TIED TO PIER REBAR

BACKFILL

DRAINPIPE IF REQUIRED SEE 18A

FOAM CUSHION ALLOWS EXPANSIVE SOIL TO RISE WITHOUT LIFTING FOUNDATION.

P.T. MUDSILL SEE 12A

CONTINUOUS REBAR ENGINEERED & TIED TO PIER REBAR

BACKFILL

DRAINPIPE IF REQUIRED SEE 18A

V-SHAPE ALLOWS EXPANSIVE SOIL TO RISE WITHOUT LIFTING FOUNDATION.

(B) PIERS FOR GRADE BEAM

(C) GRADE BEAMS
Two Types for Expansive Soils

CONCRETE BASEMENT WALL
SEE 15B

CONCRETE-BLOCK
BASEMENT WALL
SEE 15A

CONNECTION TO WOOD FLOOR:
JOISTS ON MUDSILL SEE 33A & B
JOISTS FLUSH WITH MUDSILL SEE 33C & D
JOISTS BELOW MUDSILL SEE 34

CONNECTION TO STUD
WALLS SEE 15D

BUTTRESS
SEE 17C

PILASTER
SEE 16A

CONNECTION TO
CONCRETE SLAB
SEE 21C & D

WATERPROOFING
SEE 18C

NOTE
FOR BASEMENT WALLS, VERIFY THICKNESS
OF CONCRETE OR CONCRETE BLOCK; SIZE,
AMOUNT, AND PLACEMENT OF REBAR;
STRENGTH OF CONCRETE OR GROUT; AND
CONNECTION TO FLOOR SYSTEMS
WITH AN ARCHITECT OR ENGINEER.

DRAINAGE
SEE 18B

COUNTERFORT
SEE 17A & B

Basement walls—Basement walls are one story in height (7 ft. to 9 ft.) and are generally backfilled to at least 4 ft. A basement wall must resist the lateral pressure of the backfill at both the top and bottom of the wall. Basement walls are therefore usually designed as if they were a beam spanning in the vertical direction, with the rebar located at the inside (tension) side of the wall. Because the floor must resist the lateral force of the backfill against the basement wall, the connection between the wood floor and the basement wall is especially important (see 33–34). When basement wall backfill exceeds 4 ft. in height, an engineer should be consulted about this connection. The floor system should always be in place before backfilling. Basement walls can be strengthened with pilasters (see 16), which allow the wall to be designed to span between pilasters in the horizontal (as well as the vertical) direction. Pilasters are also useful as beam supports.

SOIL PRESSURE

WOOD FLOOR

SLAB & SOIL PRESSURE ON FOOTING

Retaining walls—Retaining walls resist lateral loads from the bottom only. They rely on friction at the base of the footing and soil pressure at the outside face of the footing to resist sliding. The weight of the wall and the weight of soil on the footing resist overturning.

SOIL PRESSURE

SOIL PRESSURE ON FOOTING

OVERTURNING FORCE OF SOIL

WEIGHT OF SOIL ON FOOTING

SOIL PRESSURE ON FOOTING

WEIGHT OF WALL ON FOOTING

Sliding Forces   Overturning Forces

Buttresses and counterforts strengthen retaining walls in much the same way that pilasters strengthen basement walls (see 17). Buttresses help support retaining walls from the downhill side, and counterforts from the uphill side.

Technically, freestanding retaining walls are not a part of the building, but they are included here because they are typical extensions of the building components (foundation and basement walls) into the landscape.

FLOOR SYSTEM

INSULATION **SEE 15C**

BACKFILL AND DRAINAGE **SEE 18B**

WATERPROOFING **SEE 18C**

ALTERNATIVE LOCATION FOR INSULATION

VERTICAL REBAR PLACED AT TENSION SIDE OF WALL RESISTS BENDING FORCES.

BOND BEAMS AS REQUIRED BY ENGINEERING

VERTICAL REBAR ANCHORS WALL TO FOOTING.

SLAB **SEE 21C OR D**

FULL MORTAR JOINT ON ROUGHENED FOOTING

FOOTING **SEE 4**

A BASEMENT WALL
Concrete Block

FLOOR SYSTEM

INSULATION **SEE 15C**

BACKFILL AND DRAINAGE **SEE 18B**

WATERPROOFING **SEE 18C**

ALTERNATIVE LOCATION FOR INSULATION

VERTICAL REBAR PLACED AT TENSION SIDE OF WALL RESISTS BENDING FORCES.

HORIZONTAL REBAR AS REQUIRED BY ENGINEERING

VERTICAL REBAR ANCHORS WALL TO FOOTING.

SLAB **SEE 21C OR D**

FOOTING **SEE 4**

B BASEMENT WALL
Concrete

Heated basements must be insulated at their perimeter walls. The amount of insulation required depends on the climate. There are two ways to insulate basement walls—from the exterior or from the interior.

Exterior—Exterior insulation should be a closed-cell rigid insulation (extruded polystyrene or polyisocyanurate) that will not absorb moisture. This insulation, available in 2-ft. or 4-ft. by 8-ft. sheets, is attached directly to the basement wall with adhesive or mechanical fasteners. It may be applied either under or over the waterproofing, depending on the type.

Interior—Interior insulation may be either rigid or batt type. Petroleum-based rigid types must be covered for fire protection when used in an interior location. Other rigid insulation, such as rigid mineral fiber, need not be fire-protected. Building a stud wall with batt insulation has the advantage of providing a nailing surface for interior finishes.

Walls Parallel

Walls Perpendicular

NOTE
AN ALTERNATIVE TO THIS DETAIL IS TO BUILD THE STUD WALL 1 IN. FROM THE BASEMENT WALL.

WALL FINISH

INSULATION

30-LB. FELT STRIPS BETWEEN UNTREATED STUDS & BASEMENT WALL; EXTEND FELT BEYOND STUD OR USE P.T. STUDS.

WALL FINISH

ATTACH STUD WITH CONCRETE NAILS.

NOTE
DO NOT USE CONTINUOUS VAPOR BARRIER ON WARM SIDE OF WALL BELOW GRADE. **SEE 18C**

C BASEMENT INSULATION

D BASEMENT WALL/STUD WALL
Plan Views

1/10 OF THE DISTANCE BETWEEN VERTICAL SUPPORTS (OTHER PILASTERS, CORNERS, OR WALLS)

BACKFILL

FOR PILASTER AS A BEAM SEAT
SEE 16B

1/12 OF WALL HEIGHT

NOTE
PROPORTIONS FOR PILASTER DIMENSIONS ARE APPROXIMATE. REBAR IN WALL, PILASTER & FOOTING MUST BE ENGINEERED.

FOOTING
SEE 4

A **PILASTER**
Concrete or Concrete Block

1/2-IN. AIR SPACE AT END OF WOOD BEAM OR USE P.T. WOOD OR STEEL

NOTE
USE LAMINATED WOOD OR STEEL BEAM TO MINIMIZE SHRINKAGE.

TOP OF PILASTER

BASEMENT WALL

1/2-IN. AIR SPACE

BEAM

30-LB. FELT UNDER BEAM AT POINT OF CONTACT WITH CONCRETE OR CONCRETE BLOCK

SHIMS TO LEVEL BEAM

3-IN. MINIMUM BEARING SURFACE FOR WOOD BEAM

PILASTER

B **PILASTER BEAM SEAT**
Concrete or Concrete Block

1/2-IN. AIR SPACE AT END AND SIDES OF WOOD BEAM OR USE P.T. WOOD OR STEEL

NOTE
USE LAMINATED WOOD OR STEEL BEAM TO MINIMIZE SHRINKAGE.

NOTCH BEAM FOR MUDSILL IF REQUIRED (MAX. NOTCH EQUALS 1/4 DEPTH OF BEAM).

1/2-IN. AIR SPACE

BEAM

30-LB. FELT UNDER BEAM AT POINT OF CONTACT WITH CONCRETE OR CONCRETE BLOCK

SHIMS TO LEVEL BEAM

3-IN. MINIMUM BEARING SURFACE FOR WOOD BEAM

BASEMENT WALL

C **BEAM POCKET**
Concrete or Concrete Block

FRAMED WALL

1/2-IN. AIR SPACE

BLOCKING AS REQUIRED

BEAM WITH 1 1/2-IN. DECKING
SEE 47C & D
OR BEAM & JOIST SYSTEM SEE 33C

ATTACH BEAM TO COLUMN

4X4 WOOD OR P.T. WOOD COLUMN

WOOD COLUMN BEARS ON FOOTING. IF ATTACHMENT IS REQUIRED
SEE 6B

CONCRETE OR CONCRETE-BLOCK FOUNDATION WALL

30-LB. FELT UNDER COLUMN AT FOOTING OR USE P.T. WOOD

D **WOOD-COLUMN BEAM SUPPORT**
Basement or Crawl-Space Wall

NOTE
COUNTERFORT MUST BE PROFESSIONALLY
ENGINEERED. REINFORCEMENT IS REQUIRED
FOR TENSION AND SHEAR.

COUNTERFORT REBAR
TIED TO RETAINING
WALL & FOOTING

RETAINING WALL

8-IN.-THICK
COUNTERFORT WALL

FOOTING

DRAINPIPE

NOTE
FOOTING IS LARGE AND REINFORCED BECAUSE
COUNTERFORT USES ITS OWN WEIGHT PLUS
WEIGHT OF SOIL ABOVE FOOTING TO RESIST THE
HORIZONTAL FORCE ON THE WALL.

(A) CONCRETE COUNTERFORT

NOTE
COUNTERFORT MUST BE
PROFESSIONALLY ENGINEERED.

COUNTERFORT REBAR
TIED TO RETAINING
WALL & FOOTING

RETAINING WALL

REINFORCEMENT
REQUIRED FOR
TENSION & SHEAR

8-IN. (MIN.)-THICK
COUNTERFORT WALL,
STEPPED

FOOTING

DRAINPIPE

NOTE
FOOTING IS LARGE AND REINFORCED BECAUSE
COUNTERFORT USES ITS OWN WEIGHT PLUS
WEIGHT OF SOIL ABOVE FOOTING TO RESIST THE
HORIZONTAL FORCE ON THE WALL.

(B) CONCRETE-BLOCK COUNTERFORT

NOTE
BUTTRESS & RETAINING WALL MUST BE
PROFESSIONALLY ENGINEERED.

RETAINING WALL

8-IN. (MIN.)-THICK
BUTTRESS WALL,
SEEPED (SHOWN)
OR SLOPED

BUTTRESS REBAR
REQUIRED FOR SHEAR
IS TIED TO RETAINING
WALL & FOOTING.

DRAINPIPE

BUTTRESS FOOTING
REINFORCED & CONTINUOUS
WITH WALL FOOTING

(C) BUTTRESS
Concrete or Concrete Block

¾-IN. (MIN.) RIVER ROCK AROUND DRAINPIPE

FILTER FABRIC IF REQUIRED

4-IN. PERFORATED DRAINPIPE WITH HOLES ORIENTED DOWN. SLOPE TO DAYLIGHT OR TO STORM SEWER OR DRYWELL.

Foundation Drain

BACKFILL WITH SOIL AROUND STORM DRAIN.

4-IN. SOLID PLASTIC DRAINPIPE SLOPED TO DAYLIGHT OR TO STORM SEWER OR DRYWELL

NOTE
STORM & FOUNDATION DRAINS MAY BE COMBINED IF LOCAL CODES ALLOW.

Storm Drain

SLOPE FINISH GRADE AWAY FROM BUILDING.

WATERPROOFING SEE 18C

ASPHALT-IMPREGNATED PROTECTION BOARD RECOMMENDED FOR SOME INSULATIONS & WATERPROOFINGS

EXTERIOR OR INTERIOR INSULATION

BACKFILL WITH RIVER ROCK AGAINST WALL

FILTER FABRIC IF REQUIRED

BASEMENT WALL

SLOPE TOP OF FOOTING WITH MORTAR.

4-IN. PERFORATED DRAINPIPE WITH HOLES ORIENTED DOWN & SLOPED TO DAYLIGHT OR TO STORM SEWER OR DRYWELL

A FOUNDATION & STORM DRAINAGE

Drainage is essential in protecting a basement from groundwater, but waterproofing the basement wall from the outside is also vital. In selecting a waterproofing material, consider the method of application, the elasticity, and the cost. Below are common waterproofing and drainage materials.

Bituminous coatings—Tar or asphalt can be rolled, sprayed, troweled, or brushed on a dry surface. Often applied over a troweled-on coating of cement plaster that is called parging, some bituminous coatings may be fiberglass reinforced. They have minimal elasticity, and thin coats may not be impervious to standing water.

Modified portland-cement plaster—Plaster with water-repellent admixtures can look exactly like stucco. It is usually applied with a brush or a trowel to a moistened surface. It is inelastic, and unlike parging, it is waterproof.

Bentonite—A natural clay that swells when moistened to become impervious to water, bentonite is available as panels, in rolls, or in spray-on form. It is applied to a dry surface, and is extremely elastic.

B BASEMENT DRAINAGE

Membranes—Rubberized or plastic membranes that are mechanically applied or bonded to a moist or dry surface are moderately elastic.

Bitumen-modified urethane—The most recent development in waterproof coatings, bitumen-modified urethane is applied with a brush to a dry surface. It is elastic, protecting cracks up to ⅛ in.

Plastic air-gap materials—These drainage materials create a physical gap between the basement wall and the soil. A filter fabric incorporated in the material allows water to enter the gap and drop to the bottom of the wall. These systems are expensive, but they eliminate the need for gravel backfill.

Although waterproofing and drainage will prevent water from entering the basement, water vapor may migrate into the basement through the footing and basement wall. It's important not to trap this vapor in an insulated wall, so a vapor barrier on the warm side of a basement wall is not recommended. More common and more practical is to allow the vapor to enter the space, and to remove the vapor with ventilation or a dehumidifier.

C WATERPROOFING
Principles & Materials

One-Piece Wood Cap

- MALLEABLE OR OTHER LARGE WASHER
- WEATHER-RESISTANT WOOD CAP BEVELED ON TOP FOR DRAINAGE
- DRIP CUT IN UNDERSIDE OF CAP
- ANCHOR BOLTS AT 6 FT. O.C. MINIMUM.
- CONCRETE-BLOCK OR CONCRETE WALL

Two-Piece Wood Cap

- MALLEABLE OR OTHER LARGE WASHER
- WEATHER-RESISTANT TWO-PIECE WOOD CAP; TOP PIECE BEVELED & WITH DRIP
- ANCHOR BOLTS AT 6 FT. O.C. MINIMUM.
- CONCRETE-BLOCK OR CONCRETE WALL

Stucco Cap

- ROUNDED SHAPE PROMOTES DRAINAGE.
- STUCCO OR WALL CONTINUOUS OVER CAP. FOR STUCCO DETAILS **SEE 118-119**
- SILICONE COATING FOR MOISTURE PROTECTION
- CONCRETE-BLOCK OR CONCRETE WALL

Metal Cap

- CONTINUOUS METAL CAP WITH DRIP EDGE
- FASTEN METAL CAP TO WALL AT SIDE TO PREVENT MOISTURE PENETRATION OF TOP FLAT SURFACE.
- CONCRETE-BLOCK OR CONCRETE WALL

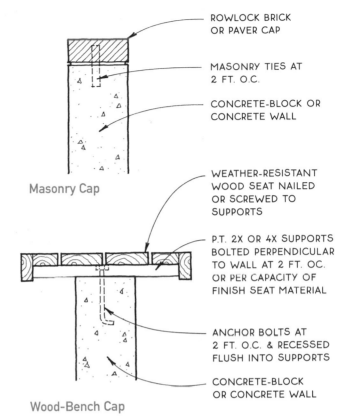

Masonry Cap

- ROWLOCK BRICK OR PAVER CAP
- MASONRY TIES AT 2 FT. O.C.
- CONCRETE-BLOCK OR CONCRETE WALL

Wood-Bench Cap

- WEATHER-RESISTANT WOOD SEAT NAILED OR SCREWED TO SUPPORTS
- P.T. 2X OR 4X SUPPORTS BOLTED PERPENDICULAR TO WALL AT 2 FT. O.C. OR PER CAPACITY OF FINISH SEAT MATERIAL
- ANCHOR BOLTS AT 2 FT. O.C. & RECESSED FLUSH INTO SUPPORTS
- CONCRETE-BLOCK OR CONCRETE WALL

NOTES

THESE DETAILS ARE FOR THE TOPS OF RETAINING WALLS, WHICH ARE USUALLY EXPOSED TO THE WEATHER. WOOD CAPS WILL ULTIMATELY DECAY, SO THEY ARE DESIGNED FOR RELATIVE EASE OF REPLACEMENT. THERE IS NOT MUCH POINT IN MOISTURE BARRIERS, SINCE THEY WILL ONLY TRAP RAINWATER AGAINST THE WOOD. RETAINING-WALL SURFACES SHOULD BE PROTECTED FROM MOISTURE PENETRATION TO PREVENT DAMAGE FROM THE FREEZE-THAW CYCLE. SEAL WITH CLEAR ACRYLIC OR SILICONE, OR WATERPROOF WITH MODIFIED PORTLAND-CEMENT PLASTER OR BITUMEN-MODIFIED URETHANE. **SEE 18C**

 CONCRETE & CONCRETE-BLOCK WALL CAPS

SLAB/BASEMENT WALL
SEE 21C & D

SLAB PERIMETER
INSULATION
SEE 22B

TURNED-DOWN
SLAB FOOTING
SEE 22 &
23C

GARAGE SLAB
SEE 24A & B, 25A

SLAB REINFORCING
SEE 21

SLAB WITH DEEP FOOTING
SEE 23A, B & D

SLAB FOOTINGS AT BEARING WALLS
& COLUMNS
SEE 23 & 24

EXPANSION JOINTS & CONTROL
JOINTS
SEE 21B

RADIANT-HEAT SLAB
SEE 25C

PLUMBING THROUGH SLAB
SEE 25B

Preparation before pouring a slab is critical to the quality of the slab itself. The primary goals in preparing for a slab are to provide adequate and even support, and to control ground moisture.

Soil—Soil is the ultimate support of the slab. Soil must be solid and free of organic material. Some soils require compaction. In termite areas, the soil is often treated chemically. Verify compaction and soil treatment practices in your local area.

Gravel—Gravel is a leveling device that provides a porous layer for groundwater to drain away from the slab. A minimum of 4 in. of gravel is recommended. Gravel must be clean and free from organic matter. Crushed and ungraded gravels must be compacted. Graded gravels such as pea gravel composed entirely of similar-sized round particles cannot and need not be compacted.

Moisture barrier—Moisture barriers prevent moisture (and retard vapor) from moving upward into a slab. Six-mil polyethylene is common and works well in Detail A. Overlap joints 12 in. and tape the joints in

areas of extreme moisture. A more substantial concrete-rated moisture barrier is necessary for Detail B because the moisture barrier is in direct contact with the concrete slab. Polyethylene may deteriorate within

CONCRETE
SLAB

SAND

MOISTURE
BARRIER

GRAVEL

SUB-SOIL

Detail A   Detail B

a very short period in this situation, and it is easily punctured during slab preparation and pouring. A more substantial concrete-rated barrier is a fiber-reinforced bituminous membrane, sandwiched between two layers of polyethylene.

Sand—Sand (shown only in Detail A), allows water to escape from concrete in a downward direction during curing. This produces a stronger slab. The American Concrete Institute recommends a 2-in. layer of sand below slabs.

Welded wire mesh—Welded wire mesh (WWM) is the most common reinforcement for light-duty slabs. The most common size is 6x6 (w1.4 x w1.4)—adequate for a residential garage, which requires a stronger slab than a house. One disadvantage to WWM is that the 6-in. grid is often stepped on and forced to the bottom of the slab as the concrete is poured.

Rebar—Rebar is stronger than welded wire mesh. A grid of #3 rebar at 24 in. o.c is also adequate for a residential garage.

Fiber reinforcement—Fiber reinforcement is a recent development in slab reinforcement. Polypropylene fiber reinforcement is mixed with the concrete at the plant and poured integrally with the slab, thereby eliminating difficulties with placement of the reinforcing material. The addition of 1.5 lb. of fiber per cubic yard of concrete produces flexural strength equal to WWM in a slab. The appearance of the slab is affected by the presence of fibers exposed at the surface.

Expansion joints—Expansion joints allow slabs to expand and contract slightly with temperature changes. They also allow slabs to act independently of building elements with which they interface. Expansion joints are appropriate at the edges of slabs that are not heated (not in the living space) or that, for some other reason, are expected to change temperature significantly over their lifetimes. Expansion joints are also used to isolate building elements that penetrate slabs such as structural columns, walls, or plumbing (see 25B).

Control joints—Control joints induce cracking to occur at selected locations. They are troweled or cut into the surface of a slab to about one-quarter of the slab depth and at 20-ft. intervals. Cold joints, which automatically occur between sections of a slab poured separately, can act as control joints.

(A) CONCRETE-SLAB REINFORCING

(B) CONCRETE-SLAB JOINTS

BACKFILL & DRAINAGE SEE 18B

WATERPROOFING SEE 18C

BASEMENT WALL

EXPANSION JOINT IF SLAB POURED IN COLD WEATHER

4-IN. (MIN.) REINFORCED SLAB

CONCRETE-RATED MOISTURE BARRIER

4-IN. (MIN.) GRAVEL

4-IN. CONTINUOUS PERFORATED DRAINPIPE SLOPED TO DAYLIGHT OR TO STORM SEWER OR DRYWELL

BACKFILL & DRAINAGE SEE 18B

WATERPROOFING SEE 18C

BASEMENT WALL

BITUMINOUS EXPANSION JOINT OR LEAVE 1-IN. SPACE BETWEEN SLAB & WALL TO RELIEVE EXCESS HYDROSTATIC PRESSURE FROM BELOW SLAB

4-IN. (MIN.) REINFORCED SLAB

CONCRETE-RATED MOISTURE BARRIER

6-IN. (MIN.) GRAVEL

4-IN. CONTINUOUS PERFORATED DRAINPIPE SLOPED TO DAYLIGHT OR TO STORM SEWER

(C) SLAB/BASEMENT WALL
Well-Drained Soil

(D) SLAB/BASEMENT WALL
Poorly-Drained Soil

P.T. MUDSILL
SEE 12A OR B

6 IN. (MIN.)
FROM SOIL
TO MUDSILL

4-IN. (MIN.) REINFORCED SLAB
CONTINUOUS WITH FOOTING

CONCRETE-RATED
MOISTURE BARRIER

4-IN. (MIN.)
COMPACTED
GRAVEL OR
PEA GRAVEL

12-IN. (MIN.)
FOOTING DEPTH

REBAR CONTINUOUS
AT PERIMETER

NOTE
AN UNINSULATED & EXPOSED PERIMETER
SLAB IS APPROPRIATE ONLY FOR UNHEATED
SPACES OR IN VERY WARM CLIMATES.

(A) **SLAB WITH TURNED-DOWN FOOTING**
Warm Climate, Well-Drained Soil

NOTE
SLABS LOSE HEAT MOST READILY AT THEIR PERIMETERS,
WHERE THEY ARE EXPOSED TO THE AIR, SO SLABS MUST
BE PROTECTED FROM HEAT LOSS BY A CLOSED-CELL RIGID
INSULATION PLACED AT THEIR EDGES. THE AMOUNT OF
INSULATION REQUIRED WILL DEPEND ON THE CLIMATE AND
ON WHETHER THE SLAB IS HEATED.
  THE POSITION OF THE INSULATION WILL DEPEND
PRIMARILY ON THE FOUNDATION TYPE. SLABS INTEGRAL
WITH TURNED-DOWN FOOTINGS ARE INSULATED AT THE
OUTSIDE BUILDING EDGE. SLABS WITH DEEP FOOTINGS
ARE OFTEN INSULATED AT THE INSIDE FACE OF THE
FOUNDATION, ALTHOUGH THEY MAY ALSO BE INSULATED AT
THE OUTSIDE BUILDING EDGE.

TURNED-DOWN
FOOTINGS
SEE 22C & D, 23C

DEEP FOOTINGS
SEE 23A, B & D

(B) **SLAB PERIMETER INSULATION**

WALL FINISH,
STUCCO-WRAPPED
INSULATION
OR SIDING
STOPPED AT TOP
OF INSULATION
WITH FLASHING
& PROTECTIVE
COATING OVER
INSULATION

4-IN. (MIN.) SLAB
CONTINUOUS WITH
FOOTING

CONCRETE-RATED
MOISTURE BARRIER

4-IN. (MIN.)
COMPACTED
GRAVEL OR
PEA GRAVEL

P.T. MUDSILL
SEE 12A OR B

CLOSED-CELL
RIGID INSULATION
TO BELOW FROST LINE

REBAR CONTINUOUS
AT PERIMETER

FOOTING BELOW
FROST LINE

(C) **SLAB WITH TURNED-DOWN FOOTING**
Insulation Outside Framing

COATING PROTECTS INSULATION
FROM ULTRAVIOLET LIGHT AND
MECHANICAL ABRASION.

CLOSED-CELL RIGID INSULATION TO BELOW
FROST LINE; THICKNESS VARIES.

TERMITE SHIELD IF REQUIRED

FRAMED WALL PROJECTED OVER
INSULATION AND COATING

P.T. MUDSILL
SEE 12A OR B

4-IN. (MIN.) SLAB
CONTINUOUS
WITH FOOTING

4-IN. (MIN.) GRAVEL

CONCRETE-RATED
MOISTURE BARRIER

FOOTING BELOW
FROST LINE

(D) **SLAB WITH TURNED-DOWN FOOTING**
Insulation Flush with Framing

FRAMED WALL

IN TERMITE REGIONS, EXTEND TERMITE SHIELD CONTINUOUSLY FROM SLAB TO EXTERIOR.

4-IN. (MIN.) REINFORCED SLAB

CONCRETE-RATED MOISTURE BARRIER

4-IN. (MIN.) COMPACTED GRAVEL OR PEA GRAVEL

CLOSED-CELL RIGID INSULATION TO BELOW FROST LINE OR 2 FT. (MIN.) **SEE 22B**

FOUNDATION WALL AND FOOTING

(A) SLAB ON GRADE/DEEP FOOTING
Vertical Interior Insulation

FRAMED WALL

IN TERMITE REGIONS, EXTEND TERMITE SHIELD CONTINUOUSLY FROM SLAB TO EXTERIOR.

4-IN. (MIN.) REINFORCED SLAB

CONCRETE-RATED MOISTURE BARRIER

CLOSED-CELL RIGID INSULATION EXTENDED 2 FT. (MIN.) UNDER SLAB

4-IN. (MIN.) COMPACTED GRAVEL OR PEA GRAVEL

FOUNDATION WALL AND FOOTING

(B) SLAB ON GRADE/DEEP FOOTING
Horizontal Interior Insulation

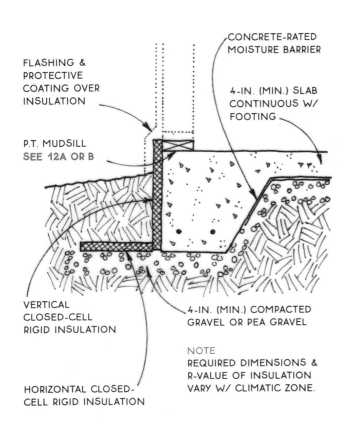

FLASHING & PROTECTIVE COATING OVER INSULATION

P.T. MUDSILL **SEE 12A OR B**

CONCRETE-RATED MOISTURE BARRIER

4-IN. (MIN.) SLAB CONTINUOUS W/ FOOTING

VERTICAL CLOSED-CELL RIGID INSULATION

4-IN. (MIN.) COMPACTED GRAVEL OR PEA GRAVEL

NOTE
REQUIRED DIMENSIONS & R-VALUE OF INSULATION VARY W/ CLIMATIC ZONE.

HORIZONTAL CLOSED-CELL RIGID INSULATION

(C) SLAB WITH TURNED-DOWN FOOTING
Frost-Protected Shallow Footing

FRAMED WALL

IN TERMITE REGIONS, EXTEND TERMITE SHIELD CONTINUOUSLY FROM SLAB TO EXTERIOR.

4-IN. (MIN.) REINFORCED SLAB

CONCRETE-RATED MOISTURE BARRIER

4-IN. (MIN.) COMPACTED GRAVEL OR PEA GRAVEL

CLOSED-CELL RIGID INSULATION TO BELOW FROST LINE OR 2 FT. (MIN.) **SEE 22B**

FOUNDATION WALL AND FOOTING

(D) SLAB ON GRADE/DEEP FOOTING
Vertical Exterior Insulation

GARAGE DOOR

4-IN. (MIN.) REINFORCED SLAB **SEE 21A**

SLOPE SLAB TOWARD DOOR AT 1/8 IN. PER FT.

RECESSED THRESHOLD CAST INTO SLAB TO CONTROL WATER

CAULKED EXPANSION JOINT

SLOPE DRIVEWAY AWAY FROM BUILDING

4-IN. (MIN.) GRAVEL

CONCRETE-RATED MOISTURE BARRIER

FOOTING CONTINUOUS WITH SLAB **SEE 22C**

GRAVEL

REBAR CONTINUOUS AT PERIMETER

(A) TURNED-DOWN FOOTING
At Garage Door

GARAGE DOOR

THICKEN SLAB EDGE AT FOUNDATION CONNECTION & TIE WITH REBAR.

4-IN. (MIN.) REINFORCED SLAB **SEE 21A**

RECESSED THRESHOLD CAST INTO SLAB TO CONTROL WATER

CAULKED EXPANSION JOINT

SLOPE DRIVEWAY

4-IN. (MIN.) GRAVEL

CONCRETE-RATED MOISTURE BARRIER

FOUNDATION WALL

FOOTING

(B) DEEP FOOTING
At Garage Door

REBAR

CONCRETE-RATED MOISTURE BARRIER

WOOD POST

GALVANIZED STEEL COLUMN BASE **SEE 6B**

P.T. SILL PLATE NAILED TO SLAB WITH CONCRETE NAILS

Wood Post

REBAR

CONCRETE-RATED MOISTURE BARRIER

30-LB. FELT UNDER P.T. SILL

NOTE
DEPTH & FLAT BEARING SURFACE OF FOOTING MUST BE SIZED TO SUPPORT VERTICAL LOADS.

Bearing Wall

(C) INTEGRAL SLAB FOOTING
Wood Post & Bearing Wall

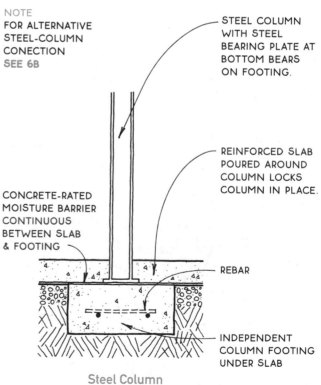

NOTE
FOR ALTERNATIVE STEEL-COLUMN CONECTION **SEE 6B**

CONCRETE-RATED MOISTURE BARRIER CONTINUOUS BETWEEN SLAB & FOOTING

STEEL COLUMN WITH STEEL BEARING PLATE AT BOTTOM BEARS ON FOOTING.

REINFORCED SLAB POURED AROUND COLUMN LOCKS COLUMN IN PLACE.

REBAR

INDEPENDENT COLUMN FOOTING UNDER SLAB

(D) UNDER-SLAB FOOTING
Steel Column

EXPANSION JOINT AT ALL EDGES OF UNHEATED GARAGE SLAB

CONCRETE OR CONCRETE-BLOCK FOUNDATION WALL 2 IN. (MIN.) ABOVE SLAB

4-IN. (MIN.) REINFORCED CONCRETE SLAB SLOPED AT 1/8 IN. PER FT. TO FRONT OF GARAGE

CONCRETE-RATED MOISTURE BARRIER

COMPACTED GRAVEL OR PEA GRAVEL

FOUNDATION WALL & FOOTING

NOTE
A STRONGER CONCRETE MIX IS REQUIRED FOR A GARAGE SLAB THAN FOR A SLAB IN LIVING SPACES. VERIFY LOCAL REQUIREMENTS.

(A) GARAGE SLAB/FOUNDATION WALL

PLASTIC-SLEEVE PIPE INSULATION ISOLATES WATER PIPES FROM SLAB.

1-IN.-THICK FIBERGLASS WRAP INSULATION ISOLATES WASTE PIPES FROM SLAB.

Hot   Cold   Waste

NOTE
USE TYPE K OR TYPE L COPPER SUPPLY PIPES. MINIMIZE BRAZED FITTINGS BELOW SLAB. HOT-PIPE INSULATION IS RECOMMENDED.

NOTE
USE ABS PLASTIC WASTE LINES. NO CLEANOUTS ARE ALLOWED BELOW SLAB. SET CLOSET FLANGE AT F.F.L. AND ANCHOR DIRECTLY & SECURELY TO SLAB.

(B) PLUMBING THROUGH SLAB

PERIMETER INSULATION REQUIRED SEE 22B, C & D

PEX TUBING AT 8 IN. O.C. (APPROX.) TIED TO REBAR OR WIRE MESH

4 IN. (MIN.) REINFORCED CONCRETE SLAB

OPTIONAL INSULATION

SLAB WITH TURNED-DOWN FOOTING OR SLAB WITH FOUNDATION WALL SEE 23B

CONCRETE-RATED MOISTURE BARRIER

CLOSED-CELL RIGID INSULATION (2 IN. MIN.) TO 4 FT. FROM PERIMETER

4 IN. (MIN.) OF GRAVEL

NOTE
CROSS-LINKED POLYETHYLENE TUBING (PEX) HAS REPLACED COPPER TUBING AS THE CONVEYOR OF HOT WATER FOR RADIANT SLABS. THIS ELASTIC TUBING IS SUPPLIED IN LONG ROLLS & CAN COVER ABOUT 200 SQ. FT. WITHOUT ANY JOINTS BELOW THE SURFACE. THE ADDITION OF INSULATION BELOW THE SLAB WILL IMPROVE THE PERFORMANCE OF THE SYSTEM.

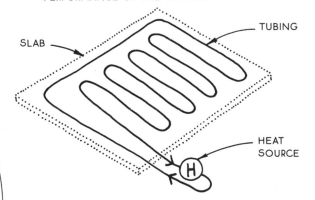

SLAB   TUBING

HEAT SOURCE

Diagram of Radiant Heat Tubing

(C) RADIANT-HEAT SLAB

chapter 2

FLOORS

The floor is the part of the building with which we have most contact. We walk on the floor and, on occasion, dance, wrestle, or lie on it. We can easily tell if the floor is not level, if it is bouncy or squeaky, and this tells us something about the overall quality of the building. The floor carries the loads of our weight, all our furniture, and most of our other possessions. It also acts as a diaphragm to transfer lateral loads (e.g., wind, earthquake, and soil) to the walls, which resist these loads. Floors insulate us from beneath and often hold ductwork, plumbing, and other utilities. So a floor must be carefully designed as a system that integrates with the other systems of a wood-frame building—the foundation, walls, stairs, insulation, and utilities. Once designed, the floor must be carefully built because so many subsequent parts of the construction process depend on a level and solid floor construction.

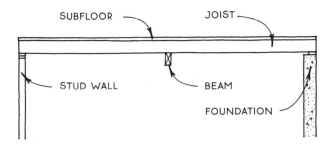

ELEMENTS OF A FLOOR SYSTEM
There are several floor-construction systems, and all of them are composed of variations of the same basic elements: support, joists, and a subfloor.

Support—Wood floor systems usually span between parallel supports. These supports may be a foundation wall, a stud-bearing wall, or a beam. The first two are covered in Chapters 1 and 3, and beams are a subject of this chapter (see 29-31).

Joists—The primary structural members of a floor system are the joists, which span between the supports. The most common materials for joists are solid-sawn lumber (see 35-42) and engineered wood I-joists (see 43-44). Joists are usually placed on 12-in., 16-in., or 24-in. centers, depending on the required span and the sizes of the joists (see 32).

Solid-Sawn
Joist

Engineered
I-Joist

Subfloor—The planar structural surface attached to the top of the joists is called the subfloor (see 48-51). The subfloor provides the level surface to which the finish floor is applied, and it also acts as a diaphragm to transfer lateral loads to the walls. Subfloors are usually made of plywood or oriented strand board (OSB) but may also be made of other materials. Some subfloors also provide mass for passive-solar heating.

FLOORS AND WALLS
It is essential to coordinate the details of a floor-framing system with those of the wall framing. There are two wall-framing systems from which to choose:

Balloon framing—Balloon framing is a construction system in which the studs are continuous through the floor levels. It is a mostly archaic system, but there are some situations where balloon framing is appropriate. These situations are discussed in the introduction to Chapter 3 (see 65-66). Balloon-framing details that pertain to floors are included in this chapter.

Platform framing—Platform framing is the dominant wood-floor construction system in this country. The platform frame floor is so named because the stud-wall structure stops at each level, where the floor structure provides a platform for the construction of the walls of the next level. This chapter concentrates on platform framing, which has two basic variations: joists with structural panels (OSB or plywood), and girders with decking.

TYPES OF FLOOR FRAMING

Throughout the history of the balloon frame and the more recent platform frame, floors have typically been made with joists (2x6, 2x8, 2x10, and 2x12) that are spaced closely (usually 16 or 24 inches on center) to support a subfloor that spans between them.

For 125 years, the joists were all solid-sawn lumber, and the subfloor started as boards, laid diagonally and later became plywood. In the past 35 years or so, solid-sawn lumber has been slowly replaced with engineered wood products—wood I-joists and other structural composite lumber (SCL). Engineered wood products are straighter, more dimensionally stable, and generally stronger than their solid-sawn counterparts. In addition, they can be made larger and longer than sawn lumber, so they can span farther.

Currently, engineered wood products have overtaken solid-sawn lumber in terms of market share for floor construction, but both materials are still widely used. Subfloors are now typically made with Oriented Strand Board (OSB) instead of the more expensive plywood.

Most of the details in this chapter are illustrated with examples showing solid-sawn lumber—primarily because the drawings are more clear using these simple forms. However, the solid-sawn details may be interpreted to be built of engineered products because the basic principles apply to all types of framing material whether solid-sawn, I-joist, or other composite materials. Because I-joists require special treatment in certain conditions, there is a section of the chapter devoted entirely to I-joists (see 43–44).

In areas where timber is plentiful, 4x girders with 2-in. tongue-and-groove subfloor decking that spans 4 ft. are often used as a floor system (see 46–47). Lower grades of decking on girders make a very economical floor over crawl spaces, and appearance grades of decking are often used for exposed ceilings. The decking itself does not technically act as a diaphragm to resist lateral loads, so it may require additional diagonal structure, especially at upper levels.

Also included in this chapter are porch and deck floors, floor insulation, and vapor barriers.

CRIB & PONY WALLS
SEE 12C & D

WOOD-BEAM OR
GIRDER/POST
CONNECTIONS
SEE 31

BEAM SPANS
SEE 29B

CONNECTIONS TO
FOUNDATION
SEE 16

BEAM TYPES
SEE 30

(A) **FLOOR BEAMS**

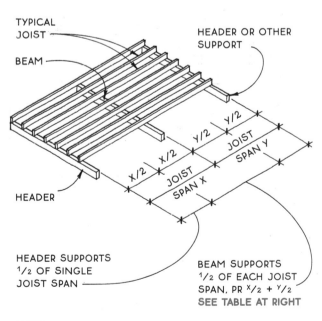

TYPICAL
JOIST

HEADER OR OTHER
SUPPORT

BEAM

JOIST
SPAN Y

JOIST
SPAN X

HEADER

HEADER SUPPORTS
1/2 OF SINGLE
JOIST SPAN

BEAM SUPPORTS
1/2 OF EACH JOIST
SPAN, PR X/2 + Y/2
SEE TABLE AT RIGHT

NOTE
THE DRAWING ABOVE AND THE TABLE AT RIGHT
ARE FOR UNIFORM FLOOR LOADS ONLY. ROOF LOADS,
POINT LOADS & OTHER LOADS MUST BE ADDED TO
FLOOR LOADS WHEN CALCULATING BEAMS & HEADERS

BEAM SPAN COMPARISON				
Beam type	Joist span ($^x/_2 + ^y/_2$)			
	8ft.	10ft.	12ft.	14ft.
	Beam Span (ft.)			
(2) 2x8 built-up beam	6.8	6.1	5.3	4.7
4x8 timber	7.7	6.9	6.0	5.3
3$^1/_8$ in. x 7$^1/_2$ in. glue-laminated beam	9.7	9.0	8.3	7.7
3$^1/_2$ in. x 7$^1/_2$ in. PSL beam	9.7	9.0	8.5	8.0
(2) $^{13}/_4$ in. x 7$^1/_2$ in. LVL (unusual depth)	10.0	9.3	8.8	8.3
4x8 steel beam (W8 x 13 A36)	17.4	16.2	15.2	14.1

This table assumes a 40-psf live load and a 15-psf dead load. The table is intended only for estimating beam sizes and comparing beam types. For calculation tables, consult the national or regional organizations listed on pp. 228–229.

(A) **FLOOR BEAMS**

Cut Timber

TIMBER BEAMS ARE AVAILABLE IN A VARIETY OF SPECIES & GRADES; DOUGLAS-FIR IS THE STRONGEST. ACTUAL WIDTHS ARE 3 1/2 IN. AND 5 1/2 IN.; ACTUAL HEIGHTS ARE 5 1/2 IN., 7 1/2 IN., ETC., TO 13 1/2 IN.

Laminated-Strand Lumber (LSL) Beam

FACTORY-MADE COMPOSITE BEAM USED FOR HEADERS, RIM JOIST, AND LIGHT-DUTY BEAMS. ACTUAL WIDTHS ARE 1 3/4 IN. AND 3 1/2 IN; ACTUAL HEIGHTS RANGE FROM 9 1/4 IN. TO 16 IN.

Parallel-Strand Lumber (PSL) Beam

FACTORY-GLUED LONG STRANDS OF VENEER MAKE VERY STRONG BEAMS. ACTUAL WIDTHS RANGE FROM 2 3/4 IN. TO 7 IN; HEIGHTS RANGE FROM 9 1/4 IN. TO 18 IN. 5 1/2 IN., 7 1/2 IN., ETC., TO 13 1/2 IN.

Laminated-Veneer Lumber (LVL) Beam

FACTORY-LAMINATED VENEERS MAKE STRONG BEAMS. USED INDIVIDUALLY OR GANGED TOGETHER. ACTUAL WIDTH IS 1 3/4 IN. (TWO PIECES MATCH THICKNESS OF 2X4 WALL) HEIGHTS RANGE FROM 5 1/2 IN. TO 24 IN.

Laminated Lumber (Glulam) Beam

FACTORY-GLUED STACK OF KILN-DRIED 2X BOARDS MAKES VERY LARGE, LONG, AND STABLE BEAMS. ACTUAL WIDTHS ARE 3 1/8 IN., 5 1/8 IN., 7 1/8 IN., ETC. HEIGHTS ARE MULTIPLES OF 1 1/2 IN. TO 36 IN. AND LARGER.

Built-Up Beam

SOLID SAWN LUMBER IS NAILED OR SCREWED TOGETHER TO FORM A SINGLE BEAM. WIDTHS ARE MULTIPLES OF 1 1/2 IN. HEIGHT FOLLOWS DIMENSION LUMBER.

Flitch Beam

A STEEL PLATE SANDWICHED BETWEEN TWO PIECES OF LUMBER ADDS STRENGTH WITHOUT SUBSTANTIALLY INCREASING THE BEAM SIZE. THE LUMBER PREVENTS BUCKLING OF THE STEEL & PROVIDES A NAILING SURFACE. WIDTHS ARE 3 IN. TO 3 1/2 IN. HEIGHTS FOLLOW DIMENSION LUMBER.

Box Beam

2X4 LUMBER IS SANDWICHED BETWEEN TWO PLYWOOD SKINS. PLYWOOD IS BOTH NAILED & GLUED TO 2X4S & AT ALL EDGES. PLYWOOD AND LUMBER JOINTS MUST BE OFFSET.

Steel Beam

THE STRONGEST OF THE BEAMS FOR A GIVEN SIZE, STEEL BEAMS ARE COMMONLY AVAILABLE IN VARIOUS SIZES FROM 4 IN. WIDE & 4 IN. HIGH TO 12 IN. WIDE & 36 IN. HIGH. THEY MAY BE PREDRILLED FOR BOLTING WOOD PLATE TO TOP FLANGE OR TO WEB.

FOR CONNECTIONS TO STEEL BEAMS **SEE 37**.

NOTE
BEAMS & JOISTS MUST BE DESIGNED AS A SYSTEM. CONNECTIONS BETWEEN JOISTS & BEAMS ARE SIMILAR FOR ALL WOOD-BEAM TYPES. **SEE 36**

 BEAM TYPES

NOTE
WOOD BEAMS MAY BE SPLICED OVER VERTICAL SUPPORTS & OFTEN MAY BE ATTACHED TO THE SUPPORT BY MEANS OF TOENAILING. SOME SITUATIONS & CODES, HOWEVER, REQUIRE A POSITIVE CONNECTION OF BEAM TO POST SUCH AS A PLYWOOD GUSSET OR METAL CONNECTOR. SPLICE BEAMS ONLY OVER VERTICAL SUPPORTS UNLESS ENGINEERED. SPLICE WILL DEPEND ON TYPE OF BEAM & TYPE OF SUPPORT.

Built-Up Beam

KEEP ONE MEMBER CONTINUOUS OVER POSTS.

Plywood Gusset

PLYWOOD GUSSETS ARE APPLIED TO BOTH SIDES OF SPLICED BEAMS. USE 5-PLY PLYWOOD.

Metal Connector

METAL CONNECTORS ARE MANUFACTURED IN MANY CONFIGURATIONS FOR MOST TYPES OF WOOD BEAM & POST JOINTS.

Metal Column

METAL LALLY COLUMN HAS INTEGRAL METAL CONNECTOR.

 WOOD BEAM OR GIRDER/POST CONNECTIONS

MID-FLOOR JOIST/JOIST CONNECTIONS
SEE 35

JOIST/BEAM CONNECTIONS
SEE 36

FLOOR/STUD WALL
CONNECTIONS
SEE 39B

BRIDGING
SEE 38

FLOOR/FOUNDATION
CONNECTION SEE 33 & 34

OPENINGS IN FLOOR
SEE 38B

FLOOR-LEVEL CHANGES
SEE 41C & D

CANTILEVERS
SEE 39A

SUBFLOORING &
UNDERLAYMENT
SEE 48

Both dimension-lumber and wood I-joists are common materials for floor structure. Both systems are flexible, and the materials are universally available. Species of lumber vary considerably from region to region, but sizes are uniform. The most common sizes for floors are 2x8, 2x10, and 2x12. Selection of floor-joist size depends on span; on spacing required for sub-flooring and ceiling finishes (usually 12 in., 16 in., or 24 in.); and on depth required for insulation (usually over a crawl space) and/or utilities (over basements and in upper floors).

The table at right compares spans at common on-center spacings for three typical species and grades of framing lumber at four different sizes of joist (2x6, 2x8, 2x10, and 2x12) and an I-joist at the two largest sizes. For information on wood I-joists, see 43 and 44; for information on wood trusses, see 45A.

This table assumes a 40-psf live load, a 10-psf dead load and a deflection of L/360. The table is for comparison and estimating purposes only.

ALLOWABLE FLOOR JOIST SPANS IN FEET

Joist size, species. and grade	Joist spacing (ft.)		
	12 in. o.c	16 in. o.c.	24 in. o.c.
2x6 hem-fir #2	10.0	9.0	7.9
2x6 spruce-pine-fir #2	10.2	9.3	8.1
2x6 Douglas fir #2	10.7	9.7	8.2
2x8 hem-fir #2	13.1	11.9	10.1
2x8 spruce-pine-fir #2	13.5	12.2	10.2
2x8 Douglas fir #2	14.1	12.7	10.4
2x10 hem-fir #2	16.8	15.1	12.3
2x10 spruce-pine-fir #2	17.2	15.3	12.5
2x10 Douglas fir #2	18.0	15.6	12.7
9.5 x 2.06-inch I-Joist	17.9	16.2	14.0
2x12 hem-fir #2	20.3	17.5	14.3
2x12 spruce-pine-fir #2	20.6	17.8	14.5
2x12 Douglas fir #2	20.8	18.0	14.7
11.9 x 2.06-inch I-joist	21.4	19.4	16.8

(A) **JOIST-FLOOR SYSTEMS**

FRAMED WALL

SUBFLOORING
SEE 48

RIM JOIST

FLOOR JOIST

P.T. MUDSILL

FOUNDATION WALL
SEE 7

NOTE
IN EARTHQUAKE OR
HURRICANE ZONES,
SECURE FLOOR JOISTS
TO MUDSILL WITH
FRAMING ANCHORS.
FOR JOIST SPAN TABLE
SEE 32.

(A) JOISTS ON MUDSILL
Perpendicular to Wall

FRAMED WALL

SUBFLOORING
SEE 48

RIM JOIST

COMMON JOIST

BLOCKING BETWEEN RIM
JOIST & FIRST COMMON
JOIST ADDS SUPPORT FOR
BEARING WALL ABOVE AND
RESISTS ROTATION OF RIM
JOIST.

P.T. MUDSILL

FOUNDATION WALL
SEE 7

(B) JOISTS ON MUDSILL
Parallel to Wall

FRAMED WALL

P.T. MUDSILL

SUBFLOORING
SEE 48

JOIST

METAL JOIST HANGER
AT EACH JOIST OR
SUPPORT WITH LEDGER
OR FRAMED WALL

ENGINEERED P.T. HEADER
BOLTED TO WALL OR
ATTACHED WITH POWDER-
DRIVEN FASTENERS

FOUNDATION WALL
SEE 7

(C) JOISTS FLUSH WITH MUDSILL
Perpendicular to Wall with Ledger

FRAMED WALL

2X8 P.T. MUDSILL
FLUSH WITH INSIDE OF
FOUNDATION WALL

SUBFLOORING

FLOOR JOIST

TOP FLANGE JOIST
HANGER AT EACH
JOIST NAILED TO AND
SUPPORTED BY MUDSILL

PROTECT ENDS OF
JOISTS FROM MOISTURE
WITH 30-LB. FELT
OR OTHER MOISTURE
BARRIER

NOTE
WALL SHEATHING ALIGNED WITH FOUNDATION
WHICH IS NATURAL WITH THIS DETAIL BUT ALSO
POSSIBLE WITH ANY DETAIL ON THIS PAGE.

(D) JOISTS FLUSH WITH MUDSILL
Perpendicular to Wall with Hanger

- FRAMED WALL
- P.T. MUDSILL **SEE 12A**
- EXTERIOR OR INTERIOR INSULATION **SEE 15C**
- 30-LB. FELT MOISTURE BARRIER BETWEEN FOUNDATION WALL & UNTREATED WOOD
- SUBFLOORING
- JOISTS PERPENDICULAR TO WALL
- BLOCKING BETWEEN JOISTS
- ENGINEERED P.T. 4X LEDGER BOLTED TO FOUNDATION WALL
- CONCRETE-BLOCK OR CONCRETE FOUNDATION WALL

(A) JOISTS BELOW MUDSILL
Perpendicular to Wall/Ledger Support

- FRAMED WALL
- P.T. MUDSILL **SEE 12A**
- EXTERIOR OR INTERIOR INSULATION **SEE 15C**
- 30-LB. FELT MOISTURE BARRIER BETWEEN FOUNDATION WALL & UNTREATED WOOD
- SUBFLOORING
- JOISTS PERPENDICULAR TO WALL W/ FULL BEARING ON 2X4 TOP PLATE
- BLOCKING BETWEEN JOISTS
- FRAMED WALL **SEE 15D**
- CONCRETE-BLOCK OR CONCRETE FOUNDATION WALL

(B) JOISTS BELOW MUDSILL
Perpendicular to Wall/Framed Wall Support

- FRAMED WALL
- P.T. MUDSILL **SEE 12A**
- EXTERIOR OR INTERIOR INSULATION **SEE 15C**
- 30-LB. FELT MOISTURE BARRIER BETWEEN FOUNDATION WALL & UNTREATED WOOD
- SUBFLOORING
- JOIST W/ FULL BEARING ON 2X4 SILL
- BLOCKING BETWEEN JOISTS
- P.T. 2X4 SILL W/ 1/2-IN. ANCHOR BOLTS AT 6 FT O.C.

NOTE
FOR DETAIL W/ JOISTS PARALLEL TO WALL **SEE 33B.**

- CONCRETE-BLOCK OR CONCRETE FOUNDATION WALL

(C) JOISTS BELOW MUDSILL
Perpendicular to Wall/Stepped Wall Support

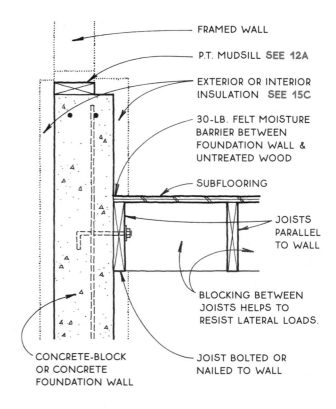

- FRAMED WALL
- P.T. MUDSILL **SEE 12A**
- EXTERIOR OR INTERIOR INSULATION **SEE 15C**
- 30-LB. FELT MOISTURE BARRIER BETWEEN FOUNDATION WALL & UNTREATED WOOD
- SUBFLOORING
- JOISTS PARALLEL TO WALL
- BLOCKING BETWEEN JOISTS HELPS TO RESIST LATERAL LOADS.
- JOIST BOLTED OR NAILED TO WALL
- CONCRETE-BLOCK OR CONCRETE FOUNDATION WALL

(D) JOISTS BELOW MUDSILL
Parallel to Wall/All Support Systems

Nailed through Joist

THE SIMPLEST BUT THE WEAKEST
METHOD IS RECOMMENDED ONLY
FOR BLOCKING.

Metal Joist Hanger

THIS IS THE STRONGEST
OF THE STANDARD
METHODS. EACH
APPROVED HANGER IS
RATED IN POUNDS.

NAIL BLOCKING TO
MAIN JOIST.

Nailed with Blocking

IN THIS FAIRLY STRONG &
SIMPLE JOINT, NAILS AT RIGHT
ANGLES EFFECTIVELY LOCK
PERPENDICULAR JOISTS IN
PLACE. IT IS RECOMMENDED
ONLY FOR SHORT JOISTS.

Doubled Hanger

DOUBLED HANGERS ARE SIZED
TO HOLD TWO PIECES OF
DIMENSION LUMBER.

NOTES

FOR METAL HANGERS, USE COMMON (NOT BOX)
NAILS. HANGER MANUFACTURERS SPECIFY NAIL
SIZE FOR EACH HANGER TYPE.

USE CONSTRUCTION ADHESIVE AT METAL JOIST
HANGERS TO REDUCE FLOOR SQUEAKING.

FOR FLOOR OPENINGS SEE 38B.

Blocked Corner

DOUBLED JOIST MAKES A
STRONG OUTSIDE CORNER FOR
CANTILEVERS SEE 39A AND
DECKS SEE 52

A JOIST/JOIST CONNECTIONS
Nailed through Joist

NOTE
SCAB MUST BE LONG ENOUGH TO QUALIFY
SPLICE AS A SINGLE JOIST SO THAT ADEQUATE
BEARING ON BEAM IS ACHIEVED. VERIFY WITH
LOCAL CODES.

BLOCKING
BETWEEN
JOISTS AS
REQUIRED

JOISTS

BLOCKING
BETWEEN
JOISTS AS
REQUIRED

SCAB
NAILED TO
SIDE OF
JOISTS

JOISTS

Lapped Joists

THIS COMMON JOINT REQUIRES SHIFTING
THE SUBFLOOR LAYOUT 1½ IN. ON
OPPOSITE SIDES OF THE BEAM TO ALLOW
THE SUBFLOOR TO BEAR ON THE JOISTS.

Spliced Joists

BUTT JOISTS TO MAINTAIN
SAME SPACING FOR NAILING
THE SUBFLOOR ON EACH SIDE
OF THE BEAM.

NOTE
LAPPED JOISTS & SPLICED JOISTS ARE COMMONLY USED OVER A CRAWL SPACE OR OTHER LOCATION
WHERE HEAD CLEARANCE BELOW THE BEAM IS NOT REQUIRED.

Ⓐ JOIST/WOOD BEAM CONNECTIONS
Beam below Joists

JOISTS

BEAM

Joist Hangers

ALIGN JOISTS ON EACH SIDE
OF BEAM TO MAINTAIN SAME
SPACING FOR SUBFLOOR
NAILING.

Joists on Ledger

A 2X2 OR 2X4 LEDGER NAILED TO THE
BEAM SUPPORTS THE JOISTS. TOENAIL
THE JOISTS TO THE BEAM OR BLOCK
BETWEEN JOISTS. NOTCH JOISTS TO
¼ OF DEPTH IF REQUIRED TO FIT OVER
THE LEDGER.

NOTE
JOIST HANGERS & JOISTS ON LEDGER ARE USED WHERE MAXIMUM HEAD CLEARANCE IS REQUIRED BELOW THE
FLOOR. THEY WORK BEST IF THE JOISTS & BEAM ARE OF SIMILAR SPECIES & MOISTURE CONTENT SO THAT ONE
DOES NOT SHRINK MORE THAN THE OTHER.

Ⓑ JOIST/WOOD BEAM CONNECTIONS
Beam Flush with Joists

2X2 WOOD STRAPS NAILED TO JOISTS OVER STEEL BEAM MAINTAIN JOIST ALIGNMENT.

JOIST

PROVIDE SPACE BETWEEN STRAP & BEAM TO ALLOW FOR JOIST SHRINKAGE.

NAILING PLATES BOLTED TO LOWER BEAM FLANGE

STEEL BEAM

Joists Bearing on Steel Flange

BLOCKING BETWEEN JOISTS AS REQUIRED

2X NAILING PLATE BOLTED TO UPPER BEAM FLANGE

STEEL BEAM

SPLICED JOISTS **SEE 36A**

BLOCKING BETWEEN JOISTS AS REQUIRED

2X NAILING PLATE BOLTED TO UPPER BEAM FLANGE

STEEL BEAM

LAPPED JOISTS **SEE 36A**

Joists on Nailing Plate

2X NAILING PLATE BOLTED TO UPPER BEAM FLANGE

JOISTS

NOTE ALLOWABLE HANGER LOADS MAY BE REDUCED DUE TO NAILING LIMITATIONS.

TOP FLANGE METAL HANGERS NAILED TO NAILING PLATE

STEEL BEAM

Joists Hung from Nailing Plate

NOTE USE ONLY IN CONDITIONS WITHOUT UPLIFT FORCES AND WHERE SCABS WILL NOT INTERFERE WITH CEILING.

1X BOARDS SCABBED TO UNDERSIDE OF JOISTS KEEP JOISTS ALIGNED & PREVENT LATERAL MOVEMENT OF STEEL BEAM.

Joists on Steel Beam

JOISTS

FACE MOUNT JOIST HANGERS ATTACHED TO NAILERS

NAILERS BOLTED TO BOTH SIDES OF WEB

Joists Hung from Double Nailer

NOTE THE DETAILS SHOWN IN **37A & B** MAY BE ADJUSTED FOR USE WITH OTHER TYPES OF JOISTS & GIRDERS DISCUSSED IN THE FOLLOWING SECTIONS.

(A) JOIST/STEEL BEAM CONNECTIONS
Beam Flush with Joists

(B) JOIST/STEEL BEAM CONNECTIONS
Beam below Joists

Block Bridging

SOLID BLOCKING FROM
SAME MATERIAL AS
JOISTS IS STAGGERED
FOR EASE OF NAILING.

Metal Bridging

METAL PIECES SHOULD
NOT TOUCH EACH OTHER.

Cross Bridging

^{5}/$_4$X3 OR ^{5}/$_4$X4 OR 2X2 OR
1X4 BOARDS ARE NAILED IN
A CROSS PATTERN BETWEEN
JOISTS. PIECES SHOULD NOT
TOUCH EACH OTHER.

NOTE
FOR DEEP JOISTS WITH LONG SPANS (OVER 10 FT.),
LOCAL CODES MAY REQUIRE BRIDGING TO PREVENT
ROTATION & TO DISTRIBUTE THE LOADING.

Ⓐ BRIDGING

JOISTS

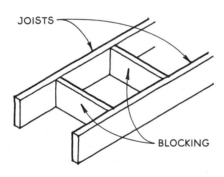

BLOCKING

DOUBLE HEADER JOISTS AT
ENDS OF OPENINGS

Small Openings

OPENINGS THAT FIT BETWEEN TWO
JOISTS FOR LAUNDRY CHUTES OR
HEATING DUCTS ARE SIMPLY MADE
BY NAILING BLOCKING BETWEEN
THE JOISTS.

PERPENDICULAR JOIST
CONNECTIONS
SEE 35

DOUBLE
TRIMMER
JOISTS AT
SIDES OF
OPENING

Large Openings

IN OPENINGS THAT ARE WIDER THAN THE JOIST SPACING, SUCH AS FOR
THE STAIRWAYS & CHIMNEYS, THE FLOOR STRUCTURE AROUND THE OPENING
MUST BE STRENGTHENED. FOR OPENINGS UP TO THREE JOIST SPACES WIDE,
DOUBLE THE JOISTS AT THE SIDES & ENDS OF THE OPENING MAY SUFFICE.
WIDER OPENINGS SHOULD BE ENGINEERED.

Ⓑ OPENINGS IN JOIST-FLOOR SYSTEM

DOUBLE SIDE JOISTS FOR
TWICE THE DISTANCE OF
THE CANTILEVER.

2X

EXTEND CANTILEVERED
JOISTS TWICE AS FAR INTO
THE BUILDING AS THE
LENGTH OF THE CANTILEVER.

CANTILEVERED
WALLS SEE 73C

2X

RIM BLOCKING
MAY BE SET 1-IN. OUT
FROM MUDSILL TO PROVIDE
SOFFIT NAILING.

DOUBLE JOISTS
AT SIDES OF
CANTILEVER.

CORNER JOINT
SEE 35

MUDSILL (FIRST-FLOOR
FRAMING) OR DOUBLE
TOP PLATE (UPPER-FLOOR
FRAMING) SUPPORTS
CANTILEVERED JOISTS.

JOIST/JOIST
CONNECTIONS
SEE 35

A **FLOOR CANTILEVERS**
Parallel & Perpendicular to Joist System

JOIST/ROOF
CONNECTIONS
(IF ATTIC FLOOR)
SEE 132

JOIST/INTERIOR-WALL
CONNECTIONS:
LOAD-BEARING WALLS
SEE 42A & B

PARTITION WALLS
SEE 42C & D

JOIST/EXTERIOR-
WALL CONNECTIONS
SEE 40, 41A & B

Joist floor-system connections to exterior walls
are straightforward. The wall framing may be one of
two types.

Platform framing—Platform framing, the most
common system in use today, takes advantage of standard materials and framing methods. The ground floor
and all upper floors can be constructed using the same
system.

Balloon framing—Balloon framing is rarely used
because it is harder to erect and requires very long
studs. It may be the system of choice, however, if the
floor structure must work with the walls to resist lateral
roof loads or if extra care is required to make the insulation and vapor barrier continuous from floor to floor.
(see 41A, B)

Joist floor-system connections to interior walls
depend on whether the walls are load-bearing walls or
partition walls. The other factor to consider is whether
edge nailing is required for the ceiling.

B **JOIST/STUD-WALL CONNECTIONS**

EXTERIOR FINISH

STUD WALL

INTERIOR FINISH

FINISH FLOOR

SUBFLOOR

RIM JOIST
(OR RIM BLOCKING)

INSULATION
& VAPOR BARRIER
SEE 63A & B

FLOOR JOIST

STUD
WALL

FINISH CEILING

(A) JOISTS AT EXTERIOR WALL
Joists Perpendicular to Wall

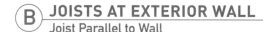

EXTERIOR FINISH

STUD WALL

INTERIOR FINISH

FINISH FLOOR

SUBFLOOR

RIM JOIST

INSULATION
& VAPOR BARRIER
SEE 63A & B

FLOOR JOIST

2X4 BLOCKING
FOR NAILING
CEILING

STUD
WALL

FINISH CEILING

(B) JOISTS AT EXTERIOR WALL
Joist Parallel to Wall

EXTERIOR FINISH

STUD WALL

INTERIOR FINISH

FINISH FLOOR

SUBFLOOR

RIM JOIST

FLOOR JOIST

BLOCKING AT SAME
SPACING AS JOISTS
ADDS STRUCTURAL
SUPPORT & PROVIDES
CEILING NAILING.

INSULATION
& VAPOR BARRIER
SEE 63A & B

STUD
WALL

FINISH CEILING

(C) JOISTS AT EXTERIOR WALL
Joists Parallel to Wall with Blocking

EXTERIOR FINISH

STUD WALL

INTERIOR FINISH

FINISH FLOOR

SUBFLOOR

RIM JOIST

RIGID INSULATION

FLOOR JOIST

SECOND RIM JOIST
ADDS STRUCTURAL
SUPPORT & PROVIDES
CEILING NAILING.

STUD
WALL

FINISH CEILING

(D) JOISTS AT EXTERIOR WALL
Doubled Rim Joists Parallel to Wall

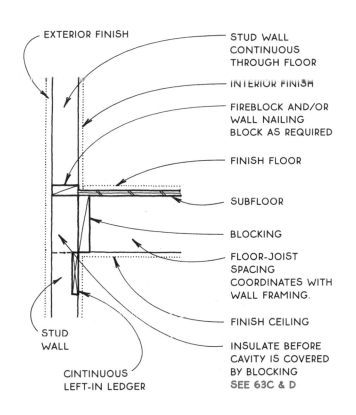

EXTERIOR FINISH

STUD WALL CONTINUOUS THROUGH FLOOR

INTERIOR FINISH

FIREBLOCK AND/OR WALL NAILING BLOCK AS REQUIRED

FINISH FLOOR

SUBFLOOR

BLOCKING

FLOOR-JOIST SPACING COORDINATES WITH WALL FRAMING.

FINISH CEILING

INSULATE BEFORE CAVITY IS COVERED BY BLOCKING SEE 63C & D

STUD WALL

CINTINUOUS LEFT-IN LEDGER

(A) JOISTS AT BALLOON-FRAMED WALL
Joists Perpendicular to Wall

EXTERIOR FINISH

STUD WALL CONTINUOUS THROUGH FLOOR

INTERIOR FINISH

FIREBLOCK AND/OR WALL NAILING BLOCK AS REQUIRED

FINISH FLOOR

SUBFLOOR

JOIST SCREWED TO STUDS

INSULATION SEE 63C & D

FINISH CEILING

VAPOR BARRIER BEHIND JOIST SEE 63C & D

(B) JOISTS AT BALLOON-FRAMED WALL
Joists Parallel to Wall

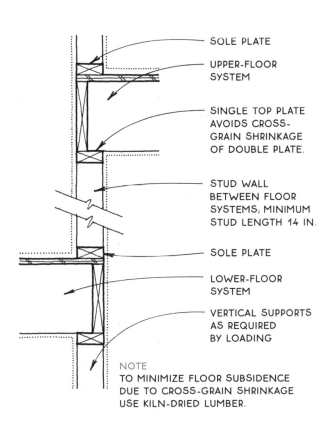

SOLE PLATE

UPPER-FLOOR SYSTEM

SINGLE TOP PLATE AVOIDS CROSS-GRAIN SHRINKAGE OF DOUBLE PLATE.

STUD WALL BETWEEN FLOOR SYSTEMS; MINIMUM STUD LENGTH 14 IN.

SOLE PLATE

LOWER-FLOOR SYSTEM

VERTICAL SUPPORTS AS REQUIRED BY LOADING

NOTE
TO MINIMIZE FLOOR SUBSIDENCE DUE TO CROSS-GRAIN SHRINKAGE USE KILN-DRIED LUMBER.

(C) LEVEL CHANGE
Platform Framing

FINISH FLOOR

UPPER-FLOOR SYSTEM

FIREBLOCK AND/OR WALL NAILING BLOCK AS REQUIRED

LET-IN LEDGER FOR JOIST BEARING

CONTINUOUS STUDS

LOWER-FLOOR SYSTEM

INTERIOR FINISH

NOTE
STUD LAYOUT MUST BE OFFSET 1½ IN. FROM JOIST LAYOUT. CONTINUOUS STUDS AVOID THE CROSS-GRAIN SHRINKING OF PLATES IN DETAIL SEE 41C.

(D) LEVEL CHANGE
Balloon Framing

Interior walls are either bearings walls, which carry loads from the roof or from floors above, or partition walls, which do not support any loads from above. Both types of wall can be fastened directly to the subfloor, but bearing walls must have their loads distributed to or through the floor system with extra framing. Both types of wall may require extra framing where they attach to floor systems, but the framing in bearing walls will generally be more substantial.

BEARING STUD WALL

FINISH FLOOR

SUBFLOOR

JOIST

BLOCKING AT 16 IN. OR 24 IN. O.C. ALIGNED WITH STUDS ABOVE & BELOW.

NOTE
BLOCKING CAN BE ELIMINATED IF BEARING WALL ALIGNS WITH JOIST.

BEARING STUD WALL (OR BEAM) BELOW; STUDS ALIGNED WITH BLOCKING & STUDS ABOVE.

A JOISTS AT BEARING WALL
Joists Parallel to Wall

BEARING STUD WALL; STUDS ALIGNED WITH JOISTS & STUDS BELOW

FINISH FLOOR

SUBFLOOR

JOIST

BLOCK IF JOIST IS SPLICED OVER BEARING WALL
SEE 36A

BEARING STUD WALL (OR BEAM) BELOW; STUDS ALIGNED WITH JOISTS (BEARING WALL IS NOT REQUIRED IF JOISTS ARE ENGINEERED TO SUPPORT TOP BEARING WALL).

B JOISTS AT BEARING WALL
Joists Perpendicular to Wall

FINISH FLOOR

SUBFLOOR

JOIST

CEILING

BLOCKING AT 16 IN. OR 24 IN. O.C. BETWEEN JOISTS

PARTITION WALL

FINISH FLOOR

SUBFLOOR

DOUBLE JOISTS BELOW PARTITION WALL

CEILING

C JOISTS AT PARTITION WALL
Joists Parallel to Wall

FINISH FLOOR

SUBFLOOR

JOIST

BLOCKING

OVERSIZED 2X BLOCKING PROVIDES CONTINUOUS NAILING FOR CEILING.

PARTITION WALL

FINISH FLOOR

SUBFLOOR

SEPARATED DOUBLE JOISTS ALLOW WIRING & PLUMBING TO ENTER WALL FROM BELOW.

CEILING

D JOISTS AT PARTITION WALL
Alternative Details

Wood I-joists are designed to work efficiently, with most of the wood located at the top and bottom of the joist where the bending stresses are greatest. Called flanges, the top and bottom are generally made of laminated or solid wood; the slender central part of the joist, the web, is made of plywood or OSB. I-joists are straighter and more precise than dimension lumber and therefore make a flatter, quieter floor. Their spanning capacity is only slightly greater than that of dimension lumber, but because they can be manufactured much deeper and longer than lumber joists (up to 30 in. deep and 60 ft. long), they are the floor-framing system of choice when long spans are required.

Wood I-joists are designed to be part of a system composed of engineered beams, joists, and sheathing. Laminated strand lumber (LSL) rim joists and laminated veneer lumber (LVL) beams are sized to integrate with the joists. In cases of extreme loading, composite beams may be substituted for I-joists. The system is completed with span-rated tongue-and-groove sheathing nailed to the joists and reinforced with construction adhesive.

BOTTOM FLANGE

TOP FLANGE

WEB

THICKNESS OF BACKER BLOCKS & WEB STIFFENERS SEE 43B

NOTE
ROUND OR RECTANGULAR HOLES FOR UTILITIES MAY BE CUT IN WEB. THE FARTHER FROM THE SUPPORT, THE LARGER THE HOLE CAN BE. 1¹/₂-IN.-DIAMETER ROUND HOLES MAY BE CUT ALMOST ANYWHERE IN THE WEB. VERIFY HOLE SIZE AND LOCATION WITH MANUFACTURER.

WIDTHS:
1¹/₂ IN., 2 IN., 3¹/₂ IN.

Ⓐ WOOD I-JOISTS

Because the web is thin, I-joists are about 50% lighter than lumber joists. But the thin web also means I-joists do not have as much strength to resist vertical crushing forces. For this reason, the web often must be reinforced with plywood or OSB web stiffeners. Nailed to the web, these stiffeners occur at connectors for deep joists, and in other conditions as required by manufacturers' specifications and local codes. When vertical loads are extreme, I-joists can be reinforced by attaching sections of 2x framing lumber called squash blocks to their sides or by fastening LSL blocking panels between them (see 44C).

When other framing members need to be attached to the side of an I-joist, backer blocks are added to the webs of the I-joists. Like web stiffeners, backer blocks are made of plywood or OSB, but their primary purpose is to provide a planar, thick nailing surface rather than to resist vertical loads (see 44D).

Like dimension lumber, wood I-joists are easily cut and joined on site. The production and fastening of backer blocks, web stiffeners, and so forth for I-joist systems can offset the construction time gained by not having to sort for defects.

WOOD BEAM OR JOIST

METAL I-JOIST HANGER

I-JOIST

I-Joist/Wood

PLYWOOD OR OSB BACKER BLOCK BOTH SIDES FLUSH WITH FLANGE

METAL I-JOIST HANGER DESIGNED TO SUPPORT BOTTOM & TOP CHORD LATERALLY

I-Joist/I-Joist

Ⓑ WOOD I-JOIST CONNECTIONS

LAMINATED STRAND
LUMBER (LSL) RIM
JOIST

SUBFLOORING

P.T. MUDSILL OR TOP
PLATE OF STUD WALL

WOOD
I-JOIST

NOTE
LSL RIM JOISTS ARE SIZED TO CORRESPOND
WITH THE DEPTH OF WOOD I-JOISTS.
DO NOT USE SAWN-LUMBER RIM.

(A) WOOD I-JOISTS AT RIM JOIST
Joists on Mudsill or Top Plate

P.T. MUDSILL

SUBFLOORING

WOOD
I-JOIST

JOIST
HANGER

NOTE
VERIFY BRIDGING REQUIREMENT
FOR TALL JOISTS.

(B) WOOD I-JOISTS AT RIM JOIST
Joists Flush with Mudsill

LSL BLOCKING
PANEL BETWEEN
I-JOISTS FOR
HEAVY LOADS

BEARING WALL

SUBFLOORING

WOOD I-JOISTS

BEARING WALL
BELOW

2X SQUASH BLOCKS AT
BOTH SIDES OF I-JOIST
FOR HEAVY LOADS

(C) WOOD I-JOISTS FOR LOADS
Squash Blocks & Blocking Panels

WOOD I-JOIST
BLOCKING BETWEEN
CUT I-JOISTS

SUBFLOORING

BEARING
WALL BELOW

BACKER BLOCKS ON BOTH
SIDES OF I-JOIST AT LOCATIONS
WHERE CONNECTIONS (SUCH AS
HANGERS) ARE MADE TO I-JOIST

(D) WOOD I-JOIST CONNECTIONS
Blocking & Backer Blocks

Top Chord Bearing

Bottom Chord Bearing

Four-by-two wood floor trusses are made up of small members (usually 2x4s) that are connected so that they act like a single large member. The parallel top and bottom chords and the webs are made of lumber held together at the intersections with toothed metal plates.

The open web allows for utilities to run through the floor without altering the truss. Round ducts from 5 in. to 16 in. in diameter can be accommodated, depending on the depth of the truss. Truss depths vary from 10 in. to 24 in., with spans up to about 30 ft. Like I-joists, floor trusses are practical for long spans and simple plans, but difficult for complicated buildings.

Floor trusses are custom manufactured for each job, and cannot be altered at the site. Bearing walls, floor openings, and other departures from the simple span should always be engineered by the manufacturer.

Ⓐ WOOD FLOOR TRUSSES

Top Chord Bearing

Bottom Chord Bearing

Wood top and bottom chords are linked with steel tubing webs in the composite truss. The tubing is pressed flat at the ends and connected to the wood chords with a metal pin. Unlike wood trusses with metal plates (see 45A above), the webs of the composite truss are entirely free to rotate (on the pins) and therefore allow the truss to return to its original shape when the load is removed.

Composite trusses are generally more heavy duty than their all-wood cousins illustrated in 45A above. The largest composite trusses are capable of spanning over 100 ft. They are made with double 2x chords, which sandwich the webs. The lightest-duty composite trusses are made with single 2x4 chords oriented flat and dadoed to receive the webs.

Like wood floor trusses, composite trusses easily accommodate ducts and other utilities, which can be run through the open webs without altering the truss. Like all trusses, composite trusses are most practical for simple plans with long spans. Once engineered and installed, they are difficult to alter.

Ⓑ COMPOSITE FLOOR TRUSSES

EXPOSED CEILING
DECKING CONNECTIONS
SEE 47C & D

VISUAL GRADES OF DRIED
T&G DECKING USED FOR
EXPOSED CEILINGS
SEE 49A

COMBINATION
SUBFLOOR-UNDERLAYMENT
SEE 48

UTILITY-GRADE 2X T&G
DECKING AS SUBFLOOR
SEE 49A

CONNECTIONS TO
FOUNDATION WALLS
SEE 47A & B

GIRDER/POST CONNECTIONS
SEE 31

Girder systems may be designed with either dimension or laminated lumber. They are most common in the Northwest, where dimension timber is plentiful. Girder floor systems are similar to joist floor systems except that girders, which are wider than joists, can carry a greater load for a given span and therefore can be spaced at wider intervals than joists. Girders are typically placed on 48-in. centers, so long-spanning subfloor materials such as 2-in. T&G decking or 1⅛-in. combination subfloor-underlayment are required (see 48).

When used over crawl spaces, girders may be supported directly on posts. Over a basement, a girder system may be supported on posts or may bear on a wall or a beam like a joist system. At upper floor levels, girder systems are often used in conjunction with an

exposed T&G decking ceiling. These exposed ceilings can make wiring, plumbing, and ductwork difficult.

This table assumes a 40-psf live load, a 10-psf dead load, and a deflection of L/360. The table is for estimating purposes only. No. 2 Douglas-fir is most prevalent in regions where girder systems are most frequently used.

GIRDER SPANS	
Size, species, grade, and spacing	Span (ft.)
4 x 6 Douglas-fir #2 @48 in. o.c.	8.6
4 x 8 Douglas-fir #2 @48 in. o.c.	11.3
4 x 10 Douglas-fir #2 @48 in. o.c.	14.4
4 x 12 Douglas-fir #2 @48 in. o.c.	17.6

Ⓐ GIRDER-FLOOR SYSTEMS

FRAMED WALL

UNDERLAYMENT & FINISH FLOOR SEE 48

4-MIL VAPOR BARRIER SEE 61

2X DECKING SPANS 4 FT.

4X GIRDER WITH FUTURE BATT INSULATION SEE 61

RIM JOIST

P.T. MUDSILL

FOUNDATION WALL SEE 7

A GIRDERS ON MUDSILL
Girders Perpendicular to Wall

FRAMED WALL

UNDERLAYMENT & FINISH FLOOR SEE 48

4-MIL VAPOR BARRIER SEE 61

2X DECKING SPANS 4 FT.

4X GIRDER WITH FUTURE BATT INSULATION SEE 61

½-IN. AIR SPACE OR 30-LB. FELT ATTACHED TO END OF GIRDER

P.T. 4X4 POST BEARING ON FOOTING

P.T. MUDSILL

FOUNDATION WALL SEE 7

B GIRDERS FLUSH WITH MUDSILL
Girders Perpendicular to Wall

FRAMED WALL

UNDERLAYMENT & FINISH FLOOR SEE 48

2X T&G DECKING EXPOSED BELOW FOR CEILING

EXPOSED OR WRAPPED GIRDER

BLOCKING APPLIED BETWEEN AND TO SIDES OF GIRDERS SUPPORTS WALL FINISH.

FILL SPACE WITH INSULATION SEE 63

FINISH WALL

NOTE

2X T&G DECKING MAY BE SANDED TO MAKE FINISH FLOOR, BUT THIS IS ADVISABLE ONLY WITH VERY DRY DECKING. DUST FILTRATION FROM UPPER TO LOWER FLOOR & SOUND TRANSMISSION BETWEEN FLOORS MAY OCCUR WITH THIS DETAIL.

C GIRDERS WITH EXPOSED DECKING
2nd Floor: Girders Perpendicular to Wall

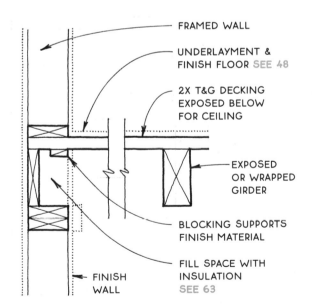

FRAMED WALL

UNDERLAYMENT & FINISH FLOOR SEE 48

2X T&G DECKING EXPOSED BELOW FOR CEILING

EXPOSED OR WRAPPED GIRDER

BLOCKING SUPPORTS FINISH MATERIAL

FILL SPACE WITH INSULATION SEE 63

FINISH WALL

NOTE

DECKING DOES NOT PROVIDE STRUCTURAL DIAPHRAGM REQUIRED AT UPPER FLOORS. USE PLYWOOD UNDERLAYMENT OR OTHER METHOD TO TRANSFER LATERAL LOADS.

D GIRDERS WITH EXPOSED DECKING
2nd Floor: Girders Parallel to Wall

Subflooring—Subflooring is the structural skin of a floor system. It spans between the joists and acts as a diaphragm to transfer horizontal loads to the walls of a structure. For joist systems, subflooring is typically tongue-and-groove (T&G) plywood, non-veneered panels such as oriented strand board (OSB) or T&G plywood combination subfloor/underlayment, which is a grade of T&G plywood that is plugged and sanded to a smooth underlayment-grade surface. In girder systems, the subflooring is typically T&G decking (see 49A).

Underlayment—Underlayment is not structural but provides a smooth surface necessary for some finish floors. It can also be used to fur up floors to match an adjacent finish floor of a different thickness. Underlayment is typically plywood, particleboard, or hardboard.

Spacing and nailing—Most plywood manufacturers specify a space of ⅛ in. between the edges of panels to allow for expansion. Panels that are sized ⅛ in. smaller in each direction are available to allow a space without compromising the 4-ft. by 8-ft. module. The procedure may be successfully avoided in dry climates. Check with local contractors for accepted local practice.

A common rule of thumb is to nail panels 6 in. o.c. at edges and 12 in. o.c. in the panel field. Glues and panel adhesives can minimize squeaks and reduce the nailing requirements for panel floor systems. Verify attachment methods with the specifications of the manufacturer. A typical plywood grade stamp is shown below.

SURFACE GRAIN OF PLYWOOD SUBFLOOR PANELS IS PERPENDICULAR TO SUPPORTS

STAGGER END JOINTS OF ALL SUBFLOOR PANELS.

OFFSET JOINTS OF SUBFLOOR & UNDERLAYMENT PANELS.

JOIST OR GIRDER

EDGE BLOCKING IS REQUIRED IF SUBFLOOR PANELS ARE NOT T&G & UNDERLAYMENT IS NOT USED.

SUBFLOORING SPANS		
Subfloor type	Thickness	Maximum span
Plywood sheathing or combination subfloor underlayment	½ in. to ⅝ in.	16 in.
	⅝ in. to ¾ in.	20 in.
	¾ in. to ⅞ in.	24 in.
	1⅛ in.	48 in.
Non-venneered panels: OSB, waferboard, particleboard	⅝ in.	16 in.
	¾ in.	24 in.

PANEL GRADE

APA—THE ENGINEERED WOOD ASSOCIATION

SPAN RATING ROOF / FLOOR

PANEL IS ⅛ IN. NARROWER & SHORTER THAN FULL SIZE

APA
RATED SHEATHING
40/20   19/32 INCH
SIZED FOR SPACING
EXTERIOR
000
PS 1-83 C-C
NER-0A397 PRP-108

THICKNESS

EXPOSURE RATING

MILL NUMBER

TECHNICAL INFORMATION

The values in this table are based on information from the APA—The Engineered Wood Association and the International Building Code (IBC). Values are for panels that are continuous over two or more spans, with the long dimension of the panel perpendicular to supports. Verify span with panel rating.

Ⓐ SUBFLOORING & UNDERLAYMENT
Plywood & Non-Veneered Panels

STAGGER JOINTS OVER GIRDERS.

GIRDER

NOTE
GLUE DECKING TO GIRDERS WITH CONSTRUCTION ADHESIVE TO MINIMIZE FLOOR SQUEAK. REFER TO WESTERN WOOD PRODUCTS USE BOOK FOR SPAN INFORMATION.

Typical T&G Decking Sections

2X6 V-JOINT IS MOST COMMONLY USED ON UPPER FLOORS TO MAKE EXPOSED CEILINGS BELOW. MOST SPECIES WILL SPAN 4 FT.

2X8 UTILITY IS USED PRIMARILY AS SUBFLOOR OVER CRAWL SPACES OR BASEMENTS & IS OFTEN INSTALLED GREEN. IT WILL SPAN 4 FT. IN MOST FLOOR SITUATIONS.

3X AND 4X LAMINATED IS USED MOSTLY AT ROOFS TO MAKE EXPOSED CEILINGS BELOW, BUT ALSO AS FLOORING. DECKING IS END MATCHED FOR RANDOM-LENGTH APPLICATION & IS AVAILABLE PREFINISHED IN 3X6, 3X8, 4X6, & 4X8 SIZES. IT SPANS UP TO 14 FT. FOR RESIDENTIAL FLOOR LOADS.

(A) SUBFLOORING
T&G Decking

CONCRETE SUBFLOOR/ COMMON JOIST
SEE 50D

CONCRETE SUBFLOOR/ FOUNDATION
SEE 50A, B & C

CONCRETE SUBFLOOR/HEADER JOIST
SEE 51A & B

NOTE:
FOR THIN-MASS FLOORS
SEE 51C & D

A small part of the subfloor may need to be concrete to support tiles or for a passive-solar mass floor at a south edge. The structure under the concrete must be lowered in order to accommodate the extra thickness of the concrete, typically 2¼ in. to 3 in. Use plywood that is rated to carry the load of wet concrete, usually ¾ in. (min.).

In the case of a tiled floor, the complications of adjusting the structure to accommodate a thick concrete subfloor may be avoided by using a ⁷⁄₁₆ in. thick glass-fiber–reinforced cement board over the surface of the typical wood subfloor. Check with the tile manufacturer for recommendations.

(A) SUBFLOORING
Concrete

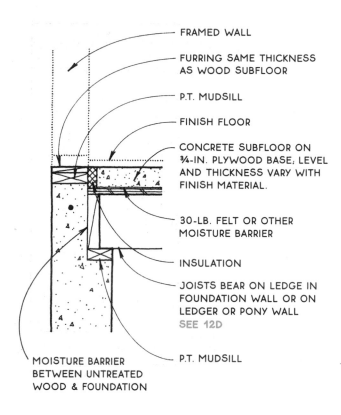

FRAMED WALL

FURRING SAME THICKNESS AS WOOD SUBFLOOR

P.T. MUDSILL

FINISH FLOOR

CONCRETE SUBFLOOR ON ¾-IN. PLYWOOD BASE; LEVEL AND THICKNESS VARY WITH FINISH MATERIAL.

30-LB. FELT OR OTHER MOISTURE BARRIER

INSULATION

JOISTS BEAR ON LEDGE IN FOUNDATION WALL OR ON LEDGER OR PONY WALL SEE 12D

P.T. MUDSILL

MOISTURE BARRIER BETWEEN UNTREATED WOOD & FOUNDATION

Ⓐ CONCRETE SUBFLOOR AT EXTERIOR
Full-Depth Joists below Mudsill

2X6 FRAMED WALL

FURRING SAME THICKNESS AS WOOD SUBFLOOR

DOUBLE RIM JOISTS

FINISH FLOOR

CONCRETE SUBFLOOR ON ¾-IN. PLYWOOD BASE; LEVEL AND THICKNESS VARY WITH FINISH MATERIAL.

30-LB. FELT OR OTHER MOISTURE BARRIER

JOISTS HUNG FROM P.T. HEADER JOIST RIPPED TO BEAR ON FOUNDATION WALL.

SPACER BLOCKS AT 16 IN. O.C.

MOISTURE BARRIER BETWEEN UNTREATED JOISTS & FOUNDATION

INSULATION

P.T. MUDSILL

NOTE:
FOR 2X4 WALL, PLACE INSULATION BETWEEN DOUBLE RIM JOIST & P.T. HEADER JOIST.

Ⓑ CONCRETE SUBFLOOR AT EXTERIOR
Full-Depth Joists/Alternative

2X6 FRAMED WALL

RIM JOIST

FURRING SAME THICKNESS AS WOOD SUBFLOOR

FURRING

FINISH FLOOR

CONCRETE SUBFLOOR ON ¾-IN. PLYWOOD BASE; LEVEL AND THICKNESS VARY WITH FINISH MATERIAL.

30-LB. FELT OR OTHER MOISTURE BARRIER

JOISTS CUT OR SIZED DOWN TO ACCOMMODATE DEPTH OF CONCRETE SUBFLOOR

P.T. MUDSILL

INSULATION

NOTE
DECREASE SPAN AND/OR SPACING OF SIZED-DOWN JOISTS SUPPORTING CONCRETE.

Ⓒ CONCRETE SUBFLOOR AT EXTERIOR
Cut-Down Joists on Mudsill

NOTE
FOR CONDITION AT EXTERIOR WALL SEE 50A & B.

NOTE
FOR CONDITION AT EXTERIOR WALL SEE 50C.

FINISH FLOOR

PLYWOOD OR OTHER WOOD SUBFLOOR

TYPICAL JOISTS

CONCRETE SUBFLOOR ON ¾-IN. PLYWOOD BASE

30-LB. FELT OR OTHER MOISTURE BARRIER

LOWERED JOISTS MAY NEED TO BE SIZED DEEPER THAN TYPICAL FULL-DEPTH JOIST TO SUPPORT CONCRETE SUBFLOOR.

CUT OR SIZED-DOWN JOIST, DECREASE SPAN AND/OR SPACING TO SUPPORT CONCRETE SUBFLOOR

Ⓓ CONCRETE SUBFLOOR AT INTERIOR
Edge Parallel to Joists/2 Details

NOTE

FOR CONDITION AT EXTERIOR WALL
SEE 50A OR B.

PLYWOOD OR OTHER
WOOD SUBFLOOR

FINISH
FLOOR

CONCRETE SUBFLOOR
ON ¾-IN. PLYWOOD
BASE

30-LB. FELT OR OTHER
MOISTURE BARRIER

JOIST ON JOIST HANGER

DOUBLE HEADER JOIST

SINGLE HEADER JOIST
NAILED TO DOUBLE
HEADER JOIST

VERTICAL SUPPORT
AS REQUIRED

JOIST ON
JOIST
HANGER

A CONCRETE SUBFLOOR AT INTERIOR
Edge Perpendicular to Joists

FINISH FLOOR

CONCRETE
SUBFLOOR ON ¾-IN.
PLYWOOD BASE

CUT-DOWN JOIST

VERTICAL SUPPORT
AS REQUIRED

FINISH FLOOR

CONCRETE
SUBFLOOR ON ¾-IN.
PLYWOOD BASE

30-LB. FELT OR OTHER
MOISTURE BARRIER

NOTCHED JOIST

BLOCKING

BEAM OR STUD-WALL
SUPPORT AS REQUIRED

B CONCRETE SUBFLOOR AT INTERIOR
Edge Perpendicular to Joists: Alternative Details

STUD WALL FRAMED
AFTER CONCRETE IS
FINISHED

DOUBLE 2X P.T. PLATE
SERVES AS SCREED

3-IN. CONCRETE
SUBFLOOR ON ¾-IN.
PLYWOOD BASE

30-LB. FELT OR OTHER
MOISTURE BARRIER

JOIST

P.T. MUDSILL (OR TOP
PLATE IF THIN-MASS
SUBFLOOR IS AT
UPPER STORY)

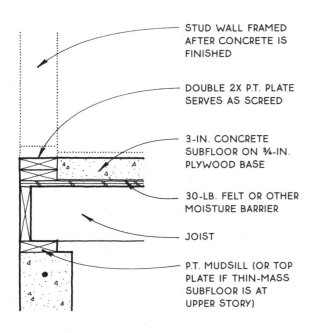

NOTE

THIS DETAIL IS USED TO PROVIDE MASS TO A LARGE
AREA OF FLOOR FOR SOLAR GAIN.

C THIN-MASS SUBFLOOR
At Exterior Wall

STUD WALL FRAMED
AFTER CONCRETE IS
FINISHED

DOUBLE 2X P.T. PLATE
SERVES AS SCREED &
ALLOWS UTILITIES TO
PASS THROUGH FLOOR
SYSTEM AT WALL.

3-IN. CONCRETE
SUBFLOOR ON ¾-IN.
PLYWOOD BASE

30-LB. FELT OR OTHER
MOISTURE BARRIER

JOIST

BLOCKING

STRUCTURE BELOW
AS REQUIRED

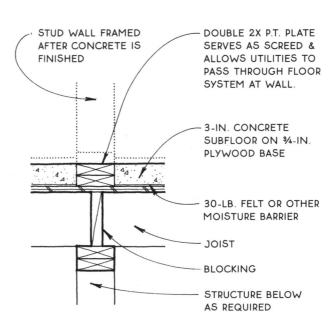

NOTE

IF THE CONCRETE IS TO BE EXPOSED, THE DOUBLE
PLATE MAY BE OMITTED FOR EASE OF TROWELING.
THE STUD WALL MAY THEN BE SHOT TO CONCRETE.
SEE 24C

D THIN-MASS SUBFLOOR
At Interior Wall

Porches and decks are traditional and useful additions to wood-frame structures. They provide a transition between indoors and out, allowing people to pause upon entering or leaving, and they extend the building to include the out-of-doors. Porch and deck floors must be constructed differently from interior floors in order to withstand the weather. The connection between porch and deck floors and the building itself is especially critical in keeping moisture out of the main structure. Because of constant exposure to the weather, this connection must be detailed in such a way that it can be repaired or replaced.

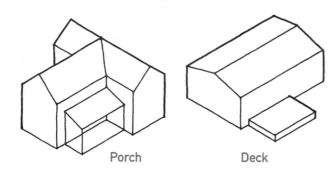

Porch   Deck

The floors of porches and decks can be grouped into two major types: those that are waterproof and thus act as a roof protecting the area below, and those that are open and allow water to pass through.

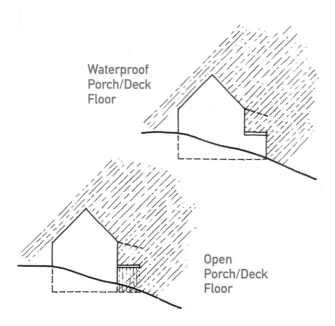

Waterproof Porch/Deck Floor

Open Porch/Deck Floor

Waterproof porch—A waterproof porch or deck floor can be treated like a flat roof. As shown in the drawing below, flashing (or the roofing material itself) must be tucked under the siding to catch water running down the side of the building, and the floor (roof) surface must be sloped away from the building (see 56A). The framing for waterproof decks over living spaces needs proper ventilation (see 205A).

EXTERIOR WALL
SIDING
FLASHING
WATERPROOF FLOOR
SLOPE
PORCH/DECK STRUCTURE

Open porch—In an open porch or deck floor, the parts that connect it to the main structure are exposed to the weather, yet need to penetrate the skin of the wall. This connection can be accomplished by keeping the porch/deck structure away from the exterior wall and attaching it only at intervals with spaced connectors (see 54B & C).

Alternatively, a continuous ledger may be bolted to the wall and flashed (see 55A & B).

EXTERIOR WALL
SIDING
SPACE ALLOWS WATER TO PASS.
PORCH/DECK STRUCTURE
CONNECTORS AT INTERVALS
SEE 54B & C

EXTERIOR WALL
SIDING
FLASHING
PORCH/DECK STRUCTURE
CONTINUOUS LEDGER
SEE 55A

(A) **PORCHES & DECKS**

Porches and decks are exposed directly to the weather in ways that the main part of the structure is not. Consequently, the wood used in porches and decks is much more susceptible to expansion and contraction, twisting, checking, and rotting. A special strategy for building porches and decks is therefore appropriate.

Weather resistance—Elements of porches and decks that are likely to get wet should be constructed of weather-resistant materials. Virtually all the material required to make a new porch or deck is now available in pressure-treated lumber. Weather-resistant woods like cedar or redwood are also appropriate.

Connectors—At least once a year, joints that are exposed to the weather will shrink and swell, causing nails to withdraw and joints to weaken. Joints made with screws or bolts will therefore outlast those made with nails. For joist connections, use joist hangers or angle clips.

Joist hangers are made of galvanized steel, which should not be adversely affected by exposure to the weather. Galvanized steel deteriorates relatively quickly, however, when combined with pressure-treated lumber, especially when moisture is added to the mix. Therefore, always use connectors with the longer-lasting hot-dip galvanized finish. Also, consider the use of weather-resistant wood species for use with galvanized hangers.

Fasteners such as nails and deck screws should be galvanized. Stainless steel screws are also available and will give the longest life.

Framing—Areas between adjacent wood members collect moisture and are especially prone to rot. Even pressure-treated lumber can rot in this situation. Avoid doubling up members in exposed situations. It is better to use a single large timber where extra strength is required, as shown in the drawing at right.

Poor   Good

Where wood must touch another surface, make the area of contact as small as possible and allow for air circulation around the joint.

Wood decking—Because decking is oriented horizontally, it has a relatively large exposed surface to collect and absorb moisture. This moisture will tend to make the decking cup. Most references suggest installing flat-grain wood decking (and rail caps) with the bark side down because boards will cup in the right direction to shed water as they season.

Unseasoned (wet)   Seasoned (dry)   Wet

However, if dry (seasoned) decking is installed with the bark side down, the boards will cup in the wrong direction when they get wet. Therefore, dry decking boards should be installed with the bark side up so that the boards will shed water if they cup.

Seasoned   Wet

Synthetic decking—There is a new generation of synthetic decking made of reclaimed hardwood and recycled plastic. This material holds up in exposed conditions, is not harmed by rot or insects, and is extremely consistent and stable. The decking is not as stiff as sawn lumber, so it requires closer joist spacing. It can be fastened to framing with conventional methods and is available in standard sizes from 1x6 to 2x8.

Because the decking does not absorb water, thermal expansion is more of a concern than warping or cupping. The decking requires no sealers or preservatives and is manufactured with a nonskid surface. It is disposable (no toxins).

Painting—Sealers and preservatives will extend the life of porches and decks. Special attention should be given to end grain and to areas likely to hold moisture. Stains will outlast paints. Special porch and deck paints are available for use where exposure to the weather is not severe.

SHEATHING

SIDING

P.T. MUDSILL

MAINTAIN 1-IN. GAP
BELOW WOOD SIDING.

OPEN DECKING

DECK JOIST

P.T. HEADER
JOIST BOLTED TO
FOUNDATION WALL

FOUNDATION WALL
SEE 7

(A) OPEN DECK/FOUNDATION WALL

SHEATHING

HORIZONTAL SIDING
OR SHINGLES

FLASHING TUCKED UNDER
TOP PIECE OF SIDING
& EXTENDED BELOW
LOWEST PIECE OF SIDING

OPEN DECKING

P.T. 2X OR 4X
BLOCK WITH
SLOPED TOP

LAG BOLT(S)
IN PREDRILLED
BLOCK

90-LB. FELT GASKET ON
FLASHING AT LAG BOLD

BLOCKING FOR LAG BOLT

P.T. MUDSILL

FOUNDATION WALL
SEE 7

(B) OPEN DECK/WOOD WALL
1st Floor : Horizontal Siding or Shingles

SHEATHING

HORIZONTAL SIDING
OR SHINGLES

FLASHING TUCKED UNDER
TOP PIECE OR SIDING
& LAPPED OVER FIRST
CONTINUOUS PIECE OF
SIDING BELOW

OPEN DECKING

PL.T. 2X OR 4X
BLOCK WITH
SLOPED TOP

LAG BOLT(S)
IN PREDRILLED
BLOCK

HEADER JOIST

90-LB. FELT GASKET ON
FLASHING AT LAG BOLT

BLOCKING FOR LAG BOLT

INTERIOR FLOOR
STRUCTURE

FRAMED WALL

(C) OPEN DECK/WOOD WALL
2nd Floor : Horizontal Siding or Shingles

NOTES

FLASHING EXTENDS 8-IN. MINIMUM PAST BOTH SIDES
OF BLOCK SPACERS.

INSTALL SPACER BLOCKS SIMULTANEOUSLY WITH
SIDING & FLASHING, THEN INSTALL DECK.

OPEN DECKING LAID DIAGONALLY ACROSS JOIST
SYSTEM ACTS AS A DIAPHRAGM, WHICH MAY
ELIMINATE THE NEED FOR BRACING PORCH SUPPORTS.

DETAILS SHOW LEVEL OF DECK SLIGHTLY BELOW
LEVEL OF FINISH FLOOR. IN SNOW COUNTRY, ADJUST
DECK LEVEL AND FLASHING HEIGHT TO ACCOUNT
FOR SNOW BUILDUP.

SPACED DECKING IS OFTEN USED FOR THE FLOOR
OF A SCREENED PORCH. IN THIS CASE, THE DECKING
MUST BE INSTALLED OVER INSECT SCREENING.

SHEATHING

SIDING

FLASHING TUCKED
1 IN. UNDER SIDING AND
WRAPPED OVER LEDGER

OPEN DECKING

HEADER
JOIST

DECK JOIST

LEDGER
NAILED TO
SHEATHING

LAG BOLTS WITH WASHERS

¾-IN. GALVANIZED
HOLLOW SPACERS FILLED
WITH SILICONE CAULK

INTERIOR FLOOR
STRUCTURE

FRAMED WALL

(A) OPEN DECK/WOOD WALL

SHEATHING

SIDING STOPPED
ABOVE DECKING

CONTINUOUS FLASHING
FROM UNDER SIDING TO
KERF IN JOISTS

OPEN DECKING

KERF IN DECK
JOISTS FOR
FLASHING DRIP

P.T. LEDGER
BOLTED TO
FRAMING

JOIST HANGER

FLASHING BEHIND LEDGER
WITH DRIP OVER SIDING

INTERIOR FLOOR
STRUCTURE

FRAMED WALL

(B) OPEN DECK/WOOD WALL
Alternative Detail

OPEN RAILING BOLTED
TO JOISTS OR AS
EXTENSION OF
VERTICAL SUPPORT
SEE 59A

OPEN DECKING

DECK JOIST SUPPORTED
BY JOIST HANGER ON
HEADER JOIST

HEADER JOIST SCREWED
OR BOLTED TO VERTICAL
SUPPORTS

SKIRTING

STUD WALL, WOOD
POST, OR OTHER
VERTICAL SUPPORT

(C) OPEN DECK/OPEN RAILING

SOLID RAILING OF
STUDS & SIDING
SEE 55A

OPEN DECKING

DECK JOIST
SUPPORTED BY
JOIST HANGER ON
HEADER JOIST

HEADER JOIST
BOLTED TO STUDS

FLASHING TUCKED
1 IN. UNDER SIDING
AND BEHIND
HEADER JOIST

DRIP

STUD WALL, WOOD
POST, OR OTHER
VERTICAL SUPPORT

(D) OPEN DECK/SOLID RAILING

CANT STRIPS AT INSIDE CORNERS AS
REQUIRED BY WATERPROOF COATING

ELASTOMERIC, BITUMINOUS, OR
OTHER WATERPROOF MEMBRANE OR
COATING; EXTEND COATING FROM
UNDER SIDING TO EDGE OF DECK.

SLIP SHEET AS REQUIRED WITH
SOME COATINGS.

SLOPE 1/4 IN. PER FT.

HEADER JOIST BOLTED
TO FRAMING MINIMIZES
MOVEMENT.

NOTES
WATERPROOFING CAN BE
PROTECTED FROM ABRASION
BY ADDITION OF WOOD OR
CONCRETE-PAVER SURFACE,
SEE 57A, B & C

SLOPE MAY BE ACHIEVED
BY SLOPING JOISTS OR,
WHERE A LEVEL SURFACE
IS REQUIRED BELOW, BY
RIPPING JOISTS OR ADDING
FURRING STRIPS.

EDGE FLASHING WITH DRIP
EXTENDS 4 IN. UNDER
WATERPROOFING.

ATTACHMENT OF RAILINGS
SEE 58 & 59

RIM JOIST DEEPER THAN
DECK JOISTS TO FORM DRIP

STUD WALL, WOOD POST, OR
OTHER VERTICAL SUPPORT

Ⓐ WATERPROOF DECKS
General Characteristics

WATERPROOF MEMBRANE
CONTINUOUS FROM
UNDER SIDING TO OUTER
EDGE OF CONCRETE

REINFORCED
LIGHTWEIGHT-CONCRETE
DECK

SLOPE 1/4 IN. PER FT.

PLYWOOD SUBFLOOR

HEADER JOIST BOLTED
TO FRAMING

NOTE
IF RAIL IS SOLID, SLOPE
CONCRETE TO SCUPPERS
FROM ALL DIRECTIONS.
SEE 57D

NOTE
ALTERNATIVE FLASHING
DETAIL BELOW WILL
PROVIDE A FORM FOR
EDGE OF CONCRETE.

EDGE FLASHING WITH DRIP
EXTENDS 4 IN. UNDER
WATERPROOF MEMBRANE.

RIM JOIST DEEPER THAN DECK
JOISTS TO FORM DRIP

STUD WALL, WOOD POST, OR
OTHER VERTICAL SUPPORT

Ⓑ LIGHTWEIGHT-CONCRETE PORCH DECK

OPEN RAIL (SHOWN) OR SOLID RAIL & SCUPPER **SEE 58 & 57D**

WATERPROOF MEMBRANE CONTINUOUS FROM UNDER SIDING TO FLASHING AT EDGE OF DECK

DUCKBOARDS **SEE 57B**

SLOPE 1/4 IN. PER FT.

EDGE FLASHING WITH DRIP

NOTE
DUCKBOARD DECKS ARE GENERALLY HELD IN PLACE BY GRAVITY. THEY SHOULD NOT BE USED IN AREAS OF EXTREMELY HIGH WINDS.

(A) DUCKBOARD DECK
Open Rail Shown

RECESSED SLEEPERS AT EDGES AGAINST WALL ALLOW WATER PASSAGE.

1X4 CEDAR, P.T. OR OTHER WEATHER-RESISTANT BOARDS SPACED 3/16 IN. APART

3/16 IN.

SLOPE OF DECK SURFACE

1X3 OR 1X4 WEATHER-RESISTANT SLEEPERS AT 12 IN. O.C. OR ACCORDING TO SPANNING CAPACITY OF SURFACE BOARDS; ORIENT IN DIRECTION OF DECK SLOPE.

BRASS OR GALVANIZED SCREWS COUNTERSUNK FROM UNDERSIDE OF SLEEPERS.

(B) DUCKBOARD DECK
Detail

WATERPROOF MEMBRANE CONTINUOUS FROM UNDER SIDING TO SCUPPER THROUGH WALL

CONCRETE PAGERS SET ON 30-LB. OR 90-LB. FELT

CEDAR SLEEPER PROVIDES GUTTER AT SOLID RAIL & RETAINS PAVERS AT OPEN RAIL & ALLOWS FOR EXPANSION OF PAVERS.

NOTE
THIS DETAIL IS NOT RECOMMENDED IN AREAS OF SEVERE FREEZING WEATHER.

SCUPPER THROUGH SOLID RAIL **SEE 57D**

(C) CONCRETE-PAVER DECK
Solid Rail Shown

THROUGH-WALL FLASHING

SCUPPER

OVERFLOW OPENING

DRIP

DOWNSPOUT

Parts of a Scupper

THROUGH-WALL FLASHING EXTENDS 4 IN. (MIN.) PAST WALL.

LOW POINT IN DECK FLOOR

SIDING FORMS DRIP OVER WALL OPENING

EXTEND FLASHING DRIP BEYOND SIDING

SCUPPER

DOWNSPOUT

Section

(D) SCUPPER

Because they make continuous contact with the porch or deck floor, solid railings are relatively simple to design and construct to resist overturning due to lateral force. For short railing spans (up to 8 ft. long) supported at both ends by a column, a wall, or a corner, the simplest framing (see the drawing below) will suffice because the top edge may be made stiff enough to span between the two rigid ends.

Longer railings or railings with one or both ends unsupported must be designed to resist lateral forces by means of a series of vertical supports firmly secured to the porch or deck floor framing (see the drawing below). This means, of course, that the porch floor framing itself must be solidly constructed.

Waterproof deck with solid railing—Waterproof decks surrounded by a solid railing must be sloped to an opening in the railing. This opening can be a flashed hole in the wall, or scupper, as shown here, or it can be a gap in the wall that accommodates a stairway or walk. (Avoid directing water to walkways in climates with freezing temperatures.) The opening should be located away from the main structure of the building, and the floor should pitch toward the opening from all directions. In some cases, a second opening or overflow should be provided to guarantee that water won't build up if the primary drain clogs.

DOUBLE TOP PLATE, SUPPORTED AT BOTH ENDS, MAY BE STIFFENED FURTHER BY RAIL CAP.

SOLE PLATE NAILED TO SIMPLE DECK CONSTRUCTION

RAILING/WALL CONNECTION SEE 105A

RAILING SEE DRAWING AT LEFT

WALL/DECK CONNECTION IS SAME AS RAILING/DECK CONNECTION SEE DRAWINGS AT LEFT

SCUPPER SEE 57D

CONTINUOUS RAILING STUD NOTCHED OVER RIM JOIST & NAILED TO JOIST SYSTEM RESISTS OVERTURNING.

BLOCKING FOR SIDING NAILING

BLOCKING FOR SUBFLOOR NAILING

NOTE
PROVIDE BLOCKING BETWEEN JOIST AT RAILING STUD IF RAILING IS PARALLEL TO JOIST SYSTEM.

The same results may be achieved in a porch or deck built over a living space by using a balloon frame system with porch-rail studs continuous through to the wall below.

Open deck with solid railing—Open decks surrounded by a solid railing are simple to drain since water will pass through the floor surface (see 55D). Care should be taken to provide adequate drainage from any surface below the deck.

A   **SOLID RAILING AT PORCH OR DECK**

Open railings are connected to the floor of a porch or deck only intermittently, where the vertical supports occur. It is through these supports that open railings gain their rigidity. When the end of the railing is supported at a wall or a column, no special connections are required. When the vertical support does not coincide with a rigid part of the structure, however, a rigid connection must be made with the floor system of the porch or deck. One logical place to locate this connection is at the inside edge of the rim joist (see the drawing below).

OPEN RAILING
BETWEEN SUPPORTS

VERTICAL SUPPORT
BOLTED TO INSIDE
OF JOIST SYSTEM

RIM
JOIST

PORCH FLOOR
STRUCTURE

SUPPORTS ARE MORE
RIGID IF CONTINUOUS
TO FOOTING.

Another logical place to secure the railing to the porch floor is at the outside of the rim joist (see the drawing below). This is usually the most practical choice for waterproof decks, since the railing does not have to penetrate the waterproof surface.

OPEN RAILING
BETWEEN SUPPORTS

VERTICAL SUPPORT
BOLTED TO OUTSIDE
OF JOIST SYSTEM

RIM
JOIST

PORCH FLOOR
STRUCTURE

BALUSTERS MAY ALSO
BE ATTACHED TO THE
JOIST TO STIFFEN THE
RAILING EVEN MORE.

However the railing is attached to the porch, its rigidity depends ultimately on the solid construction of the porch framing. Pressure-treated joists will contribute to the floor's longevity, and metal hangers and clips will add rigidity. Block between joist bays when the railing is parallel to the joist system.

Waterproof deck with open railing—Waterproof decks surrounded by an open railing should be sloped away from the wall(s) of the building. Drainage may be distributed around all open edges, as shown below, or it can be collected in a scupper.

RAILING/WALL
CONNECTION
SEE 105A

TRADITIONAL
PORCH RAILING
SEE 60C

PORCH
FLASHING
SEE 56

Open deck with open railing—Open decks surrounded by an open railing are relatively simple to drain. Be sure to provide adequate drainage from the surface below the deck.

Ⓐ OPEN RAILING AT PORCH OR DECK

A wood porch with an open railing and a tongue-and-groove wood floor has been a tradition throughout the United States for the entire history of wood-frame construction and is still in demand. A tongue-and-groove porch floor is actually a hybrid between a waterproof deck and an open deck because although it is not waterproof, it is also not truly open like the spaced decking of open porch or deck floors. Moisture is likely to get trapped in the tongue-and-groove joint between floor boards and cause decay. To avoid this problem, the floors of these porches are often painted annually. Weather-resistant species or wood that has been pressure-treated will provide the most maintenance-free porch.

The tongue-and-groove wood porch was traditionally built without flashing. But for a longer lasting porch, the connection between the porch floor and the main structure should be flashed for the same reason as for all open porch and deck floors.

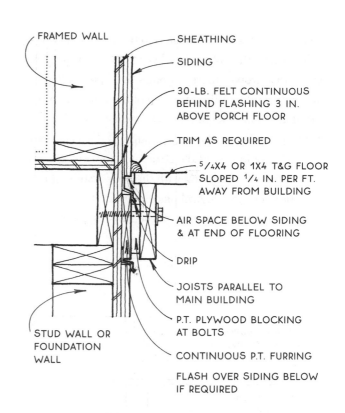

FRAMED WALL

SHEATHING

SIDING

30-LB. FELT CONTINUOUS BEHIND FLASHING 3 IN. ABOVE PORCH FLOOR

TRIM AS REQUIRED

5/4X4 OR 1X4 T&G FLOOR SLOPED 1/4 IN. PER FT. AWAY FROM BUILDING

AIR SPACE BELOW SIDING & AT END OF FLOORING

DRIP

JOISTS PARALLEL TO MAIN BUILDING

P.T. PLYWOOD BLOCKING AT BOLTS

CONTINUOUS P.T. FURRING

FLASH OVER SIDING BELOW IF REQUIRED

STUD WALL OR FOUNDATION WALL

Ⓐ TRADITIONAL WOOD PORCH
Floor Characteristics

Ⓑ TRADITIONAL WOOD PORCH
Connection to Main Structure

OPEN RAILING
SEE 59

CONTINUOUS COLUMN IN PORCH RAILING

TRIM

5/4X4 OR 1X4 T&G FLOOR SLOPED 1/4 IN. PER FT. AWAY FROM BUILDING

TRIM AS REQUIRED

SKIRTING

JOIST

SOLID RAILING STUDS CONTINUOUS FROM TOP TO BASE OF RAIL

SHEATHING

SIDING

TRIM AS REQUIRED

FURRING JOIST ALLOWS NAILING & REPLACEMENT OF FLOORING WITHOUT REMOVAL OF SIDING.

FLASHING CONTINUOUS OVER FURRING JOIST

5/4X4 OR 1X4 T&G FLOOR SLOPED 1/4 IN. PER FT. AWAY FROM BUILDING

PRESSURE-TREATED JOIST NAILED TO FURRING JOIST THROUGH FLASHING

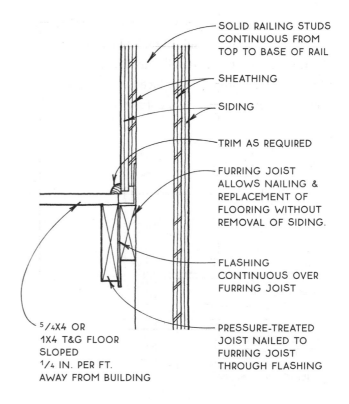

Ⓒ TRADITIONAL WOOD PORCH
Open Railing

Ⓓ TRADITIONAL WOOD PORCH
Closed Railing

ROOF INSULATION
SEE 197

WALL INSULATION
SEE 120

PORCH & DECK FLOORS OVER HEATED SPACE SEE 197

FLOOR INSULATION AT UPPER FLOORS SEE 63

HEATED CRAWL SPACES SEE 15C

FLOORS OVER UNHEATED CRAWL SPACE (SEE NOTES ON THIS PAGE)

SLAB INSULATION SEE 22B

FLOORS OVER OTHER UNHEATED AREAS SEE NOTES ON THIS PAGE

FLOOR INSULATION AT FOUNDATION SEE 62

Floor insulation—Building codes in most climates require at least R-11 for floors over unheated spaces.

Installation—Floors over vented crawl spaces and other unheated areas are typically insulated with fiberglass batts because the ample depth of the floor structure can accommodate this cost-effective but relatively bulky type of insulation. The batts are easiest to install if weather and other considerations permit them to be dropped in from above. To support the batts, a wire or plastic mesh or wood lath can first be stapled to the underside of the joists, or plastic mesh can be draped very loosely over the joists.

SUPPORT FIBERGLASS-BATT INSULATION WITH WIRE OR PLASTIC MESH, OR WITH WOOD LATH OR WIRE AT 12 IN. O.C.

When crawl-space floor insulation must be installed from below, spring wires are cheap, easy, and effective.

SPRING WIRES PUSHED INTO PLACE AT 24 IN. O.C. SUPPORT INSULATION.

Floor insulation over open areas that are exposed to varmints and house pets should be covered from below with solid sheathing (see 88A).

Vapor retarder—A vapor retarder is not always required in the floor structure over a crawl space because the temperature differential between the interior space and the crawl space is not always enough to cause condensation. A floor over a heated basement or crawl space (see 8) would not require a vapor retarder. When conditions do require a vapor retarder or when an air-infiltration barrier (AVB) is desired, a 4-mil air/vapor barrier may be placed on the warm side of the insulation, as shown in the drawing below.

VAPOR RETARDER CAN GO ON TOP OF SUBFLOOR IF UNFACED BATT INSULATION IS BELOW, OR
VAPOR RETARDER CAN BE INTEGRAL WITH OR ON TOP SIDE OF INSULATION.

A vapor retarder placed on the subfloor is more continuous than one on the top side of the batts, and it also will not trap rainwater during construction. Floor vapor retarders in any position are likely to accumulate multiple nail penetrations and should be coordinated with the finish floor. For more on vapor retarders and air-infiltration barriers, see 120.

Perimeter insulation—Floors whose perimeter completes the thermal envelope, such as upper floors that are located over a heated space, need only be insulated at their perimeter, not throughout the entire floor. The continuity of insulation and air/vapor barriers at this location requires serious consideration (see 62B, C & D and 63).

(A) **FLOOR INSULATION**

FRAMED WALL WITH FUTURE WALL INSULATION, VAPOR RETARDER, MOISTURE BARRIER & SIDING

SUBFLOOR

VAPOR RETARDER ON TOP OF SUBFLOOR CAN BE SEALED TO WALL VAPOR RETARDER AT BOTTOM PLATE.

UNFACED FIBERGLASS-BATT INSULATION FILLS JOIST OR GIRDER CAVITIES. SEE 61

P.T. MUDSILL

FOUNDATION WALL

Ⓐ FLOOR INSULATION AT FOUNDATION
Uninsulated Basement or Crawl Space

FRAMED WALL WITH FUTURE WALL INSULATION, VAPOR RETARDER, MOISTURE BARRIER & SIDING

SUBFLOOR

UNFACED FIBERGLASS BATT INSULATION FILLS JOIST CAVITIES. SEE 61

RIGID INSULATION SEALED AT EDGES

JOIST ON MUDSILL SEE 33A & B

INSULATED FRAMED WALL SEE 15C & D

P.T. MUDSILL WITH SILL GASKET

FOUNDATION WALL

Ⓑ FLOOR INSULATION AT FOUNDATION
Heated Basement/Joist on Mudsill

FRAMED 2X6 WALL CANTILEVERED 2 IN. WITH FUTURE WALL INSULATION, VAPOR RETARDER, MOISTURE BARRIER & SIDING

SUBFLOOR

2X8 P.T. MUDSILL WITH SILL GASKET

JOIST HUNG FROM MUDSILL SEE 33D

RIGID INSULATION WITH PROTECTION ABOVE GRADE SEE 15A, B & C

FOUNDATION WALL

Ⓒ FLOOR INSULATION AT FOUNDATION
Heated Basement/Joist Flush with Mudsill

FRAMED WALL WITH FUTURE WALL INSULATION, VAPOR RETARDER, MOISTURE BARRIER & SIDING

SUBFLOOR

P.T. MUDSILL WITH SILL GASKET

RIGID INSULATION SEALED AT EDGES

JOISTS ON FRAMED WALL SEE 34B

INSULATED FRAMED WALL SEE 15C & D

FOUNDATION WALL

NOTE
INSULATION IS NOT CONTINUOUS SO THIS DETAIL NOT RECOMMENDED FOR EXTREME CLIMATES UNLESS WALLS ARE SUPERINSULATED. SEE 121B

Ⓓ FLOOR INSULATION AT FOUNDATION
Heated Basement/Joists Flush with Mudsill

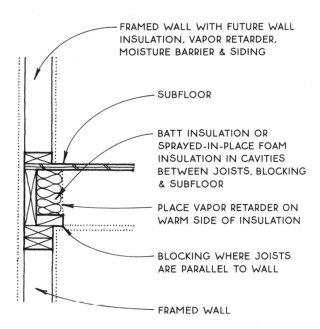

- FRAMED WALL WITH FUTURE WALL INSULATION, VAPOR RETARDER, MOISTURE BARRIER & SIDING
- SUBFLOOR
- BATT INSULATION OR SPRAYED-IN-PLACE FOAM INSULATION IN CAVITIES BETWEEN JOISTS, BLOCKING & SUBFLOOR
- PLACE VAPOR RETARDER ON WARM SIDE OF INSULATION
- BLOCKING WHERE JOISTS ARE PARALLEL TO WALL
- FRAMED WALL

NOTE
BECAUSE JOISTS PERPENDICULAR TO THE WALL PENETRATE THE WALL CAVITY, IT IS DIFFICULT TO GET A TIGHT SEAL AGAINST AIR INFILTRATION. FOR ALTERNATIVE DETAIL SEE 63B.

A UPPER-FLOOR INSULATION
Platform Framing

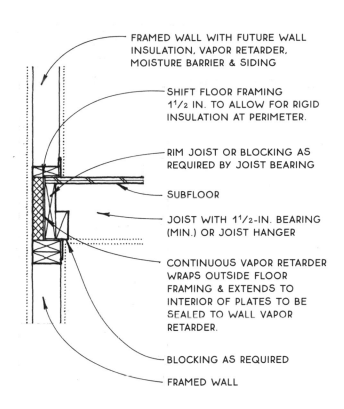

- FRAMED WALL WITH FUTURE WALL INSULATION, VAPOR RETARDER, MOISTURE BARRIER & SIDING
- SHIFT FLOOR FRAMING 1½ IN. TO ALLOW FOR RIGID INSULATION AT PERIMETER.
- RIM JOIST OR BLOCKING AS REQUIRED BY JOIST BEARING
- SUBFLOOR
- JOIST WITH 1½-IN. BEARING (MIN.) OR JOIST HANGER
- CONTINUOUS VAPOR RETARDER WRAPS OUTSIDE FLOOR FRAMING & EXTENDS TO INTERIOR OF PLATES TO BE SEALED TO WALL VAPOR RETARDER.
- BLOCKING AS REQUIRED
- FRAMED WALL

B UPPER-FLOOR INSULATION
Platform Frame: Alternative Detail

- 2X4 OR 2X6 FRAMED WALL WITH FUTURE WALL INSULATION, VAPOR RETARDER, MOISTURE BARRIER & SIDING
- FIRE/NAILING BLOCK
- SUBFLOOR
- VAPOR RETARDER CONTINUOUS BEHIND JOIST; SEAL TO WALL VAPOR RETARDER ABOVE & BELOW.
- INSULATE WALL BEHIND JOIST BEFORE JOIST IS INSTALLED.
- CONTINUOUS HEADER JOIST SCREWED TO WALL

NOTE:
BECAUSE THE JOISTS DO NOT PENETRATE THE WALL CAVITIY, IT IS POSSIBLE TO PROVIDE A GOOD SEAL AGAINST AIR INFILTRATION. HOWEVER, THIS DETAIL DOES NOT PROVIDE THE LATERAL STRUCTURAL STRENGTH OF ALTERNATIVE DETAIL. SEE 63D

 C UPPER-FLOOR INSULATION
Balloon Framing/Joists Perpendicular to Wall

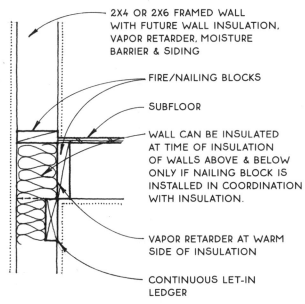

- 2X4 OR 2X6 FRAMED WALL WITH FUTURE WALL INSULATION, VAPOR RETARDER, MOISTURE BARRIER & SIDING
- FIRE/NAILING BLOCKS
- SUBFLOOR
- WALL CAN BE INSULATED AT TIME OF INSULATION OF WALLS ABOVE & BELOW ONLY IF NAILING BLOCK IS INSTALLED IN COORDINATION WITH INSULATION.
- VAPOR RETARDER AT WARM SIDE OF INSULATION
- CONTINUOUS LET-IN LEDGER

NOTE:
BECAUSE JOISTS PERPENDICULAR TO THE WALL PENETRATE THE WALL CAVITY, IT IS DIFFICULT TO GET A TIGHT SEAL AGAINST AIR INFILTRATION FOR ALTERNATIVE DETAIL. SEE 63C

D UPPER-FLOOR INSULATION
Balloon Frame: Alternative Detail

WALLS

The walls of a building serve several important functions: They define the spaces within the building to provide privacy and zoning, and they enclose the building itself, keeping the weather out and the heat or cold in. Walls provide the vertical structure that supports the upper floors and roof of the building, and the lateral structure that stiffens the building. Walls also encase the mechanical systems (electrical wiring, plumbing, and heating). To incorporate all of this within a 4-in. or 6-in.-deep wood-framed panel is quite an achievement, so numerous decisions need to be made in the course of designing a wall system for a wood-frame building. There are two preliminary decisions to make that establish the framework for the remaining decisions.

WALL THICKNESS

Should the walls be framed with 2x4s or 2x6s? The 2x6 wall has become increasingly popular in recent years, primarily because it provides more space for insulation and allows for other minor energy-saving advantages (such as the ability to run electricity in a notched base, as shown in 73A). These advantages all come at some cost. A 2x6 wall with studs spaced 24 in. o.c. (the maximum spacing allowed by codes) uses about 20% more material for studs and plates than a 2x4 wall with studs with a code-allowed spacing of 16 in. o.c. On the outside, the sheathing has to be ½ in. thick (⅛ in. thicker than sheathing on a standard 2x4 wall). Inside, the drywall also has to be ⅛ in. thicker to span the 24-in. spacing between 2x6 studs. Thicker insulation costs more too. So, overall, 2x6 framing makes a superior wall, but one that costs more. Framing the exterior walls with 2x6s and interior walls

with 2x4s is a typical combination when the energy-efficient 2x6 wall is selected. Stud spacing of 2x4 and 2x6 walls may vary with loading, lumber grades, and finish materials; in this book, however, studs are assumed to be 16 in. o.c. in 2x4 walls and 24 in. o.c. in 2x6 walls unless noted otherwise.

FRAMING STYLE

Should the walls be built using platform framing or balloon framing? Balloon framing, with studs continuous from mudsill to top plate and continuous between floors, was developed in the 1840s and is the antecedent of the framed wall. In recent years, balloon framing has been almost completely superseded by the more labor-efficient and fire-resistant platform frame construction, with studs extending only between floors. There are still situations, however, where a variation of the balloon frame system is useful. One such situation is where the continuity of studs longer than the normal ceiling height is essential to the strength of a wall. Examples include parapet walls and eave (side) walls that must resist the lateral thrust of a vaulted roof (as in a 1½-story building).

Balloon-framed gable-end walls also provide increased stability in high-wind areas (see 160).

Another reason for using balloon framing is to minimize the effects of shrinkage that occurs across the grain of joists in a platform-framed building. This could be important with continuous stucco siding that spans two floors without a control joint, or in a multiple-story hybrid building system where the floors in the balloon-framed part would not shrink equally with the floors in the platform-framed part.

DESIGNING A WALL SYSTEM

Once the stud size and spacing and the framing system have been selected, it is time to consider how to brace the building to resist the forces of wind, earthquakes, and eccentric loading. Will diagonal bracing be adequate, or should the building be braced with structural sheathing and/or shear walls? This question is best answered in the context of the design of the building as a whole, considering the other materials that complete the wall system. How is the wall to be insulated? Where are the openings in the wall for doors and windows? Will there be an air-infiltration barrier? What material will be used for the exterior finish? The details relating to these issues are addressed in this chapter, along with some suggestions for their appropriate use. How these various details are assembled into a complete wall system depends on local climate, codes, tradition, and the talent of the designer.

SIZING HEADERS

Headers are structural members over openings in walls for windows or doors. Header size depends on wood species and grade, loading, header design, and rough-opening span. Following is a rule of thumb for sizing a common header type, the 4x header (see 68B):

For a single-story building with a 30-lb. live load on the roof and 2x4 bearing walls, the span in feet of the rough opening should equal the depth (nominal) in inches of a 4x header. For example, openings up to 4 ft. wide require a 4x4 header and up to 6 ft. wide, a 4x6 header.

ADVANCED FRAMING

Advanced framing minimizes the amount of structural material that is required to hold up the building. The greatest impact on framing efficiency can be made in the walls because wall construction has evolved in such a way that the typical wall is overbuilt. Floors and roofs are constructed reasonably efficiently because the design challenge has been to span horizontally with an economy of materials. Standard framed walls, however, contain numerous extraneous and oversized elements. The elimination and downsizing of wall members not only saves lumber, it also lowers the effect of thermal bridging, thus saving energy. Advanced framing of walls is discussed in this chapter (see 74–76).

ABOUT THE DRAWINGS

Construction terms vary regionally, and the names for the components that frame wall openings (see 68A) are the least cast in stone. Studs called "trimmer studs" in one locality are called "jack studs" in another; and the bottom plate may go by either "bottom plate" or "sole plate." Consult local builders and architects for common usage.

For clarity, insulation is not generally shown in the exterior walls except in the insulation section (120–125).

HEADERS
SEE 68, 69, 70A & C

OPENINGS
SEE 68A

INTERSECTING
WALLS
SEE 70A & B

RAKE WALLS
SEE 72

CONNECTIONS
WITH ROOF
& CEILING
SEE 132-134

CONNECTIONS
WITH FLOORS
SEE 40-42

LATERAL
BRACING
SEE 77

CORNERS
SEE 70A & D, 71

BLOCKING,
BACKING,
FIRESTOPPING
SEE 73A & B

CANTILEVERED
WALLS
SEE 73C & D

RESOURCE-EFFICIENT
ADVANCED FRAMING
SEE 74

NOTE
IN THIS CHAPTER ALL 2X4 WALLS ARE SHOWN
WITH STUDS AT 16 IN. O.C.; ALL 2X6 WALLS ARE
SHOWN WITH STUDS AT 24 IN. O.C.; UNLABELED
WALLS MAY BE EITHER 2X4 OR 2X6.

Ⓐ WALL FRAMING

DOUBLE TOP PLATE

LAP DOUBLE TOP PLATE 4 FT. (MIN.)

CRIPPLE STUDS

HEADER

TRIMMER STUD

KING STUD

COMMON STUDS

SUBFLOOR

DOOR ROUGH OPENING TYP. 6 FT. 10 1/2 IN. FOR 6 FT. 8 IN. DOOR

HEADER

TRIMMER STUD

KING STUD

SILL

WINDOW ROUGH OPENING

WINDOW HEADER TYP. ALIGNS WITH DOOR HEADER.

CRIPPLE STUDS

DOOR ROUGH OPENING

SOLE PLATE

WINDOW ROUGH OPENING

(A) OPENINGS IN A STUD WALL

DOUBLE TOP PLATE

CRIPPLE STUDS AT SAME SPACING AS COMMON STUDS

4X HEADER AT SAME WIDTH AS STUDS

TRIMMER STUD

KING STUD

(B) 4X HEADER
2x4 Bearing Wall

DOUBLE TOP PLATE

CRIPPLE STUDS AT SAME SPACING AS COMMON STUDS

DOUBLE 2X HEADER WITH 1/2-IN. OR 3/8-IN. PLYWOOD SPACER

TRIMMER STUD

KING STUD

NOTE
HEADER BUILDS TO THICKNESS OF WALL & PROVIDES NAILING AT ALL SURFACES.

(C) TYPICAL DOUBLE 2X HEADER
2x4 Bearing Wall

DOUBLE TOP PLATE

DOUBLE (OR SINGLE) 2X10 HEADER WITH 2X4 SCABBED TO BOTTOM (ELIMINATES THE NEED FOR CRIPPLE STUDS IN AN 8-FT. WALL)

1/2-IN. PLYWOOD OR WOOD LATH SHIMS AT INSIDE SURFACES (OR RIGID INSULATION)

TRIMMER STUD

KING STUD

(A) 2X10 HEADER
2x4 Bearing Wall

DOUBLE TOP PLATE

CRIPPLE STUDS AT SAME SPACINIG AS COMMONG STUDS

DOUBLE LVL OR SINGLE LSL HEADER AT SAME WIDTH AS 2X4 WALL

TRIMMER STUD

KING STUD

NOTE
LSL IS NOT AS STRONG AS DOUBLE LVL.

(B) DOUBLE LVL OR LSL HEADER
2x4 Bearing Wall

DOUBLE TOP PLATE

CRIPPLE STUDS AT SAME SPACING AS COMMON

DOUBLE FLAT 2X4 HEADER

TRIMMER STUD

KING STUD

(C) FLAT 2X4 HEADER
2x4 Partition Wall

TOP PLATE MUST BE CONTINUOUS ACROSS OPENING.

CRIPPLE STUDS AT SAME SPACING AS COMMON STUDS

1/2-IN. CDX PLYWOOD (MIN.) NAILED TO ONE SIDE OF FRAMING WITH 8D COMMON NAILS AT 3 IN. O.C. STAGGERED 1/2 IN. TO AVOID SPLITTING FRAMING

TRIMMER STUD

KING STUD

NOTE
THIS HEADER, WHICH WAS DEVELOPED BY N.A.H.B. (SEE RESOURCES), CAN BE SIZED TO SPAN UP TO 8 FT.

(D) OPEN-BOX PLYWOOD HEADER
2x4 Bearing Wall

DOUBLE TOP PLATE

NOTCH CRIPPLE STUDS
FOR 2X HEADER.

2X HEADER AT OUTSIDE
OF WALL

2-IN. OR 4-IN. SPACE
AT INSIDE OF HEADER
FOR INSULATION

2X4 OR 2X6
HEADER PLATE

TRIMMER STUD

KING STUD

Ⓐ INSULATED HEADER
2x4 or 2x6 Exterior Wall

DOUBLE TOP PLATE OVERLAPS
AT CORNERS TO LOCK TWO
WALLS TOGETHER.

2X4 STUDS
AT 16 IN. O.C.
TYPICAL

Ⓑ 2X4 CORNER
At Double Top Plate

DOUBLE TOP PLATE

CRIPPLE STUD AT
SAME SPACING AS
COMMON STUDS

BUILT-UP HEADER
OF 2X'S WITH
2X3 SPACER
BETWEEN

$2\frac{1}{2}$-IN.
INSULATION
SPACE

2X3 SPACER

TRIMMER STUD

KING STUD

Ⓒ INSULATED DOUBLE 2X HEADER
2x6 Bearing Wall/Alternative Detail

CORNER STUDS BUILT UP WITH
2X4 BLOCKING BETWEEN
PROVIDES NAILING AT
INSIDE CORNER.

SOLE
PLATE

NOTE
THIS DETAIL WORKS
FOR BOTH INSIDE &
OUTSIDE CORNERS.

Ⓓ 2X4 CORNER
At Sole Plate

DOUBLE TOP PLATE OVERLAPS
AT CORNERS, LOCKING
TWO WALLS
TOGETHER

TOP PLATE OF
INTERSECTING
WALL OVERLAPS
CONTINUOUS
TOP PLATE OF
PRIMARY WALL.

CONTINUOUS
TOP PLATE OF
PRIMARY WALL

COMMON STUDS
IN PRIMARY WALL

BLOCKING AT 16 IN.
O.C. PROVIDES
NAILING &
ALLOWS SPACE
FOR INSULATION

END STUD OF
INTERSECTING
WALL

2X6 STUDS AT 24 IN.
O.C. OR 2X4 STUDS
AT 16 IN. O.C. TYPICAL

Ⓐ **2X4 OR 2X6 CORNER**
At Double Top Plate

Ⓑ **INTERSECTING 2X WALLS**
At Double Top Plate

EXTRA STUD ADDED PERPENDICULAR TO
CORNER STUD PROVIDES NAILING AT
INSIDE CORNER & ALLOWS SPACE FOR
4-IN.-THICK INSULATION AT CORNER.

TOP PLATE OF
INTERSECTING
WALL OVERLAPS
CONTINUOUS TOP
PLATE OF PRIMARY
WALL

CONTINUOUS TOP
PLATE OF PRIMARY
WALL

COMMON STUDS
IN PRIMARY WALL

SOLE
PLATE

2X4 OR 2X6 STUDS AT 16 IN.
OR 24 IN. O.C. TYPICAL

2X6 OR 2X8 BACKER
STUD PROVIDES
NAILING AND ALLOWS
SPACE FOR INSULATION

END STUD OF
INTERSECTION WALL

Ⓒ **2X4 OR 2X6 CORNER**
At Sole Plate

Ⓓ **INTERSECTING 2X WALLS**
At Double Top Plate/Alternative Detail

A wall that extends to a sloped roof or ceiling is called a rake wall and may be built one of two ways:

Platform framing—Platform framing is commonly the method of choice when a horizontal structural element such as a floor or ceiling ties the structure together at the level of the top plate or when the top plate itself is short enough to provide the necessary lateral strength (see 72B).

Balloon framing—Balloon framing allows for ease of construction and economy of material and stabilizes a tall wall because the studs are continuous from sole plate to roof (see 72C). Balloon framing can also be employed to stiffen a wall that projects above the roof such as a parapet or railing (see 72D). Balloon framing is greatly preferred in general from a structural perspective where lateral forces are extreme, such as in high-wind areas.

For details of rake walls with truss-framed roofs, see 156.

RAKE-WALL STUDS ALIGNED WITH WALL STUDS BELOW ARE TOENAILED TO TOP PLATE & TO RAFTER (SHOWN WITH DASHED LINES FOR CLARITY)

CEILING JOIST

OVERLAPPING DOUBLE TOP PLATE

(A) RAKE WALL
Notes

(B) RAKE WALL
Platform Framing

SINGLE TOP PLATE SLOPED TO MATCH PITCH OF ROOF

FIREBLOCKING AS REQUIRED

STUD CONTINUOUS FROM SOLE PLATE

TOP SURFACE OF SLOPED TOP PLATE FLUSH WITH INSIDE CORNER OF DOUBLE TOP PLATE

NOTE
TIE CORNER TOGETHER WITH SHEATHING OR METAL STRAPS.

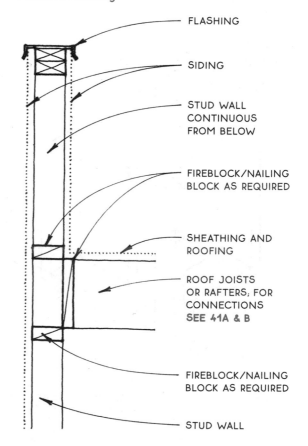

FLASHING

SIDING

STUD WALL CONTINUOUS FROM BELOW

FIREBLOCK/NAILING BLOCK AS REQUIRED

SHEATHING AND ROOFING

ROOF JOISTS OR RAFTERS; FOR CONNECTIONS SEE 41A & B

FIREBLOCK/NAILING BLOCK AS REQUIRED

STUD WALL

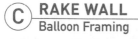

(C) RAKE WALL
Balloon Framing

(D) PARAPET WALL FRAMING
Roof Joists Shown Perpendicular to Wall

FIRESTOPPING RETARDS THE SPREAD OF FIRE IN WALL CAVITIES & MAY ALSO SERVE AS BLOCKING. **SEE 73B**

BLOCKING SUPPORTS PIPING & OTHER UTILITIES WITHIN THE WALL CAVITY. IT PROVIDES A SOLID NAILING SURFACE FOR CHANGES IN MATERIAL SUCH AS WAINSCOTING & IT ALSO SUPPORTS CABINETS, PLUMBING FIXTURES, TRIM, TOWEL BARS, BALUSTRADES & OTHER ACCESSORIES THAT ARE ATTACHED TO THE FINSH SURFACE OF THE WALL. WHEN POSSIBLE, BLOCKING IS APPLIED FLAT TO ALLOW INSULATION AT EXTERIOR WALLS.

NOTCHING BASE OF 2X6 WALL ALLOWS ELECTRICAL WIRES TO RUN WITHOUT COMPRESSING INSULATION AT CENTER OF WALL (NOT ALLOWED IN 2X4 WALL).

A BLOCKING & NOTCHING

FIRESTOPPING MAY BE STAGGERED FOR BASE OF NAILING.

CONTINUOUS STUDS

NOTE
CODES VARY, BUT FIRESTOPPING IS USUALLY REQUIRED AT STAIRS ALONGSIDE THE STRINGERS; BETWEEN FLOORS & BETWEEN THE TOP FLOOR & THE ATTIC IN BALLOON-FRAME BUILDINGS (THE PLATES IN PLATFORM-FRAME BUILDINGS AUTOMATICALLY PROVIDE FIREBLOCKING BETWEEN FLOORS); BETWEEN WALL CAVITIES & CONCEALED HORIZONTAL SPACES SUCH AS SOFFITS & DROP CEILINGS; IN TALL WALLS EVERY 10 FT. VERTICALLY.

FIRESTOPPING IS USUALLY 2X FRAMING LUMBER BUT CAN ALSO BE OTHER MATERIALS SUCH AS LAYERS OF PLYWOOD OR GYPSUM WALLBOARD WHEN APPROVED BY LOCAL CODES.

B FIRESTOPPING

IT IS OCCASIONALLY DIFFICULT OR IMPOSSIBLE TO CANTILEVER THE FLOOR FRAMING TO SUPPORT A PROJECTION FROM THE BUILDING. WHERE LOADS ARE NOT GREAT, IT IS POSSIBLE TO SUPPORT THE PROJECTION WITH CANTILEVERED WALLS.

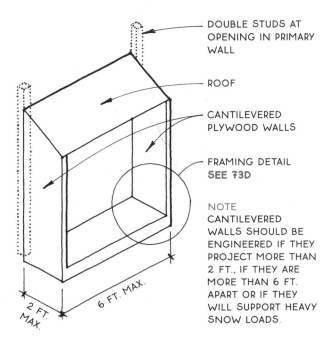

DOUBLE STUDS AT OPENING IN PRIMARY WALL

ROOF

CANTILEVERED PLYWOOD WALLS

FRAMING DETAIL **SEE 73D**

NOTE
CANTILEVERED WALLS SHOULD BE ENGINEERED IF THEY PROJECT MORE THAN 2 FT., IF THEY ARE MORE THAN 6 FT. APART OR IF THEY WILL SUPPORT HEAVY SNOW LOADS.

2 FT. MAX.

6 FT. MAX.

C CANTILEVERED WALLS

CORNER NAILING STUD ATTACHED AFTER CANTILEVERED WALL IS NAILED

DOUBLED STUDS AT OPENING IN PRIMARY WALL; 16D TOENAILS OR METAL FRAMING ANGLES ADVISABLE AT TOP & BOTTOM

CANTILEVERED WALL IS SUPPORTED BY NAILING THROUGH PLYWOOD TO DOUBLED STUDS IN PRIMARY WALL.

STUDS OF CANTILEVERED WALL

EXTEND SHEATHING DOWN TO LAP FLOOR-SYSTEM FRAMING.

SOLE PLATE OF CANTILEVERED WALL

FLOOR-SYSTEM FRAMING

BUILDING LINE

D CANTILEVERED-WALL FRAMING
Detail at Base

REDUCED FRAMING IN
STRUCTURAL HEADERS
WHERE THEY ARE REQUIRED
SEE 76

SINGLE TOP
PLATE

INTERSECTING WALLS
SEE 75B & D

JOISTS ALIGNED
OVER STUDS ALLOWS
FOR SINGLE TOP
PLATE

RIM JOIST
USED AS HEADER
ELIMINATING
STRUCTURAL
HEADERS IN
OPENINGS BELOW.

STANDARD WALL
FRAMING
SEE 67

ROOF STRUCTURE
ALIGNED OVER
STUDS ALLOWS
FOR SINGLE TOP
PLATE

BALLOON-FRAMED
RAKE WALLS
SEE 72C

ELIMINATE
STRUCTURAL
HEADERS AT
OPENINGS
WHERE THEY ARE
NOT REQUIRED

STUDS ALIGNED
BETWEEN FLOORS

SUPERINSULATED
CORNER
SEE 75A & C

Advanced framing—Advanced framing minimizes
the amount of framing that extends from the interior
to the exterior of a wall, thus lowering the effect of
thermal bridging. By limiting the amount of framing,
more volume in the wall can be occupied by insulation,
which increases thermal performance of the overall
assembly. Advanced framing alone can increase the
thermal performance of framed walls by only about

7%, but, given that it uses less material than standard
framing and also helps to conserve a precious resource,
it should be considered for every framed building.
Details of advanced framing are illustrated on 75–76.
The goal when designing an energy-efficient header
is to allow for the most insulation while providing for
nailing at both the exterior and interior of the opening.

(A) ADVANCED WALL FRAMING

SINGLE TOP PLATE

METAL STRAP TIE TWO WALLS TOGETHER

2X6 STUDS AT 24 IN. O.C. TYPICAL

A **SUPERINSULATED 2X6 CORNER**
Outside Corner Only at Top Plate

CONTINUOUS SINGLE TOP PLATE OF PRIMARY WALL

METAL STRAP TIES TWO WALLS TOGETHER.

SINGLE TOP PLATE OF INTERSECTING WALL

BACK-UP CLIPS FOR GYPSUM WALLBOARD ON INTERSECTING WALL LEAVE WALL CAVITY BETWEEN SUTDS CLEAR FOR INSULATION.

STUDS OF PRIMARY WALL

B **INTERSECTING 2X WALLS**
At Top Plate

BACKUP CLIPS AT INSIDE CORNERS OF GYPSUM WALLBOARD ELIMINATE NEED FOR EXTRA STUD, ALLOWING FOR FULL THICKNESS OF INSULATION.

SOLE PLATE

NOTE
BACKUP CLIPS CAN ALSO BE USED IN 2X4 WALLS.

C **SUPERINSULATED 2X6 CORNER**
Outside Corner Only at Sole Plate

BACK-UP CLIPS LEAVE CAVITY BETWEEN STUDS CLEAR FOR INSULATION.

COMMON STUDS IN PRIMARY WALL

END STUD OF INTERSECTING WALL

CONTINUOUS SOLE PLATE OF PRIMARY WALL

SOLE PLATE OF INTERSECTING WALL

D **INTERSECTING 2X WALLS**
At Sole Plate

SHEATHING

BATT INSULATION AS IN TYPICAL WALL

DOUBLE 2X HEADER FOR HEAVY LOADING
SEE 76

2½ IN. OF RIGID INSULATION

KING STUD OR TRIMMER STUD FOR HEAVY LOADS

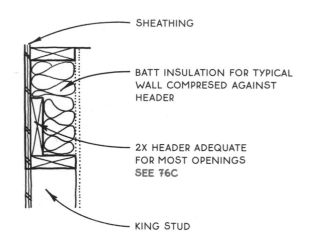

SHEATHING

BATT INSULATION FOR TYPICAL WALL COMPRESED AGAINST HEADER

2X HEADER ADEQUATE FOR MOST OPENINGS
SEE 76C

KING STUD

When a structural header is required over an opening in an exterior wall, the header itself occupies space that could otherwise be filled with insulation. Because a deep (tall) header is more effective structurally than a wide one, the header does not usually have to fill the entire width of the wall. In fact, the taller and thinner the header, the more space there will be for insulation. The headers illustrated on this page provide both structure and space for insulation. The box header

(see 69D) also provides space for insulation because it uses sheathing as structure.

The elimination of the trimmer studs that usually support a header at its ends also allows for more insulation in the wall. The header can usually be supported by the king stud as illustrated in the two examples below. (Backing may need to be added to the king studs when wide casings are used.)

(A) SUPERINSULATED HEADERS
General

SHINGLE TOP PLATE

BUILT-UP HEADER
SEE 70C

KING STUD

MANUFACTURED METAL BRACKET SUPPORTS HEADER AT END ELIMINATING NEED FOR TRIMMER STUD.

(B) SUPERINSULATED HEADER
Relatively Heavy Loads

SINGLE TOP PLATE

HEADER SIZED FOR LIGHT LOADS LET INTO 2X6 KING STUD AND NAILED

KING STUD

(C) SUPERINSULATED HEADER
Relatively Light Loads

Most wood buildings are sheathed with plywood, OSB, or other structural panels that provide the necessary lateral stability when fastened directly to the stud frame (see 78–80). Where lateral forces on walls are extreme, such as in areas subject to hurricanes or earthquakes, specially designed shear walls are commonly required to withstand these forces (see 82–87).

When neither structural panels nor shear walls are required, there are two good methods of bracing the building for lateral stability: the let-in wood brace (see 77B) and the kerfed-in metal brace (see 77C).

The old-fashioned method of bracing with diagonal blocking between studs is not recommended because the nails may withdraw under tension and the many joints tend to open up as the blocking shrinks.

Bracing is often referred to as "corner bracing," and indeed, the International Residential Code begins its discussion of every allowed wall bracing method with the phrase "located at each end…" While it is true that the corners are the most effective location for a limited amount of wall bracing, it is also possible to successfully brace a building at locations other than the corners. If this were not true, there would be no corner windows. Braces may be located anywhere along a wall, and the bracing effect will be transferred to the rest of the wall through the continuous top and bottom plates. Increased nailing, stronger sheathing, and other methods can also augment bracing. A good structural engineer will be able to design walls of just about any configuration to resist lateral forces.

The methods shown here are located at a corner only for clarity of illustration.

(A) LATERAL BRACING
Notes

TOP OF BRACE IS LET INTO TOP PLATE & FASTENED SECURELY.

NOTCH STUD & NAIL OR STAPLE BRACE & EACH STUD.

BOTTOM OF BRACE IS LET IN & FASTENED SECURELY TO STUD.

NOTE
LET-IN BRACES SHOULD BE MADE OF STRUCTURALLY SOUND 1X4 OR 1X6 LUMBER. THEY SHOULD BE FROM TOP PLATE TO SOLE PLATE & 45° TO 60° FROM THE HORIZONTAL.

(B) LET-IN WOOD BRACE

TOP OF BRACE IS NAILED SECURELY IN KERF AT TOP PLATE.

KERF STUD & NAIL BRACE AT EACH STUD.

BOTTOM OF BRACE FITS IN KERF IN SOLE PLATE.

NOTE
METAL BRACING SET IN A SAW KERF & NAILED TO EACH STUD IS ENGINEERED TO EQUAL THE CODE REQUIREMENTS OF A 1X4 WOOD LET-IN BRACE. SURFACE MOUNTED TYPES (WITHOUT KERF) MUST BE INSTALLED IN OPPOSING DIRECTIONS IN AN "X" OR "V" CONFIGURATION. ALL TYPES MUST BE INSTALLED AT 45° TO 60° FROM THE HORIZONTAL.

(C) KERFED-IN METAL BRACE

Structural sheathing performs two functions—it provides lateral bracing, and it forms a structural backing for siding materials. OSB is currently the most common structural sheathing, but the use of plywood, gypsum board (which also contributes fire resistance) and other panel products is also widespread. OSB and plywood both have a strength axis along the length of the panel because of the orientation of wood fibers, but this axis is only important in relation to its bending strength between studs. The panel's shear strength—its ability to resist lateral forces—is not affected by its orientation.

Panels may be installed either vertically or horizontally. Vertically applied sheathing does not usually require blocking because all panel edges are aligned with framing members. Horizontally applied panels, if engineered to provide lateral resistance, must have blocking between studs for nailing. Horizontal OSB and plywood panels provide a stronger backing for siding than do panels with a vertical orientation.

In earthquake or hurricane zones or where walls are very tall or penetrated by many openings, structural sheathing may require engineering, or shear walls (see 82) may be required.

The capacity of panel products such as OSB and plywood to span between studs is related to thickness. The following chart applies generally:

STUD SPACING	PANEL THICKNESS
16 in. o.c.	3/8 in.
24 in. o.c.	1/2 in.

Nails or other approved fasteners should be sized and spaced according to the following schedule. Verify with manufacturer and local codes.

PANEL THICKNESS	NAIL SIZE	PANEL EDGE NAILING	FIELD NAILING
1/2 in. or less over 1/2 in.	6d 8d	6 in. o.c.	12 in. o.c.

(A) STRUCTURAL SHEATHING
Notes

PANEL NAILNG
SCHEDULE
SEE 78A

1/8-IN. SPACING BETWEEN
ALL PANEL EDGES

8-FT. OR 9-FT. PANEL ON
SECOND STORY, DEPENDING
ON CEILING HEIGHT

9-FT. PANEL LAPS RIM JOIST
& TIES FRAMING TO
FOUNDATION IN HIGH-WIND
OR EARTHQUAKE REGIONS.

ALTERNATIVE 8-FT. PANEL
WITH FILLER STRIP AT
RIM JOIST.

NOTE
IN CERTAIN CASES, SUCH AS
WHEN MOST OF A WALL
IS COVERED WITH DOORS
& WINDOWS, STRUCTURAL
SHEATHING MUST BE
PROFESSIONALLY ENGINEERED
AS BRACING. TYPE OF SHEATHING,
SIZE & SPACING OF NAILS
AND/OR TIE-DOWNS SHOULD
BE SPECIFIED.

(B) STRUCTURAL SHEATHING
Multiple-Story Building

NOTE
IN REGIONS NOT SUBJECT TO HIGH RISK OF HURRICANE OR EARTHQUAKE, HORIZONTAL PANELS WITHOUT BLOCKING & WITH FILLER STRIPS AT BASE MAY BE ACCEPTABLE.

PANEL NAILING SCHEDULE
SEE 78A

LEAVE 1/8-IN. SPACE BETWEEN ALL PANEL EDGES.

IN HIGH-WIND OR HIGH-RISK SEISMIC ZONES, USE 9-FT. VERTICAL PANEL CUT TO EXTEND FROM TOP OF FRAMING TO MUDSILL.

IN OTHER REGIONS, 8-FT. VERTICAL PANEL TO RIM JOIST WITH FILLER STRIP BELOW IS ADEQUATE.

MUDSILL DETAILS
SEE 12A & B

A STRUCTURAL SHEATHING/SINGLE-STORY BUILDING
Distance from Mudsill to Top Plate over 8 Ft.

STAGGER VERTICAL JOINTS BETWEEN STRUCTURAL PANELS.

WHEN NOT ENGINEERED AS BRACING, SHEATHING PANELS MAY PAN BETWEEN STUDS WITHOUT BLOCKING DEPENDING ON STUD SPACING, PANEL THICKNESS & SIDING MATERIAL. 3/8-IN. SHEATHING IS RECOMMENDED FOR STUDS AT 16 IN. O.C. & 1/2-IN. SHEATHING FOR STUDS AT 24 IN. O.C. VERIFY SPAN RATING ON PANELS.

NOTE
HORIZONTAL PANELS SHOWN IN THIS DETAIL MAY BE REPLACED WITH VERTICAL PANELS.
SEE 79A

PANEL NAILING SCHEDULE
SEE 78A

UPPER EDGE OF PANEL ALIGNS WITH LOWER TOP PLATE.

LEAVE 1/8-IN. SPACE AT ALL PANEL EDGES.

BLOCKING BEHIND PANEL JOINTS IS REQUIRED WHEN HORIZONTAL PANELS ARE ENGINEERED FOR LATERAL BRACING.

NOTE:
THIS DETAIL IS APPROPRIATE ONLY IF STUDS ARE PRECUT AT 90 3/4 IN. OR LESS & THE SUBFLOOR SITS DIRECTLY ON THE MUDSILL, SEE 33C & D, OR IF A SLAB FOUNDATION IS USED, SEE 22

MUDSILL DETAILS
SEE 12A & B

B STRUCTURAL SHEATHING/SINGLE-STORY BUILDING
Distance from Mudsill to Top Plate 8 Ft. or Less

TOP OF WALL
SEE 80B & C

SINGLE-PANEL
SIDING

CORNER
SEE 112

BASE DETAILS
SEE 80B & C

STUD WALL

In single-wall construction, a single panel of plywood or composite board siding provides both structural and weathering functions. This is an inexpensive, low-quality type of construction most appropriate for garages and sheds, but also used for residential construction. Panels are installed vertically, usually over a moisture barrier.

Precut studs (from 88½ in. to 92⅜ in.) allow 8-ft. panels to cover the framing on the exterior if the subfloor sits directly on the mudsill (see 80B) or if there is a slab floor. Adding trim to the base allows the use of 8-ft. panels with taller studs and/or different subfloor connections (see 80C).

Taller (9-ft. and 10-ft.) panels are also available.

(A) SINGLE-WALL CONSTRUCTION
Structural Sheathing

ROOF SYSTEM

TOP OF PANEL
FASTENED TO
TOP PLATE

STUD WALL

CONTINUOUS
MOISTURE BARRIER
FROM TOP OF PANEL
TO BELOW MUDSILL

8 FT. PANEL

BOTTOM OF PANEL
LAPS FOUNDATION
½ IN. (MIN.).

JOIST-BELOW-MUDSILL
FOUNDATION SYSTEM, SEE 33C & D,
OR
SLAB FOUNDATION, SEE 20.

(B) SINGLE-WALL CONSTRUCTION
8-Ft. Panel Typical

ROOF SYSTEM

TOP OF PANEL
FASTENED TO
TOP PLATE

STUD WALL

CONTINUOUS
MOISTURE BARRIER
FROMO TOP OF PANEL
TO BELOW MUDSILL

8 FT. PANEL

BOTTOM OF PANEL
AT OR BELOW
BOTTOM PLATE

FLASHING SEE 105B

WOOD WATER TABLE
LAPS FOUNDATION
½ IN. (MIN.).

(C) SINGLE-WALL CONSTRUCTION
8-Ft. Panel with Water Table

TONGUE-AND-GROOVE EDGE HELPS KEEP 2-FT. PANELS IN PLANE OF WALL.

HORIZONTAL 2FT. X 8FT. PANELS PROVIDE WATER-RESISTANT NON-STRUCTURAL SHEATHING.

FULL-SIZE PANELS (4FT. X 8FT., 9FT, OR 10FT.) CAN PROVIDE STRUCTURAL SHEATHING AND/OR FIRE RESISTANCE.

SHEATHING PANELS MAY SPAN BETWEEN STUDS WITHOUT BLOCKING SINCE SIDING MUST BE NAILED TO STUDS IN ANY CASE.

STAGGER VERTICAL JOINTS BETWEEN PANELS.

Many sheet materials that can be used for sheathing do not provide adequate lateral bracing. In addition to providing a base for a moisture barrier and siding, such nonstructural sheathings may also provide insulation or fire protection.

Insulative sheathings range in thickness from ½ in. to 1½ in. They include fiberboards, foam plastic, and rigid fiberglass boards. R-values vary. Verify that the permeability of the sheathing is coordinated with the permeability of the vapor retarder (see 88A).

Siding must be nailed through nonstructural sheathings directly into the studs beneath them. The need for lateral bracing is often satisfied by applying plywood or other structural panels to the corners of a building, with less-expensive nonstructural sheathing elsewhere.

Fire-protective sheathings are often required at walls on or near property lines, between attached dwellings, and between garages and living space. Type-X gypsum wallboard applied directly to the studs will satisfy most codes. Water-resistant gypsum board applied to the exterior of framed walls can also serve as an underlayment for various siding materials.

Gypsum board can also satisfy code requirements for shear strength. In this application, 4-ft.-wide panels may be applied vertically or horizontally (if covered with a moisture barrier) and must be nailed at 4 in. o.c. at the 4-ft. ends and 8 in. o.c. elsewhere. The panels do not have to be blocked at edges.

While gypsum sheathing can provide fire protection, water resistance, and structural strength, it has severe limitations for the attachment of siding materials. It is not a nailing base, so any siding material applied over it must be connected through the gypsum to the framing behind or to furring strips or another sheathing material applied over or under the gypsum.

A GYPSUM SHEATHING

B NONSTRUCTURAL SHEATHING

In most cases, minimum code requirements for let-in bracing or structural sheathing will sufficiently stiffen the walls of a light wood-frame building to resist the typical lateral loads of wind or eccentric loading. The stiffened walls act like the sides of a shoe box working in concert with the lid to maintain the overall shape of the box.

In more extreme conditions such as zones with a high risk of earthquakes or severe winds, lateral bracing measures beyond standard structural sheathing or let-in bracing must be taken. For small simple buildings in these zones, codes typically require increased nailing, strapping, and anchoring, as well as extra framing members.

But it is common to have conditions where even these increased code requirements are not adequate. Such conditions generally involve a building in which numerous wall openings reduce the ability of the wall to resist the lateral forces. In these cases, more extreme measures must be taken to resist lateral loads, and these usually involve calculations by an engineer to design diaphragms coupled with shear walls.

The following diagram summarizes how diaphragms and shear walls work together to resist lateral forces. For simplicity, the diagram shows a wind acting in a single direction perpendicular to the building wall, but in reality, the direction of lateral forces cannot be pre-dicted, so lateral resisting systems must be designed for the eventuality of forces in all directions.

The lateral force follows a continuous path through the structure: (1) the force of wind on the windward wall is transferred through studs to the top (and base) of the wall, (2) the diaphragm collects the loads from the top of the windward wall and transfers them to the top of the shear walls at either side, and (3) the shear walls at opposite ends of the diaphragm transfer the loads down to the foundation.

The diagrams on these pages use wind forces to illustrate how lateral forces follow a continuous path through diaphragm and shear walls. Although these structural elements are designed essentially the same to resist the forces of wind or earthquakes, these two forces act differently on buildings. Simply stated, wind forces act on the top of a building and earthquake forces act on the bottom. The relatively light weight of wood-frame buildings works to their advantage in the case of earthquakes, but works against them in the case of high winds.

Diaphragm—A diaphragm is a horizontal structure such as a floor or roof composed of sheathing, framing members, and a structural perimeter. In the case of a floor, the framing members are joists, and the structural perimeter is composed of rim joists and/or blocking (see 32). In the case of a roof, the framing members are common rafters (or trusses), and the structural perimeter is composed of end rafters (or trusses) and frieze blocks (see 129). A diaphragm acts as a horizontal beam to collect lateral forces and transfer these forces to the shear walls.

1.) FORCE OF WIND

2.) LOAD TRANSFERS TO TOP OF SHEAR WALL

3.) LOAD TRANSFERS TO FOUNDATION

HORIZONTAL RIGIDITY PREVENTS DEFLECTION.

TOP OF SHEAR WALL HOLDS EDGES OF DIAPHRAGM FIRMLY IN PLACE.

(A) **SHEAR WALLS**

Shear walls—Shear walls are extremely strong framed walls that connect the horizontal diaphragm to the foundation. They act like regular braced or structurally sheathed walls to resist the action of lateral forces except that they are much stronger. Their greater strength comes from increased nailing, thicker sheathing, more framing members at their edges, and more substantial anchoring.

Shear walls act as beams cantilevered from the foundation (or upper floor) to resist forces parallel to them. They are connected at their base to the foundation (or to another shear wall) and at their top to a diaphragm.

At their base, shear walls must resist both sliding and overturning. Horizontal forces can slide the wall off the foundation if adequate shear connections are not provided. Sliding forces are resisted by anchor bolts, by nailing, and/or by framing anchors at upper floors (see 85).

LATERAL FORCES FROM DIAPHRAGM

DEFLECTED SHAPE

ANCHOR BOLTS, FRAMING ANCHORS, AND/OR NAILING PREVENT SLIDING

Horizontal forces applied to the top of a shear wall can cause overturning unless the bottom corners are adequately tied (with hold-downs) to resist uplift (see 85 & 86A). While the force is applied, one edge of the wall will be in tension while the opposite edge is in compression.

Longer shear walls are inherently better because they have a longer base to resist sliding and because the hold-downs are farther apart to resist overturning.

Connections—Because shear walls involve a large number and variety of components and connections, it is critical that each connection be designed and constructed to resist the forces that pass through it. Depending on their location, connections may be called upon to resist vertical and horizontal forces in several directions. When designing and building to resist extreme conditions, it is especially important to pay close attention to manufacturers' instructions for the installation of connectors. A shear wall is only as strong as its weakest connection.

Distribution—Shear walls are generally located within each (principal) exterior wall of a building, but may also be located strategically at interior walls. For earthquake resistance, shear walls should generally be balanced on all four sides of the building; for wind resistance, however, shear walls should be longer (or stronger, see 85B) at the short walls in order to resist the larger wind forces imposed on the long walls.

LATERAL FORCES FROM DIAPHRAGM

DEFLECTED SHAPE

LEEWARD EDGE UNDER COMPRESSION

HOLD-DOWN ANCHOR TO FOUNDATION COUNTERACTS TENSION ON WINDWARD EDGE TO PREVENT OVERTURNING.

SHEAR WALLS NEED NOT EXTEND TO CORNERS.

SHEAR WALLS SHOULD BE LOCATED NEAR OR AT THE PERIMETER OF THE BUILDING

Plan

SHEAR WALLS SHOULD BE DISTRIBUTED EVENLY AROUND THE BUILDING'S PERIMETER.

Ⓐ **SHEAR WALLS**

NOTE
FOR GARAGE PORTAL FRAME, **SEE 87C.**

SHEAR WALLS CONNECT
TO FLOOR DIAPHRAGM.
SEE 86B

DRAG STRUT TIES
SHEAR WALL TO
DIAPHRAGM.
SEE 87B

LARGE WALLS ON
UPPER LEVELS MAY
USE STANDARD
CODE-PRESCRIBED
SHEATHING TO
PROVIDE LATERAL
RESISTANCE.

SHEAR WALLS ACT
COLLECTIVELY TO
RESIST LATERAL
FORCES IN A
SINGLE PLANE.

OPENINGS IN WALL
LIMIT SHEAR WALL
LOCATION AND SIZE.

SHEAR WALLS
CONNECT TO ROOF
DIAPHRAGM AT EAVE
AND RAKE.
SEE 86C & D

SHEAR WALLS AT
UPPER FLOORS
ANCHORED TO LOWER
SHEAR WALLS
SEE 87A

SHEAR WALLS
ANCHORED TO
FOUNDATION AT
BASE CORNERS.
SEE 86A

SMALL PROJECTIONS
MAY BE STABILIZED
BY FLOOR AND ROOF
DIAPHRAGMS, AND
THUS MAY NOT
REQUIRE SHEAR WALLS.

SHEAR WALLS ON
UPPER LEVELS CAN
BE OFFSET FROM
THOSE AT LOWER
LEVELS TO
ACCOMMODATE
OPENINGS.

Because lateral forces such as wind are assumed to act perpendicularly to the walls of a building, they can theoretically be resisted by shear walls in each of the four walls of a simple building. Forces acting in a north-south direction, for example, can be resisted by shear walls located in the east and west walls of the building (and vice versa). When the wind blows on a diagonal (as it usually does), shear walls in all four walls will be in play.

Because they connect diaphragm to the foundation, shear walls cannot be placed where there are openings in the wall. Therefore, in walls with many openings, there may need to be several shear wall segments in order to provide ample resistance to lateral forces.

Shear walls are most effective when they are wide relative to their height and their base anchors are far apart. For this reason, codes have specified that shear walls must have a height-to-width ratio of 3.5:1 or less. The practical effect of this limitation is a minimum shear wall width of approximately 2 ft. for a wall 8 ft. tall.

In a building with more than one floor, the need for shear walls is greater on floors nearest the ground. This is because the lower floors are required to resist the forces from upper floors in addition to their own. It is not unusual to have a two-story wood-frame building with engineered shear walls on the ground floor and standard code-prescribed sheathing on the upper floor.

The calculation of shear wall values is fairly complicated—involving different factors for earthquake or wind forces—and is thus usually performed by a licensed engineer.

Ⓐ **SHEAR WALLS IN CONTEXT**

DOUBLE TOP PLATE ACTS AS A STRUT.

DOUBLE STUDS AT EDGES ACT AS CHORDS THAT STIFFEN EDGE AND PROVIDE THICK ANCHORAGE FOR HOLD-DOWNS AT BASE.

BLOCKING AS REQUIRED PREVENTS BUCKLING OF PANEL EDGES.

HOLD-DOWNS AT BASE CONNECT TO FOUNDATION OR OTHER SHEAR WALLS TO PREVENT OVERTURNING.

ANCHOR BOLTS PREVENT SLIDING.

(A) COMPONENTS OF A SHEAR WALL

Once the lateral forces have been determined, there are seven basic considerations that need to be taken into account when designing a shear wall:

Proportion—Most codes specify a maximum height-to-width ratio of 3.5:1. This generally means that shear walls cannot be less than 2 ft. wide.

Hold-downs—Extreme forces at the lower corners of shear walls necessitate metal hold-downs to connect the shear-wall chord to the foundation or to lower shear walls (see 85A & 86A). There are a variety of types and capacities of hold-downs.

Anchor bolts—To prevent sliding, anchor bolts are used to connect the base of a shear wall to the foundation. At framed floors, framing anchors and nailing are used to prevent sliding. Hold-downs also resist sliding but are not generally considered in engineering calculations.

Sheathing strength—The strength of the rated sheathing must match the required capacity of the shear wall. Sheathing on both sides of the shear wall will double its capacity. All panel edges must be blocked to prevent buckling of the panel.

Chord strength—At the boundaries of the shear wall where stress is greatest, chords must be stronger than standard studs. A minimum of two studs is required by most codes (see 85A).

Strut strength—Like chords, struts are at the boundary of shear walls where stresses are greatest. Typical framing (i.e., single sole plate and double top plate) is usually sufficient as struts. Splices in struts should be avoided if possible.

Nailing—Size and spacing of nails must be specified. More nailing is required at the edges of panels than in the field of the panel. Increased nailing acts to increase wall strength (see 78A).

(B) SHEAR WALL DESIGN CONSIDERATIONS

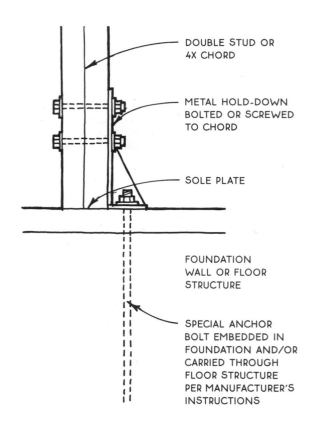

DOUBLE STUD OR
4X CHORD

METAL HOLD-DOWN
BOLTED OR SCREWED
TO CHORD

SOLE PLATE

FOUNDATION
WALL OR FLOOR
STRUCTURE

SPECIAL ANCHOR
BOLT EMBEDDED IN
FOUNDATION AND/OR
CARRIED THROUGH
FLOOR STRUCTURE
PER MANUFACTURER'S
INSTRUCTIONS

(A) SHEAR WALL HOLD-DOWNS

PLYWOOD FLOOR
DIAPHRAGM

SPECIFIED NAILING
AT DIAPHRAGM EDGE

RIM JOIST
OR BLOCKING

SHEAR WALL
SHEATHING LAPS
RIM JOIST,

OR

FRAMING ANCHOR
TIES DIAPHRAGM
TO SHEAR WALL STRUT.

DOUBLE TOP PLATE
ACTING AS A SHEAR
WALL STRUT

(B) SHEAR WALL/FLOOR DIAPHRAGM

PLYWOOD ROOF
DIAPHRAGM

SPECIFIED NAILING
AT DIAPHRAGM EDGE

FRIEZE BLOCK

ALTERNATIVE FRIEZE
BLOCK LOCATION

SHEAR WALL
SHEATHING LAPS
FRIEZE BLOCK,

OR

FRAMING ANCHOR
TIES DIAPHRAGM TO
SHEAR WALL STRUT.

DOUBLE TOP PLATE
ACTING AS A SHEAR
WALL STRUT

(C) SHEAR WALL/ROOF DIAPHRAGM
At Eave

PLYWOOD ROOF
DIAPHRAGM

LOOKOUT
SEE 145A

SPECIFIED NAILING
AT DIAPHRAGM EDGE

END RAFTER

SHEAR WALL
SHEATHING LAPS
END RAFTER,

OR

FRAMING ANCHOR
TIES DIAPHRAGM
TO SHEAR WALL STRUT.

DOUBLE TOP PLATE
ACTING AS A SHEAR
WALL STRUT

(D) SHEAR WALL/ROOF DIAPHRAGM
At Rake

When shear walls are required on upper floors, they must be tied, through the floor diaphragm, to the shear walls below. If upper and lower shear walls align, their corners may be tied with hold-downs (see 86A) with the lower hold-downs inverted. If the shear walls do not align, their edges may be tied to the diaphragm with a combination of twist straps (for uplift) and framing anchors (for horizontal shear).

Drag struts are sometimes required to tie the diaphragm to the shear walls, especially if the diaphragm is not bounded by shear walls at each end. A drag strut consists of a long metal strap firmly attached to the diaphragm above the shear wall. The drag strut extends into the diaphragm in a line parallel to the shear wall to pull or "drag" the force from the diaphragm to the shear wall.

(A) SHEAR WALL/SHEAR WALL
Tie between Floors

(B) DRAG STRUT

Garages with wide doors and limited walls are typical of buildings requiring shear walls. These conditions are so typical that several companies have developed proprietary premanufactured walls specifically for garages. The shear walls are strapped to the door header and work in conjunction with it. Garage shear walls are also commonly site-built.

Engineers can design reinforced windows so the window can extend virtually from wall to wall in small buildings and building extensions. A shear panel below the window opening is strapped to stiff single-piece or built-up columns at the corners. The columns effectively cantilever up from the panel, stiffening the entire wall.

(C) GARAGE PORTAL FRAME

(D) REINFORCED WINDOW

Once the walls are framed and sheathed, they must be protected from moisture. This involves the installation of a moisture barrier. The moisture barrier must be coordinated with an air barrier (to control air infiltration), a vapor retarder (to control water vapor), and insulation.

A moisture barrier (also called a weather barrier or water-resistive barrier) is a membrane directly under the siding that prevents any water penetrating the siding from reaching the sheathing or the framing. An effective moisture barrier stops liquid water but lets water vapor through, thereby letting the wall breathe.

A vapor retarder (formerly known as a vapor barrier) is a membrane on the warm side of the wall (usually the interior) that retards the passage of water vapor from the warm inside air into the cooler wall, where it could condense (see 120).

An air barrier limits the infiltration of air through the wall. Either a moisture barrier or a vapor retarder may be detailed to seal the wall against air infiltration, thereby becoming an air barrier as well (see 120).

Coordinating these components is critical to avoid trapping water vapor in the wall cavity. The principle to follow is that the permeability (the degree to which water vapor will pass through a material) must be higher for materials on the cool side of the wall (usually the outside) than for materials on the warm side of the wall (usually the inside). For example, foil-faced rigid insulation, which has a very low permeability, should not be placed on the exterior in a cool climate. The chart below rates the permeability of common materials.

MATERIAL	PERMEABILITY (perms per STM-E96)
Foil-faced insulation	0
4-mil PVC	0.08
Extruded polystyrene	0.3–1.0
½-in. CDX plywood	0.4–1.2
½-in. OSB	0.7
Kraft paper	1.8
15-lb. felt	5.6
½-in. gypsum board	20
Building or house wraps	88–107

(A) MOISTURE, VAPOR & AIR BARRIERS
Notes

OVERLAP 2 IN. TO 4 IN. AT HORIZONTAL JOINTS.

OVERLAP 4 IN. AT VERTICAL JOINTS.

ALIGN BOTTOM OF EDGE OF MOISTURE BARRIER WITH BOTTOM EDGE OF SHEATHING. SEE SPECIFIC SIDING TYPE FOR DETAILS.

A moisture barrier under the siding is a sensible second line of defense to prevent water from reaching the frame of the building. Many products such as 15-lb. felt and bitumen-impregnated paper (which come in 3-ft.-wide rolls, as shown here) have been used historically and are suitable for this purpose.

A moisture barrier acting also as an air infiltration barrier under the siding must retard the passage of air and be impermeable to water, but allow vapor to pass. Polyolefin membranes, commonly called building or house wraps, meet these specifications and are the most prevalent barriers. They are very lightweight and come in rolls up to 12 ft. wide, allowing a single-story building to be covered in one pass. Building wraps can provide better protection against air infiltration than felt and kraft paper because the wide rolls require fewer joints, and these joints are taped.

(B) MOISTURE & AIR INFILTRATION BARRIERS
Installation

SHEATHING

ROUGH FRAMING

1.) STAPLE MOISTURE BARRIER TO SILL & FOLD 6 IN. DOWN, EXTENDING 6 IN. TO EACH SIDE. DO NOT STAPLE LOWER EDGE; IT WILL LAP WALL MOISTURE BARRIER.

2.) STAPLE MOISTURE BARRIER TO JAMBS OF ROUGH OPENING & FOLD 6 IN. OVER SHEATHING & 6 IN. ABOVE & BELOW ROUGH OPENING.

3.) REPEAT STEP 2, BUT FOR TOP OF ROUGH OPENING. LEAVE OUTER EDGES UNSTAPLED FOR FUTURE INTEGRATION WITH WALL MOISTURE BARRIER.

NOTE
IT IS EXTREMELY IMPORTANT TO WRAP ROUGH OPENINGS WITH A MOISTURE BARRIER TO PROTECT THE FRAMING BECAUSE THIS IS WHERE LEAKS ARE MOST LIKELY TO OCCUR. THE METHOD SHOWN HERE IS ADEQUATE FOR LIMITED EXPOSURE SITUATIONS BECAUSE ALL LAYERS OVERLAP TO DIRECT WATER AWAY FROM THE STRUCTURAL FRAME OF THE BUILDING. SIMPLER METHODS MAY BE EMPLOYED WHERE EXPOSURE TO RAIN IS NOT LIKELY TO OCCUR, AND MORE EXTREME METHODS (SEE 89B) SHOULD BE EMPLOYED WHERE EXPOSURE IS SEVERE. FOR THE METHOD SHOWN HERE, MANY BUILDERS PREFER TO USE THIN MOISTURE BARRIERS THAT WILL NOT BUILD UP WITH THE FOLDS & WITH SEVERAL LAYERS.

(A) WINDOW/DOOR ROUGH-OPENING WRAP

MOISTURE BARRIER CUT AND TEMPORARILY RAISED AT HEAD OF ROUGH OPENING. THIS FLAP OF BARRIER WILL LATER BE LAPPED OVER HEAD FLASHING OR NAILING FLANGE. SEE 93, 94, 95A

MOISTURE BARRIER CONTINUOUS AROUND SIDES OF ROUGH OPENING.

WOOD STOP AT INSIDE OF ROUGH SILL FORMS BARRIER, FORCING WATER TO THE EXTERIOR.

FLEXIBLE PEEL-AND-STICK FLASHING MEMBRANE PROTECTS THE SEALS TO BASE OF ROUGH OPENING AND LAPS OVER AND SEALS TO THE MOISTURE BARRIER.

PLASTIC OR SHEET-METAL SILL PAN PROVIDES ALTERNATIVE MOISTURE PROTECTION IN SEVERE CONDITIONS. FASTEN PAN ONLY THROUGH SIDES AND FACE FLANGES AND LAP SIDES WITH PEEL-AND-STICK FLASHING.

(B) WINDOW/DOOR ROUGH-OPENING WRAP
Alternative Details for Severe Exposure to Rain

HEAD JAMB

SASH

SIDE JAMB

CASING

SILL

Traditional Window

CASING ATTACHES TO EXTERIOR FRAME OF BUILDING.

JAMB

SASH

STOP

JAMB EXENDER ADJUSTS JAMB WIDTH TO WALL THICKNESS.

Head Jamb

SILL SEE BELOW

CASING

JAMB

SASH

STOP

JAMB EXTENDER

Side Jamb

Modern windows derive from the traditional wooden window shown above. Older windows have a wooden sash that holds the glass, which is usually divided into small panes by muntin bars. This sash is hinged or slides within a wooden frame that is fixed to an opening in the wall. At the bottom of the frame is a wood sill, sloped to shed water. The sides and top of the frame are called jambs.

These components and their terminology have been handed down to the modern window, but modern windows are better insulated and better sealed, and usually need less maintenance than the traditional prototypes.

Today's window is made in a factory and is shipped ready to install in a rough opening. Several popular types, classified by their method of operation, include casement, double-hung, sliding, hopper, awning, and fixed. Each of these types is made in wood, vinyl, metal, fiberglass, or a combination of these materials. Sizes and details vary with the manufacturer. Double-hung, sliding, and fixed windows are generally made in larger sizes than the hinged types. Optional trim packages are available with most.

STOOL APPLIED AFTER WINDOW INSTALLED

SASH

CASING DIES ON TOP OF SILL.

SILL WITH DRIP EDGE

OPTIONAL APRON APPLIED AFTER WINDOW IS INSTALLED.

SIDE JAMB EXTENDS BELOW SILL TO SUPPORT WINDOW ON FRAMING.

Sill

SHEATHING

EXTERIOR WALL FINISH

FLASHING SEE 103B & C

CASING

HEADER SUPPLIES STRUCTURE TO WALL ABOVE WINDOW OPENING. SEE 68-70

INSULATION FILLS IN VOID BETWEEN WINDOW JAMB & ROUGH OPENING TO INSULATE BETTER & TO RETARD AIR INFILTRATION.

SASH

SUPPORT WINDOW ON FRAMING ACCORDING TO MANUFACTURER'S SPECIFICATIONS.

MOISTURE-BARRIER WRAP PROTECTS FRAMING FROM WATER LEAKS AROUND WINDOW. SEE 89

All windows require a coordinated installation in wood-frame walls, as follows:

Header—Size the header so that loads from above do not bear on the window itself, restricting operation.

Window wrap—Wrap the framing at the rough opening with a moisture barrier to protect it from any leaks around the edges of windows and doors.

Sill pan—At windows exposed to severe weather, add under the window a continuous metal or plastic pan that drains to the exterior (see 89B).

Shim and support—Shim the window at the sill and affix the shims to the framing so that the window is level and rests firmly on the framing.

Insulation—Place batt or spray foam insulation around the edges of the installed window to reduce both heat loss and air infiltration.

Air barrier—An air barrier, if used, must be sealed to the window unit. The moisture/air barrier may be sealed to the window nailing flange at the wall's outside surface, or the vapor/air barrier may be sealed to the jamb's inside edge at the wall's inside surface.

Wood windows—Wood windows (see 92–95) are pleasing for their warm, natural look. Along with the excellent thermal properties of wood, the aesthetic appeal of the wood window is its strongest asset.

The major disadvantages of wood windows are the initial high cost and the ongoing need for maintenance. Wood is susceptible to deterioration from the weather, so periodically refinishing the exterior surfaces is necessary. Every effort should be made to protect all-wood windows from rain by locating them under overhangs.

Wood windows clad with aluminum and vinyl were developed to minimize maintenance. The cladding decreases their need for maintenance yet retains the aesthetic advantages of wood on the interior.

Vinyl windows—Made of extruded PVC that is either screwed or heat-welded at mitered corners, vinyl windows (see 93B and 94B) have come to dominate the window market. Their cost and expected maintenance are low, while their insulative properties are relatively high. They are available in all typical operating types.

Vinyl windows are not available with exterior casings, but decorative casings are often added (see 93B). One disadvantage of vinyl windows is the limited range of available colors. The vinyl cannot be painted, and only very light colors such as white and tan are available because dark colors tend to absorb heat, causing warping.

Fiberglass windows—Newly developed fiberglass windows have none of the disadvantages of competing materials, but they are currently quite expensive. Fiberglass does not deteriorate in the weather like wood and does not expand with heat like vinyl. It is a relatively good insulator and is so durable that manufacturers offer lifetime warranties. Fiberglass windows have factory-applied finishes, ranging from light to very dark, and can be painted.

Metal windows—Until recently, aluminum windows were the most common low-cost window. But energy codes and the popularity of vinyl windows have virtually eliminated aluminum windows from the residential market except in very mild climates. Aluminum is still available for commercial applications. The ubiquitous storefront windows are available in polished aluminum, anodized bronze, and a spectrum of baked-enamel colors.

Unclad wood windows are attached to the building through the casing. This is the traditional way that windows have been fastened to wood buildings. The nail holes are typically filled, and the casings painted. It is also possible to cover the nails with a dripmold or with a backband that may be nailed from the side or the face, depending on the profile of the backband. The backband is mitered at the corners and dies on the sill.

When attaching a window through the casing, it is important to support the weight of the window unit from below. Shim the sill and/or the extensions of the side jambs below the sill.

Some manufacturers also recommend blocking and nailing the units through the jamb. In this case, the nails can be covered by the stops.

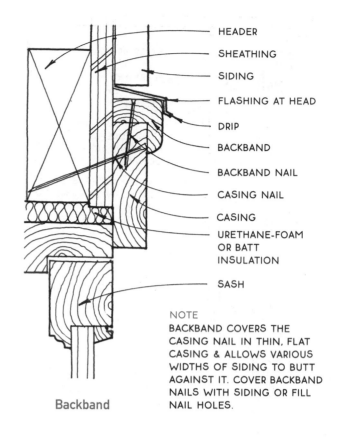

HEADER

SHEATHING

SIDING

FLASHING AT HEAD

DRIP

BACKBAND

BACKBAND NAIL

CASING NAIL

CASING

URETHANE-FOAM
OR BATT
INSULATION

SASH

NOTE
BACKBAND COVERS THE
CASING NAIL IN THIN, FLAT
CASING & ALLOWS VARIOUS
WIDTHS OF SIDING TO BUTT
AGAINST IT. COVER BACKBAND
NAILS WITH SIDING OR FILL
NAIL HOLES.

Backband

Typical Backband Profiles

HEADER

SHEATHING

SIDING

FLASHING AT HEAD

DRIP

CASING NAIL
(FILL NAIL HOLE)

BRICKMOLD

URETHANE-FOAM
OR BATT
INSULATION

SASH

NOTE
TRADITIONAL BRICKMOLD
CASING HAS DEEP PROFILE
TO ALLOW VARIOUS WIDTHS
OR SIDING TO BUTT
AGAINST IT.

Brickmold Casing

HEADER

SHEATHING

SIDING

FLASHING WITH DRIP
(OPTIONAL)

WOODEN DRIPMOLD

CASING NAIL

CASING

URETHANE-FOAM
OR BATT
INSULATION

SASH

NOTE
WOODEN DRIPMOLD
CAN TAKE THE PLACE OF
FLASHING DRIP AT THE HEAD
OF WINDOWS & DOORS.
IT MAY ALSO BE USED
IN CONJUNCTION WITH
FLASHING. IT IS OFTEN
USED WITH SHINGLE SIDING.

Dripmold at Head

(A) WOOD WINDOWS
Attachment through Casing

HEADER SEE 68-70

SHEATHING

WINDOW WRAP
SEE 89

SIDING

FLASHING IF EXPOSED TO
WEATHER
SEE 103B & C

CASING
SEE 92

Head Jamb

SIDING

SHEATHING

WINDOW WRAP
SEE 89

CAULK
SEE 106

CASING
SEE 92

Side Jamb

STOOL IS APPLIED
AFTER WINDOW IS
ATTACHED TO BUILDING.

SUPPORT SILL OF WIDE
WINDOWS ON FRAMING &
ATTACH THROUGH SHIMS
FROM BELOW.

FIT SIDING INTO GROOVE
PLOWED INTO UNDERSIDE
OF SILL, OR APPLY APRON
ON TOP OF SIDING.

WINDOW WRAP SEE 89

SHEATHING

Sill

MODERN WINDOWS ARE USUALLY MANUFACTURED
WITH NAILING FINS THAT ACT AS FLASHING & PROVIDE
NAILING FOR ATTACHING THE WINDOW TO THE BUILDING.
WINDOWS WITH NAILING FINS CAN BE USED BOTH
WITH & WITHOUT CASINGS.

HEADER

SHEATHING

SIDING

MOISTURE BARRIER
LAPS NAILING FIN
AT HEAD (FIN LAPS
MOISTURE BARRIER AT
SIDES & SILL).

FLASHING WITH DRIP

NAIL THROUGH FIN
INTO FRAMING.

URETHANE-FOAM
OR BATT INSULATION

METAL, VINYL, OR WOOD
JAMB & SASH (CLAD
WOOD SHOWN)

NOTE:
CAULK BETWEEN
NAILING FIN
& MOISTURE
BARRIER.

**Nailing Fin
without Casing**

HEADER

SHEATHING

SIDING

FLASHING WITH DRIP
AT HEAD

DECORATIVE CASING
RABBETED OVER
NAILING FIN

MOISTURE BARRIER
LAPS NAILING FIN
AT HEAD (FIN LAPS
MOISTURE BARRIER AT
SIDES & SILL).

SECONDARY FLASHING
OR DRIP IN CASING AT
HEAD

NAIL THROUGH FIN
INTO FRAMING.

URETHANE-FOAM
OR BATT INSULATION

METAL, VINYL, OR WOOD
JAMB & SASH (CLAD
WOOD SHOWN)

**Nailing Fin
with Casing**

 A **UNCLAD WOOD WINDOWS**
Attachment through Casing

B **WOOD, METAL, OR VINYL WINDOWS**
Attachment through Nailing Fin

HEADER SEE 68-70

SHEATHING

WINDOW WRAP
SEE 89

SIDING

NAILING FIN ATTACHED
TO FRAME OF BUILDING

FLASHING IF EXPOSED
TO WEATHER
SEE 103B & C

Head Jamb

SHEATHING

WINDOW WRAP
SEE 89

SIDING

NAILING FIN ATTACHED
TO FRAME OF BUILDING

CAULK AT JAMB
SEE 106

Side Jamb

SIDING

NAILING FIN ATTACHED
TO FRAME OF BUILDING

SHEATHING

WINDOW WRAP
SEE 89

SIDING

Sill

HEADER SEE 68-70

SHEATHING

WINDOW WRAP SEE 89

SIDING & OPTIONAL
CASING

NAILING FIN ATTACHED
TO FRAME OF BUILDING

FLASHING AT HEAD IS
RECOMMENDED IF WINDOW
IS EXPOSED TO WEATHER.
SEE 103B & C

JAMB EXTENDER WITH
CASING OR INTERIOR FINISH
WRAPPED TO WINDOW

Head Jamb

SHEATHING

WINDOW WRAP
SEE 89

SIDING & OPTIONAL
CASING

CAULK AT JAMB
SEE 106

NAILING FIN ATTACHED
TO FRAME OF BUILDING

JAMB EXTENDER WITH
CASING OR INTERIOR FINISH
WRAPPED TO WINDOW

Side Jamb

SHIM WINDOW TO
BOTTOM OF ROUGH
OPENING FOR LEVELING
& SUPPORT.

NAILING FIN ATTACHED
TO FRAME OF BUILDING

WINDOW WRAP
SEE 89

SHEATHING

SIDING

Sill

(A) CLAD WOOD WINDOWS
Attachment through Nailing Fin

(B) VINYL & FIBERGLASS WINDOWS

HEADER SEE 68-70

SHEATHING

WINDOW WRAP
SEE 89

SIDING

FLASHING IF EXPOSED TO
WEATHER SEE 103B & C

CASING

DOUBLE OR SINGLE
GLAZING INSTALLED WITH
CAULK OR GLAZING TAPE

INTERIOR STOP FOR EASY
GLASS REPLACEMENT

Head Jamb

SHEATHING

SIDING

CAULK AT JUNCTION OF
CASING & SIDING
SEE 106

CASING

GLAZING

STOP

JAMB

Side Jamb

STOOL

INTERIOR STOP

GLAZING INSTALLED WITH
CAULK OR GLAZING TAPE

SET GLASS ON RESILIENT
SETTING BLOCKS AT SILL.

SLOPED EXTERIOR STOP
AT EXPOSED LOCATIONS

SLOPED SILL WITH DRIP
AT EXPOSED LOCATIONS

APRON

SIDING

SHEATHING

Sill

Where fixed windows are acceptable, a great deal of expense may be saved by custom-building the windows on the job without sash. In this case, the glass is stopped directly into the window frame, and caulk or glazing tape seals the glass to the casing just as it would to the sash. Ventilation must be provided for the space by means other than operable windows.

When designing and installing site-built fixed windows, the following guidelines are useful:

1. Allow ⅛ in. minimum clearance at the top and sides of the glass.

2. Rest the base of the glass on setting blocks spaced one-quarter of the width from each end.

3. Glass can be set closer to the interior of the building than shown in 95A by using exterior stop.

4. Support the sill of wide or heavy windows by shimming it from the framing.

Ⓑ SITE-BUILT FIXED WINDOWS

Storm sash made today are usually fitted to aging single-glazed windows. The storm sash protects the existing window from the weather and also improves the thermal performance of the window.

Usually made of aluminum, storm sash are custom fit to the exterior face of the existing window. Many are operable from the interior and are fitted with screens. Depending on how they are installed, storm sash can either significantly extend the useful life of old windows or actually contribute to their deterioration. A proper installation depends on numerous factors including the climate and the detailing of the original window.

New custom wood windows can be manufactured with single glazing if fitted with storm sash. This can be useful for historic work or when attempting to make simple inexpensive sash for a microclimate that requires them. The storm sash provide the thermal performance required by code at the same time they protect the most precious part of the assembly—the sash itself—from the weather. Storms located at fixed sash can be left in place year-round, while storms at operable windows can be exchanged for screens during the summer.

Ⓐ SITE-BUILT FIXED WINDOWS

Ⓒ STORM SASH

HEAD JAMB

SIDE JAMB

SILL

Traditional Exterior Door

Head Jamb

- HEADER SEE 68-70
- SHEATHING WRAPPED WITH MOISTURE BARRIER
- SIDING
- FLASHING IF EXPOSED TO WEATHER SEE 103B & C
- CASING ATTACHES TO EXTERIOR FRAME OF BUILDING.
- INSULATION
- RABBETED JAMB

Side Jamb

- CASING ATTACHED FIRMLY TO FRAMING
- RABBETED JAMB SIZED TO WIDTH OF WALL (FRAMING + SHEATHING + INTERIOR FINISH)
- ADD SHIM & SCREW JAMB TO FRAMING BEHIND HINGES OF HEAVY DOORS.
- EDGE OF SILL BELOW

Sill

- EDGE OF CASING
- BOTTOM OR RAIL OF DOOR
- SUBFLOOR
- FINISH FLOOR
- WOOD OR METAL THRESHOLD WITH WEATHERSTRIP
- SILL WITH DRIP SEE 100A
- SIDING
- SHEATHING
- RIM JOIST

NOTE
FINISH ALL EDGES OF EXTERIOR DOORS TO PREVENT SWELLING.

Modern doors have been derived from traditional prototypes; they are better insulated and better sealed, and usually require less maintenance than their ancestors. Exterior hinged doors are made of wood (plywood, composite, or solid wood), fiberglass (fiberglass skin over a wood frame with a foam core), or insulated steel. Wood is the most beautiful, fiberglass the most durable, steel the most inexpensive.

Most exterior doors swing inward to protect them from the weather. Nearly all manufacturers sell their doors prehung (hinged to a jamb and with exterior casing attached). Sills and thresholds are the most variable elements in manufactured prehung doors. Most doors come with an extruded metal sill and integral threshold, which is installed on top of the subfloor (see 100B). Wood sills must be thicker than metal for strength, so they work best with finish flooring materials that are ¾ in. thick or more (see sill drawing at right).

Because of the torsional forces exerted by the hinges on the jamb when the door is open, doors that swing need to have their jambs fastened directly and securely to the building's frame. The best way to accomplish this is to nail the jamb directly to the supporting stud, using shims to make the jamb plumb. It is common practice to attach a prehung door through the casing with long screws through the hinge and jamb into the stud.

 EXTERIOR HINGED DOORS
Attachment to Walls

HEAD JAMB

SIDE JAMB

SILL

Sliding Door

HEADER **SEE 68-70**

SHEATHING

DOOR WRAP IF EXPOSED TO WEATHER **SEE 89**

NAILING FIN ON SHEATHING & UNDER MOISTURE BARRIER

SIDING

CAULK **SEE 106**

FLASHING IF EXPOSED TO WEATHER **SEE 103B & C**

INSULATE ROUGH-OPENING CAVITY.

JAMB EXTENDER TO MAKE JAMB FLUSH WITH INTERIOR WALL FINISH

Head Jamb

SHEATHING

DOOR WRAP IF EXPOSED TO WEATHER **SEE 89**

NAILING FIN ON MOISTURE BARRIER

SIDING

CAULK **SEE 106**

INSULATE ROUGH-OPENING CAVITY.

Side Jamb

SLIDING DOOR

FIXED DOOR

SCREEN DOOR

FINISH FLOOR

SUBFLOOR CARRIES WEIGHT OF DOOR UNIT.

SEAL BELOW SILL.

SHEATHING

WRAP SILL UNLESS PROTECTED FROM WEATHER. **SEE 89**

SIDING

Sill

Sliding doors, whether they are wood, vinyl, fiberglass, or aluminum, fasten to a building more like a window than like a hinged door. Because the weight of a sliding door remains within the plane of the wall, there is no lateral loading on the jamb of the door unit. Sliding doors are therefore supported on the sill and can be attached to the building like windows—through the casing or with a nailing fin. As with sliding windows, most sliding-door manufacturers recommend not fastening the nailing fin at the head because header deflection can impede door operation.

Sliding doors are trimmed to the finish materials of the wall in the same way as swinging doors and windows (see 92–94).

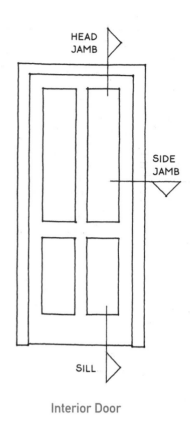

HEAD JAMB

SIDE JAMB

SILL

Interior Door

HEADER
SEE 68-70

INTERIOR FINISH

CASING

JAMB WITH APPLIED STOP
SEE BELOW

Head Jamb

INTERIOR FINISH

CASING

JAMB WITH APPLIED STOP
SIZED TO WIDTH OF WALL
(FRAMING + 2 + INTERIOR
FINISH)

ADD SHIM & SCREW JAMB
TO FRAMING BEHIND
HINGES OF HEAVY DOORS
OR
NAIL BEHIND STOP OR
HINGES OF STANDARD
DOORS.

Side Jamb

Because they do not have to be sealed against the weather, interior doors are much simpler than exterior doors. Interior doors are used primarily for privacy and to control air flow. The doors themselves are typically made of wood or composite wood products. They are 1⅜ in. thick, and have either panels, like the one shown above, or a flush plywood veneer over a hollow core or solid core.

Hinged interior doors are usually prehung on a jamb without casings. The jamb on the hinged side is first nailed to the frame of the building, using shims to make it plumb. The jambs at the head and opposite side are then shimmed for proper clearance and nailed.

Some doors are hinged to a split jamb that will expand to accommodate some variation in wall thickness. Interior doors do not have sills and rarely have a threshold unless the floor material changes at the door.

EDGE OF CASING

EDGE OF STOP

BOTTOM RAIL OF DOOR

UNDERCUT DOOR FOR
CLEARANCE & FOR AIR
FLOW.

FINISH FLOOR

SUBFLOOR

Sill

(A) **INTERIOR HINGED DOORS**

HEAD JAMB

SIDE JAMB

POCKET FRAME

SILL

Pocket Door

HEADER SET HIGHER THAN STANDARD TO ALLOW FOR TRACK.

INTERIOR FINISH

JAMB

CASING PROJECTS BELOW HEAD JAMB & IS FITTED WITH TRIM TO COVER TRACK HARDWARE.

ADJUSTABLE TRACK HARDWARE

Head Jamb

INTERIOR FINISH

CASING

POCKET-DOOR FRAME SIZED TO WIDTH OF WALL

NOTE
STANDARD WIDTH IS 4⁹/₁₆ IN. SIZED FOR 2X4 WALL WITH ¹/₂-IN. GYPSUM WALLBOARD ON BOTH SIDES.

Side Jamb

EDGE OF CASING

BOTTOM RAIL OF DOOR

UNDER-CUT DOOR FOR CLEARANCE AND FOR AIR FLOW

FINISH FLOOR

SUBFLOOR

NOTE
SOME POCKET DOORS HAVE GUIDES AT THE BASE OF THE POCKET.

Sill

Pocket doors—Pocket doors slide on a track attached to the head jamb and are sold as a kit, with the door and pocket separate and the pocket broken-down for ease of transport. The pocket is assembled at the site, and the head jamb (which much be set higher than 6 ft. 8 in. to allow for the track) is leveled, shimmed, and attached to the frame of the building. Next the pocket itself and the opposite jamb are shimmed and nailed. The heavier and wider the door and the better the quality of the hardware, the less likely the door is to derail. Pocket doors can't be made to seal as tightly as hinged doors. The walls are flimsy at the pocket, and wiring or plumbing can't be put in this section of wall.

Bypass doors—Bypass doors, such as sliding closet doors, slide on a track, like pocket doors, but have a double track and two doors that are not concealed in a pocket in the wall. Nylon guides on the floor keep the bottom of the doors in line. As with pocket doors, the header of a bypass door should be set higher than normal, and the casing should be designed to cover the track hardware. The jambs are like those for hinged doors but without stops.

Bifold doors—Bifold doors have two hinged halves that fold to one side, with a track at the top. Installation notes for bypass doors apply, except that casing trim must be kept above the top of the doors to allow the doors to fold.

 POCKET DOORS, BYPASS DOORS & BIFOLD DOORS

CASING (DIES ON TOP OF SILL)

SIDE JAMB

DOOR

WOOD OR METAL THRESHOLD

FINISH FLOOR

SUBFLOOR

BLOCKING BELOW EDGE OF SUBFLOOR

RIM JOIST

SHEATHING

SIDING

TRADITIONAL WOOD SILL WITH DRIP SLOPES AT 10° & REQUIRES THAT TOP OF RIM JOIST & COMMON JOISTS BE SHAVED OFF FOR INSTALLATION. SILL EXTENDS TO OUTSIDE EDGES OF DOOR CASINGS.

CASING TO BOTTOM EDGE OF SILL

JAMB

DOOR

WOOD OR METAL THRESHOLD

FINISH FLOOR

SUBFLOOR

BLOCKING BELOW EDGE OF SUBFLOOR

RIM JOIST

OPTIONAL SUB-SILL EXTENDS TO OUTSIDE EDGES OF CASINGS.

FLATTENED WOOD SILL SLOPES AT 7° & IS INSTALLED ON TOP OF JOIST SYSTEM. OUTSIDE EDGE IS FLUSH WITH JAMB (SHOWN) OR CASING.

NOTES
ADJUST PROFILE OF SILLS FOR OUTSWINGING DOORS.
WEATHERSTRIP BOTTOM OF DOOR.
WOOD SILLS ARE NOT COMPATIBLE WITH SLAB SUBFLOORS.

 A **WOOD SILLS**

CASING

SIDE JAMB

DOOR

INTEGRAL METAL THRESHOLD

FINISH FLOOR

SUBFLOOR

RIM JOIST

SHEATHING

METAL OR WOOD SILL SUPPOT
OR
SILL SUPPORTED BY CONCRETE WALK OR TERRACE.

EXTRUDED SILLS OF ALUMINUM OR POLYCARBONATE ARE THE MOST COMMON FOR ALL MODERN DOORS. THE THRESHOLD IS INTEGRAL. THE SILL MUST BE SUPPORTED AT OUTER EDGE. EXTRUDED SILLS MAY ALSO BE USED IN SLAB-ON-GRADE CONSTRUCTION.

B **EXTRUDED SILLS**

SOLE PLATE

SHEATHING

PLASTIC OR METAL PAN FITS IN DOOR ROUGH OPENING (USE NO FASTENERS THROUGH PAN).

INTERIOR FLANGE COORDINATES WITH SILL & FINISH FLOOR.

BOTTOM FLANGE OF PAN LAPS SHEATHING & DOOR WRAP.

NOTE
MOISTURE BARRIER (NOT SHOWN FOR CLARITY) CONTINUOUS AROUND SIDES OF ROUGH OPENING & LAPS SIDES OF SILL PAN, **SEE 89.**

AT DOOR LOCATIONS EXPOSED TO THE WEATHER, A GALVANIZED METAL DOOR-SILL PAN FIT INTO THE DOOR ROUGH OPENING WILL PROTECT THE STRUCTURE OF A WOODEN FLOOR SYSTEM BELOW.

 C **DOOR-SILL PAN**

HEAD
JAMB

SIDE
JAMB

SILL

Garage Door

CEILING LINE

DOOR IN RAISED
POSITION

DOOR TRACK

SECTIONAL DOOR

GARAGE SLAB

HEAD
ROOM

DOOR
HEIGHT
TYP.
6 FT. 8 IN.
OR
7 FT.

Head Jamb

HEADER SEE 68-70

2X CASING

JAMB SIZED TO
WALL THICKNESS

STOPMOLD COVERS
JAMB/CASING JOINT
& MAY BE FITTED WITH
VINYL OR RUBBER
SEAL.

GARAGE DOOR

Side Jamb

TRACK MOUNTS TO
2X CASING

NOTE:
VERIFY SIDE
CLEARANCE FOR
TRACK.

STOPMOLD

ROLLERS MOUNT
TO GARAGE DOOR.

Sill

BOTTOM SECTION
OF GARAGE DOOR

RUBBER OR VINYL
FLOOR SEALS
(OPTIONAL)

SLAB EDGE AT
GARAGE DOOR
SEE 25A

Residential garage doors have evolved from swinging and sliding types to almost exclusively the overhead variety. They are manufactured primarily with a solid-wood frame and plywood or particleboard panels. Paneled metal, fiberglass, and vinyl doors are available in some regions. There are two operating types, sectional and one-piece, both which can be manual or fitted with automatic openers.

Sectional doors—Sectional doors are by far the more common (see 101B). They are hinged horizontally—usually in four sections—and roll up overhead. The advantages are that a sectional door is totally protected by the structure when in the open position, and that it closes to the inside face of the jamb, making the design of the jamb opening somewhat flexible.

One-piece doors—One-piece doors pivot up. The door fits within the jamb and extends to the outside of the building when in the open position. This exposes the open door to the weather. The advantage of this type of door over a sectional door is the greater design flexibility afforded by the single-piece door. Hardware for this type of door is not usually available locally.

 A GARAGE DOORS

B SECTIONAL GARAGE DOOR

INTERSECTION
WITH ROOF
SEE CH. 4

ABUTTING MEMBERS
SUCH AS BEAMS,
JOISTS, OPEN
RAILINGS SEE 105A

WALL CONNECTION
WITH PORCH OR DECK
SEE 52-60

SEALANTS
SEE 106

HEAD FLASHING AT
WINDOWS & DOORS
SEE 103B & C

DOOR-PAN FLASHING
SEE 100C

ABUTTING WALLS
SUCH AS SOLID
PORCH RAILINGS
SEE 105B

ADJOINING FLAT
DECK/ROOF
SEE 56-57

HORIZONTAL JOINTS
IN MATERIAL SUCH
AS PLYWOOD
EDGES, WATER
TABLES, MATERIAL
CHANGES
SEE 104

WOOD WALL CAP
SEE 105D

Flashing is essential to keeping water away from the structure and the interior of a building. It is used wherever there is a horizontal or sloped penetration of the outer building skin or a juncture of dissimilar materials that is likely to be exposed to the weather. Flashing provides a permanent barrier to the water and directs it to the outer surface of the building, where gravity carries the water down to the ground. Of course, the best protection against water penetration of walls is an adequate eave, but wind-driven rain may make this strategy occasionally unreliable.

Wall flashing, which provides the first line of defense against water, should be taken very seriously, especially because walls, unlike roofs, are not intended to be replaced regularly. Wall flashing is likely to be in place for the life of the building.

Two physical properties affect the flow of water on vertical surfaces. The first property, gravity, can be used to advantage in directing water down the wall of a building. The other property, surface tension, creates capillary action that results in water migrating in all directions along cracks in and between materials. In

many cases, the negative effects of surface tension can be avoided by the proper use of a drip.

A drip is a thin edge or undercut at the bottom of a material placed far enough away from the building surface so that a drop of water forming on it will not touch the wall but will drop away (see 103A). Drips may be made of flashing or may be cut into the building material itself.

In the case of vertical joints, a sealant may be required to counter the effects of surface tension. Except for vertical joints that cannot be flashed effectively, a well-designed flashing (see 103–105) is always preferable to a bead of sealant.

Common flashing materials include galvanized steel, baked enamel steel, aluminum, copper, stainless steel, and lead. Because flashing materials may be affected in different ways by different climates, air pollutants, and building materials, the selection of appropriate materials is specific to each job. It is also important to isolate different metals when flashing to prevent corrosive interaction (galvanic action) between them. Consult with local sheet-metal shops for appropriate materials for specific applications.

Ⓐ **WALL FLASHING**

FLASHING

NOTE
THE DETAIL AT RIGHT
IS PREFERRED TO THE
DETAIL AT LEFT BECAUSE
IT IS LESS SUSCEPTIBLE
TO PHYSICAL DAMAGE.

PAINT TENDS TO CLOG FLASHING
DRIPS, BUT IT ALSO TENDS TO SEAL
THE CRACK BETWEEN FLASHING &
THE MATERIAL THE FLASHING COVERS.
FLASHING SUCH AS THIS SHOULD
BE USED ONLY AT LOCATIONS WITH
MINIMAL EXPOSURE.

(A) FLASHING DRIPS

SIDING

MOISTURE BARRIER

HEAD FLASHING
SEE 103C

HEAD CASING

ROUGH-OPENING
WRAP
SEE 89

SHEATHING

MOISTURE BARRIER

HEAD FLASHING

SIDING

HEAD CASING

Section

(B) WINDOW/DOOR HEAD FLASHING

THE BEST HEAD
FLASHING IS SOLDERED
AT THE END SO THAT
THE END PROFILE
MATCHES THE SIDE
PROFILE.

LOWER EDGE OF
FLASHING EXTENDS PAST
HEAD CASING AT LEVEL
OF DRIP.

CASING

Soldered Head Flashing

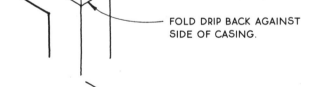

TWO MORE PRACTICAL
SOLUTIONS ARE TO CUT
THE FLASHING FLUSH
WITH THE CASING, OR,
BETTER, TO TRIM & FOLD
THE FLASHING ON SITE,
AS SHOWN BELOW.

TRIM FLASHING LONGER
THAN HEAD CASING &
NOTCH BACK TO CASING
AT FOLD IN FLASHING.

FOLD DRIP BACK AGAINST
SIDE OF CASING.

FOLD HORIZONTAL PART
OF FLASHING DOWN
OVER SIDE OF CASING.

SURFACE OF SIDING TO
BE APPLIED LATER.

Folded Head Flashing

(C) WINDOW/DOOR HEAD FLASHING
At End of Flashing

SIDING PANEL

CONTINUOUS HORIZONTAL Z METAL FLASHING WITH 2-IN. (MIN.) OVERLAPS AT JOINTS.

SIDING PANEL

MOISTURE BARRIER CONTINUOUS UNDER HORIZONTAL SIDING JOINT

Isometric

SHEATHING (OR STUD WALL FOR SINGLE-WALL CONSTRUCTION)

CONTINUOUS MOISTURE BARRIER

Z METAL FLASHING

SIDING PANELS

Section

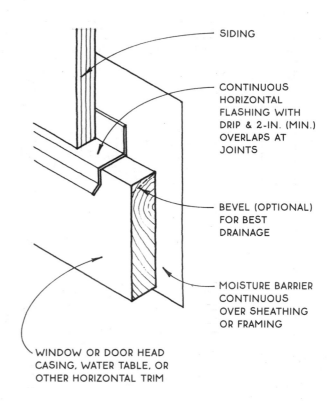

SIDING

CONTINUOUS HORIZONTAL FLASHING WITH DRIP & 2-IN. (MIN.) OVERLAPS AT JOINTS

BEVEL (OPTIONAL) FOR BEST DRAINAGE

MOISTURE BARRIER CONTINUOUS OVER SHEATHING OR FRAMING

WINDOW OR DOOR HEAD CASING, WATER TABLE, OR OTHER HORIZONTAL TRIM

(A) **HORIZONTAL WALL FLASHING**
Z Metal at Panel Joint

(B) **HORIZONTAL WALL FLASHING**
Joint between Dissimilar Materials

Step 1   Step 2

MOISTURE BARRIER ON SHEATHING

FLASHING

WATER TABLE OR OTHER HORIZONTAL TRIM

Outside Corner

Step 1   Step 2

MOISTURE BARRIER ON SHEATHING

FLASHING

WATER TABLE OR OTHER HORIZONTAL TRIM

Inside Corner

NOTE
IT IS PRUDENT TO COVER THE VERTICAL END OF THE FLASHING WITH A SMALL PIECE OF MOISTURE BARRIER OR A DAB OF SEALANT TO MINIMIZE THE POTENTIAL FOR LEAKS.

(C) **HORIZONTAL WALL FLASHING**
Corner Details

Any horizontal member such as a handrail, a trellis, or a joist that butts into an exterior wall poses an inherently difficult flashing problem at the top edge of the abutting members. Where such a connection is likely to get wet, the best approach is to avoid the problem by supporting the member independent of the wall. A handrail, for example, could be supported by a column near the wall but not touching it. A trellis could be self-supported.

If a horizontal member must be connected to a wall in a location exposed to the weather, two things can be done to protect the structure of the wall. First, do not puncture the surface of the siding with the member, and do everything possible to attach the member to the surface of the siding with a minimum number of fasteners. Second, place an adequate gasket, such as 30-lb. or 90-lb. felt, behind the siding at the location of the attachment. This will help seal nails or screws that pass through the siding to the structure of the wall.

SHEATHING

MOISTURE BARRIER

30-LB. (MIN.) FELT GASKET TO SEAL AROUND NAIL OR SCREW

SIDING

NAIL OR SCREW

HORIZONTAL MEMBER SUCH AS HANDRAIL OR TRELLIS ATTACHED TO SURFACE OF SIDING

Ⓐ FLASHING ABUTTING MEMBERS

THIS HORIZONTAL JOINT IS BEST PROTECTED WITH A FLASHING MADE TO FIT OVER THE SHEATHING AND MOISTURE BARRIER OF THE FRAMED WALL.

WALL CAP + 2 IN.

2 IN.

4 IN.

6 IN.

WIDTH OF FRAMED WALL

Flashing Detail

WALL CAP
SEE 105C

Ⓑ FLASHING ABUTTING WALLS

WOOD CAP WITH SLOPED TOP

P.T. FURRING SCREWED TO UNDERSIDE OF WOOD CAP

DRIP

TRIM FASTENED THROUGH SIDING TO FURRING & WALL

SIDING

MOISTURE BARRIER CONTINUOUS OVER TOP OF WALL

SHEATHING

WALL FRAMING

NOTE
THIS DETAIL HAS A CONTINUOUS MOISTURE BARRIER OVER THE TOP OF THE WALL WITHOUT PENETRATIONS. THE MOISTURE BARRIER MAY BE REPLACED WITH METAL FLASHING.

Ⓒ WOOD WALL CAP

WINDOW HEAD
SEE 103B & C

TOP EDGE
SEE 107B

BOTTOM EDGE
SEE 107C

TOP EDGE
SEE 107B

TOP EDGE
SEE 107B

DOOR HEAD
SEE 103B & C

SHEATHING
SEE 78-81

DETAILS OF
SIDING TYPES
SEE 108-119

VERTICAL EDGE
SEE 107A

MOISTURE
BARRIERS
SEE 88

BOTTOM EDGE
SEE 107C

OUTSIDE CORNER
SEE 104C

INSIDE CORNER
SEE 104C

Many of today's common exterior wall finishes have been protecting walls from the weather for hundreds of years. Others such as plywood, hardboard, and vinyl have been developed more recently. Regardless of their history, when applied properly, each is capable of protecting the building for as long as the finish material itself lasts.

If possible, the best way to protect both the exterior finish and the building from the weather is with adequate overhangs. But even then, wind-driven rain will occasionally get the building wet. It is important, therefore, to detail exterior wall finishes carefully at all but the most protected locations.

The introduction of effective moisture barriers under the siding has the potential to prolong the life of walls beyond the life of the siding alone. While the siding is still the first line of defense against weather, it is possible to view one of its primary functions as keeping sunlight from causing the deterioration of the moisture barrier, which ultimately protects the walls of the building.

Where the moisture barrier stops—at the edges and the openings through the wall—special attention must be paid to the detailing of exterior wall finishes.

Sealants—In this country alone, there are more than 200 manufacturers of 20 different types of caulks and sealants. However, the appropriate use of sealants for wood-frame buildings is limited for two reasons. First, sealants are not really needed—there are 200-year-old wooden buildings still in good condition that were built without the benefit of any sealants. Second, the lifespan of a sealant is limited—manufacturers claim only 20 to 25 years for the longest-lasting sealants. Therefore, it is best practice to not rely heavily on the use of sealants to keep water out of buildings.

However, some situations in wood-frame construction do call for the use of a sealant or caulk. These are mostly cases where the sealant is a second or third line of defense against water intrusion or where it is used to retard the infiltration of air into the building. In all instances, it is recommended that the caulk or sealant not be exposed to the direct sunlight.

(A) **EXTERIOR WALL FINISHES**

A VERTICAL EDGE IS A LIKELY PLACE FOR WATER TO LEAK AROUND THE EXTERIOR WALL FINISH INTO THE STRUCTURE OF A BUILDING. A CONTINUOUS MOISTURE BARRIER BEHIND THE VERTICAL JOINT IS CRUCIAL. A SEALANT CAN HELP DETER THE MOISTURE, BUT WILL DETERIORATE IN THE ULTRAVIOLET LIGHT UNLESS PLACED BEHIND THE WALL FINISH, WHERE IT WILL BE PROTECTED.

AT THE UPPER EDGES OF WALL FINISHES (AT EAVES & RAKES, UNDER WINDOWS & DOORS & AT OTHER HORIZONTAL BREAKS), DIRECT MOISTURE AWAY FROM THE TOP EDGE OF THE FINISH MATERIAL TO THE FACE OF THE WALL.

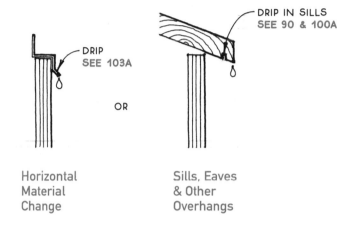

DRIP IN SILLS
SEE 90 & 100A

DRIP
SEE 103A

OR

Horizontal Material Change

Sills, Eaves & Other Overhangs

WINDOW OR DOOR CASING OR OTHER VERTICAL TRIM

SEALANT

WALL STRUCTURE

MOISTURE BARRIER CONTINUOUS BEHIND SIDING & VERTICAL TRIM

SIDING

Plan Section

A SECOND BEAD OF SEALANT MAY BE USEFUL AT OUTER EDGE IF SIDING IS TO BE PAINTED.

(A) EXTERIOR WALL FINISHES
At Vertical Edges

(B) EXTERIOR WALL FINISHES
At Top Edges

THE BOTTOM EDGE OF THE WALL FINISH IS MORE LIKELY TO GET WET THAN THE TOP. ALLOW WATER TO FALL FROM THE BOTTOM EDGE OF THE WALL FINISH IN A WAY THAT AVOIDS CAPILLARY ACTION.

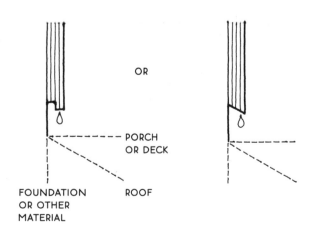

OR

PORCH OR DECK

FOUNDATION OR OTHER MATERIAL

ROOF

(C) EXTERIOR WALL FINISHES
At Bottom Edges

BUTT SIDING TO VERTICAL CASINGS & OTHER TRIM WITH SEALANT SEE 107A

OUTSIDE CORNERS TRIMMED WITH TWO-PIECE CORNER BOARDS AT LEAST AS DEEP AS DEEPEST PART OF SIDING

OR

METAL CORNERS ALSO AVAILABLE FOR MOST BEVEL TYPE HORIZONTAL SIDING

OR

SOME PROFILES MAY BE MITERED.

AT INSIDE CORNERS, SQUARE CORNER BOARD WIDER THAN DEEPEST PART OF SIDING FORMS SURFACE FOR SIDING TO BUTT AGAINST.

TRIM AT HORIZONTAL TOP EDGES RABBETED TO FIT OVER TOP EDGE OF SIDING

OR

FURRED-OUT TRIM LAPS OVER TOP EDGE OF SIDING.

RABBET AT BOTTOM OF SIDING FORMS DRIP AT BOTTOM EDGE.

ROOFING

RAKE TRIM

SPACER AS THICK AS THICKEST PART OF SIDING

SIDING

Elevation

Section

Rake Details

Drop · Shiplap · T & G · Bevel · Clapboard

Horizontal Siding Profiles

Types—Siding joints may be tongue and groove, rabbeted, or lapped. Common profiles (names may vary regionally) are illustrated at bottom right.

Application—Boards are typically applied over a moisture barrier and sheathing, and should generally be back-primed before installation. Boards are face-nailed with a single nail near the bottom of each board but above the board below to allow movement. Siding is joined end to end with miter or scarf joints and sealant over a stud.

Finish—Horizontal wood siding is usually painted or stained. Clear lumber siding is sometimes treated with a semitransparent stain.

Horizontal wood siding is common in both historic and modern buildings. The boards cast a horizontal shadow line unique to this type of siding.

Materials—Profiles (see below right) are commonly cut from 4-in., 6-in., and 8-in. boards. Cedar, redwood, and pine are the most typical. Clear grades are available in cedar and redwood. Many profiles are also made from composite hardboard or cementboard. These materials are much less expensive than siding milled from lumber and are almost indistinguishable from it when painted.

(A) HORIZONTAL SIDING
Wood, Hardboard, Cement Board

FURRING STRIPS STOP ABOVE HORIZONTAL FLASHING TO CONNECT AIR SPACES

VERTICAL FURRING STRIPS CREATE AIR SPACE BETWEEN SIDING AND MOISTURE BARRIER

FURRED OUT TRIM AT TOP OF WALL MAINTAINS GAP FOR VENTILATION OF AIR SPACE

WEATHER BARRIER LAPS HORIZONTAL FLASHING

FELT PAPER COVERS FURRING STRIPS

CONTINUOURS CORRUGATED PLASTIC SCREEN/VENT AT EAVE OR RAKE

CONTINUOUS CORRUGATED PLASTIC SCREEN/VENT AT BASE OF WALL

Rain Screen Siding—Rain screen siding strategy recognizes that some moisture will penetrate the wall and provides an easy path for this moisture to escape the wall assembly. A rain screen wall can be understood as two layers of protection with an air space in between. An outer layer sheds most of the weather, and an inner layer takes care of what little moisture gets through. The critical element—one that is not present in (most) other siding systems—is the air space between the two layers. This air space provides a capillary break and promotes the rapid escape of moisture with a clear path to the base of the wall for water to drain by gravity and by allowing ventilation to remove moisture in the form of water vapor.

Materials—The inner layer can be made of the same materials as the moisture barrier in most siding systems: tar paper, building wrap, or rigid foam insulation in conjunction with flashing (and tape or sealant). The air space is created by vertical furring strips, usually ⅜ in. to ½ in. thick aligned over the studs. The outer layer is usually made with horizontal wood siding (clapboards), but can be made of any material that sheds water and is capable of spanning between the vertical furring strips. Screening is required at the top and bottom of the wall to keep insects out of the air space.

Application—Materials are applied with nails or staples as with standard siding materials. Special care should be taken that materials lap properly to shed water. The inner layer, called the drainage plane, must be especially carefully detailed and constructed to keep moisture out of the framing. Back-priming and end-priming of wood siding materials is very important to prolong the life of the material and of the finish.

Finish—Rain screen siding can be finished with any paint or stain designed for use on standard siding. Because the system breathes and does not trap moisture within the wall, finishes will typically outlast the same finish applied to a standard wall.

Ⓐ RAIN SCREEN SIDING

LAP INSIDE CORNERS. FIRST PIECE MAY BE HELD AWAY FROM CORNER TO ALLOW FOR MOISTURE BARRIER.

TRIM MAY BE ELIMINATED AT HORIZONTAL TOP EDGES IF SIDING IS CUT CAREFULLY TO FIT UNDER SILLS OR EAVES.

OR

MATCHED SIDING MAY BE TRIMMED WITH SECOND LAYER, OR BOARD SIDING WITH HORIZONTAL BATTEN.

SIDING BUTTS TO VERTICAL CASINGS & OTHER TRIM WITH SEALANT. **SEE 107A**

OUTSIDE CORNERS LAPPED

OR

TRIMMED WITH LAPPED BATTENS IN BOARD & BATTEN

BOTTOM EDGE PROJECTS BELOW SHEATHING TO FORM DRIP AT FOUNDATION.

OR

RABBET OR BEVEL ON REAR SIDE FORMS DRIP AT HORIZONTAL SURFACES.

Vertical wood siding falls into two major groups. One group, such as the tongue-and-groove and channel patterns shown below, has its side edges rabbeted or grooved and lies flat on the wall, one board thick. The other group, including board and batten, has square edges and uses a second layer to cover the edges of the first layer. The thicker patterns in the second group may require careful coordination with casings and trim. Both groups require ⅝-in. (min.) plywood or OSB sheathing or horizontal nailing strips to strengthen the wall. Where end joints occur, siding is sealed and joined with a scarf joint or a miter joint sloped to the exterior.

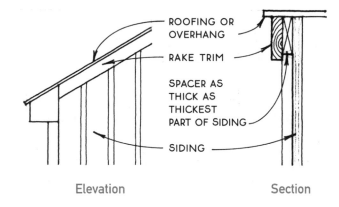

ROOFING OR OVERHANG

RAKE TRIM

SPACER AS THICK AS THICKEST PART OF SIDING

SIDING

Elevation　　　Section

Rake Details

CHANNEL

TONGUE AND GROOVE FLUSH (SHOWN) AND V-GROOVE

BOARD AND BATTEN

REVERSE BOARD AND BATTEN

VERTICAL EDGES (CASINGS) ARE TRIMMED WITH SIDE CHANNEL INSTALLED BEFORE SIDING & INTO WHICH SIDING SLIDES (RAKE RIMMED WITH SAME CHANNEL).

ALL SIDING PIECES ARE ATTACHED THROUGH SLOTS THAT ALLOW FOR EXPANSION & CONTRACTION. LOCATE NAILS IN THE CENTER OF THE SLOT; NAIL LOOSELY SO PIECES CAN MOVE WITH TEMPERATURE CHANGES.

TOP EDGES (SOFFIT TRIM, EAVE TRIM & UNDER SILLS) TRIMMED WITH UNDER SILL TRIM INTO WHICH SIDING SLIDES. SPECIAL TOOL PUNCHES TABS AT CUT TOP EDGE OF SIDING; TABS LOCK INTO TRIM, WHICH MAY NEED TO BE FURRED DEPENDING ON LOCATION OF HORIZONTAL CUT IN SIDING.

SIDING HOOKS ON PIECE BELOW.

OUTSIDE CORNERS ARE A VARIATION OF THE BASIC CHANNEL & COVER THE ENDS OF THE SIDING.

INSIDE CORNERS ARE TRIMMED WITH DOUBLE CHANNEL INSTALLED BEFORE SIDING & INTO WHICH SIDING SLIDES.

STARTER STRIP PROVIDES CONTINUOUS ANCHORAGE FOR BOTTOM ROW.

THE BASIC PIECE HOOKS OVER THE PIECE BELOW & IS NAILED AT THE TOP EDGE. SIDES, TOPS & RAKES ARE TRIMMED WITH J-SHAPED CHANNELS INTO WHICH THE SIDING SLIDES.

Vinyl sidings were developed in an attempt to eliminate the maintenance required of wood sidings. Most aluminum-siding manufacturers have moved to vinyl.

Material—There are several shapes available. Most imitate horizontal wood bevel patterns, but there are some vertical patterns as well. Lengths are generally about 12 ft., and widths are 8 in. to 12 in. The ends of panels are factory-notched to allow for lapping at end joints, which accommodates expansion and contraction. Color is integral with the material and ranges mostly in the whites, grays, and imitation wood colors. The vinyl will not dent like metal, but will shatter on sharp impact, especially when cold. Most manufacturers also make vinyl soffit material, and some also make decorative trim. Vinyl produces extremely toxic gasses when involved in a building fire.

Installation—Vinyl has little structural strength, so most vinyl sidings must be installed over solid sheathing. Proper nailing with corrosion-resistant nails is essential to allow for expansion and contraction. Because vinyl trim pieces are rather narrow, many architects use vinyl siding in conjunction with wood trim, as suggested in the isometric drawing above.

Ⓐ **VINYL SIDING**

TOP EDGES ARE SOMETIMES LEFT WITHOUT TRIM BECAUSE THEY CAN EASILY BE CUT TO A CLEAN SQUARE EDGE THAT IS BUTTED AGAINST A SOFFIT, EAVE, OR OTHER HORIZONTAL SURFACE, OR TRIM MAY BE ADDED.

HORIZONTAL JOINTS BETWEEN SIDING PANELS OR BETWEEN PANELS & OTHER MATERIAL SHOULD BE BLOCKED IF THEY DO NOT OCCUR OVER A PLATE OR FLOOR FRAMING.

BOTTOM EDGES AT THE BASE OF A WALL EXTEND 1/2 IN. (MIN.) BELOW THE SHEATHING TO FORM A DRIP.
SEE DETAIL AT RIGHT

MUDSILL

DRIP

LAP PANELS TO FORM A DRIP EDGE

OR

BUTT PANELS AND FLASH WITH METAL Z FLASHING, **SEE 104A**

OUTSIDE CORNERS HAVE ONE PANEL RABBETED IF CORNER IS NOT COVERED WITH CORNERBOARDS.

VERTICAL JOINTS BETWEEN SIDING PANELS SHOULD ALWAYS FALL OVER A STUD.

INSIDE CORNERS MAY BE BUTTED & CAULKED OR HAVE CORNER BOARDS ADDED.

BUTT JOINT COVERED WITH BATTEN

MANUFACTURED LAP JOINT

Materials—Plywood siding is available in 4-ft.-wide panels, 8 ft., 9 ft., and 10 ft. tall. Typical thicknesses are 3/8 in., 1/2 in. and 5/8 in. The panels are usually installed vertically to avoid horizontal joints, which require blocking and flashing. Textures and patterns can be cut into the face of the plywood to resemble vertical wood-siding patterns.

Installation—Manufacturers suggest leaving a 1/8-in. gap at panel edges to allow for expansion. All edges should be treated with water repellent before installation. It is wise to plan to have window and door trim because of the difficulty of cutting panels precisely around openings. Fasten panels to framing following the manufacturer's recommendation.

Single-wall construction—Since plywood, even in a vertical orientation, will provide lateral bracing for a building, it is often applied as the only surface to cover a building. This is called single-wall construction and has some unique details (see 80 and 113).

Ⓐ **PLYWOOD SIDING**

Most of the details for double-wall plywood construction also apply to single-wall construction. But with single-wall construction, the moisture barrier is applied directly to the framing, making it more difficult to achieve a good seal. The wide-roll, polyolefin moisture/air infiltration barriers work best (see 88B). Also, the bottom edge of the plywood is flush against the foundation, so a drip detail is impossible (see right).

MUDSILL

NO SHEATHING BENEATH PLYWOOD, SO PLYWOOD DOES NOT FORM DRIP AT BOTTOM EDGE. SEALANT MAY BE BETTER THAN NOTHING IN SOME SITUATIONS.

Flashing—Windows and doors that are attached through the casing and need head flashing because of exposure to rain or snow are very difficult to flash. As shown in the drawings below, a saw kerf must be cut into the siding at the precise location of the flashing. The flashing and siding must be installed simultaneously before the door or window is attached.

HEADER

ROUGH OPENING

Step 1

PLYWOOD

HEADER

SAW KERF

Step 2

HEAD FLASH & FURRING AT HEAD

Step 3

SEE SECTION

INSTALLED WINDOW OR DOOR WITH HEAD FLASH

Step 4

Flashing a Header

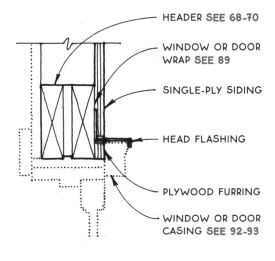

HEADER SEE 68-70

WINDOW OR DOOR WRAP SEE 89

SINGLE-PLY SIDING

HEAD FLASHING

PLYWOOD FURRING

WINDOW OR DOOR CASING SEE 92-93

Section

Ⓐ **SINGLE-WALL PLYWOOD SIDING**

COVER HORIZONTAL EDGES WITH TRIM FASTENED TO A SPACER. LOCATE SHINGLE FASTENERS VERY HIGH ON LAST COURSE.

SHINGLES BUTT TO VERTICAL TRIM.

1/4-IN. SPACE BETWEEN ADJACENT SHINGLES IN FIELD (NOT AT CORNERS OR EDGES)

OUTSIDE CORNERS ARE WOVEN SO ALTERNATE ROWS HAVE EDGE OF SHINGLE EXPOSED. EDGE IS TRIMMED FLUSH WITH ADJACENT SHINGLE ON OPPOSITE FACE OF CORNER. CORNER BOARDS CAN ALSO BE USED AS TRIM AT OUTSIDE CORNERS. SEE 110

NOTE
SHORT HORIZONTAL EDGES SUCH AS APRONS MAY BE COVERED WITH A PIECE OF TRIM FASTENED TO THE SLOPED SURFACE OF THE SHINGLES. FOR RAKE TRIM. SEE 115A & B

FASTENERS 1 IN. (MIN.) ABOVE COURSE LEVEL OF NEXT COURSE

JOINTS BETWEEN SHINGLES OFFSET 1 1/2 IN. (MIN.) FOR THREE ADJACENT COURSES.

DOUBLE BOTTOM COURSE PROJECTS 1/2 IN. BELOW SHEATHING TO FORM DRIP.

INSIDE CORNERS ARE WOVEN LIKE OUTSIDE CORNERS. SHINGLES ARE TRIMMED TO BUTT AGAINST SHINGLE ON OPPOSITE FACE. TOP SHINGLE ALTERNATES FROM ROW TO ROW. CORNERBOARDS CAN ALSO BE USED AS TRIM AT INSIDE CORNERS. SEE 110

Shingles are popular because they can provide a durable, low-maintenance siding with a refined natural appearance. Shadow lines are primarily horizontal but are complemented with minor verticals. Material costs are relatively moderate but installation costs may be very high.

Materials—Shingles are available in a variety of sizes, grades, and patterns. The most typical is a western red cedar shingle 16 in. long. Redwood and cypress shingles are also available. Because shingles are relatively small, they are extremely versatile, with a wide variety of coursings and patterns.

Installation—Shingles are applied over a moisture barrier to a plywood or OSB wall sheathing so at least two layers of shingles always cover the wall. Standard coursing allows nail or staple fasteners to be concealed by subsequent courses. With shingles there is less waste than with other wood sidings.

Finish—Enough moisture gets between and behind shingles that paint will not adhere to them reliably. Left unfinished, they endure extremely well, but may weather differentially, especially between those places exposed to the rain and those that are protected. Stains and bleaching stains will produce more even weathering.

Preassembled shingles—Shingles are also available mounted to boards. These shingle boards increase material cost, decrease installation cost, and are most appropriate for large, uninterrupted surfaces. Corner boards are required at corners.

(A) **WOOD SHINGLE SIDING**

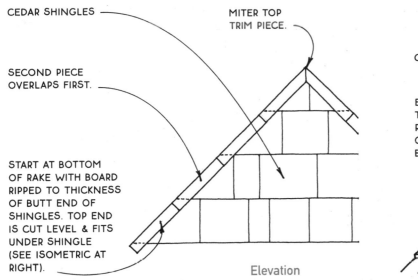

CEDAR SHINGLES

MITER TOP TRIM PIECE.

SECOND PIECE OVERLAPS FIRST.

START AT BOTTOM OF RAKE WITH BOARD RIPPED TO THICKNESS OF BUTT END OF SHINGLES. TOP END IS CUT LEVEL & FITS UNDER SHINGLE (SEE ISOMETRIC AT RIGHT).

Elevation

CEDAR SHINGLES

EQUAL SIZED TRIM PIECES RIPPED FROM 2X CEDAR LAP AT BOTTOM

Isometric

ONE METHOD OF FINISHING THE TOP EDGE OF A SHINGLE WALL IS TO LAP THE SHINGLE COURSES WITH TRIM PIECES RIPPED FROM A CEDAR 2X. IF THE COURSING IS EQUAL, ALL THE TRIM PIECES, EXCEPT FOR THE MITERED TOP PIECES, WILL ALSO BE EQUAL.

(A) SHINGLE SIDING AT RAKE
Lapped Trim

RIP SHINGLES TO DESIRED WIDTH & APPLY AT SAME COURSING AS BODY OF WALL.

Shingled Trim

SPACER

1X TRIM LAPS TOP EDGE OF SHINGLES.

1x Trim

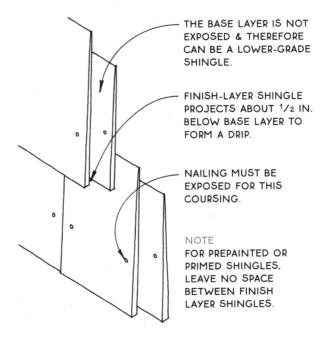

THE BASE LAYER IS NOT EXPOSED & THEREFORE CAN BE A LOWER-GRADE SHINGLE.

FINISH-LAYER SHINGLE PROJECTS ABOUT 1/2 IN. BELOW BASE LAYER TO FORM A DRIP.

NAILING MUST BE EXPOSED FOR THIS COURSING.

NOTE
FOR PREPAINTED OR PRIMED SHINGLES, LEAVE NO SPACE BETWEEN FINISH LAYER SHINGLES.

DOUBLE COURSING, AN ALTERNATIVE COURSING METHOD, CALLS FOR TWO LAYERS APPLIED AT THE SAME COURSE. A PREPAINTED OR PRIMED SHINGLE CALLED SIDEWALL SHAKE IS COMMONLY USED.

(B) SHINGLE SIDING AT RAKE
Shingled & 1x Trim

(C) DOUBLE-COURSED SHINGLES

BRICK & SIDING
CORNER SEE 117A

FOUNDATION WALL
SEE 117B

CORNERS SEE 117A

WINDOW & DOOR
OPENINGS SEE 117C

FASCIA

SOFFIT

TOP OF WALL IS DETAILED TO KEEP WATER OFF THE
HORIZONTAL SURFACE OF THE TOP BRICK. THIS CAN
USUALLY BE ACCOMPLISHED WITH THE DETAILING OF
THE ROOF ITSELF. COVER THE JOINT BETWEEN BRICK
& ROOF WITH WOOD TRIM. CAULK THE JOINT AS FOR
VERTICAL JOINTS, BELOW.

RAKE TRIM
LAPS BRICK.

ATTACH TO FRAMING
WITH LOOKOUTS.

SEALANT BETWEEN
WOOD & BRICK

RAKE IS USUALLY TRIMMED WITH WOOD
SUFFICIENTLY WIDE TO COVER THE STEPPING OF BRICK
CAUSED BY SLOPE. DETAIL AS FOR TOP OF WALL.

Brick veneer covers wood-frame construction across
the country. Where it is not subjected to moisture and
severe freezing, it is the most durable exterior finish.

Materials—Bricks come in a wide variety of sizes,
with the most common (and the smallest) being the
modular brick (2¼ in. by 3⅝ in. by 7⅝ in.). These
bricks, when laid in mortar, can follow 8-in. modules
both horizontally and vertically. Colors vary from cream
and yellows to browns and reds, depending on the clay
color and method of firing. Bricks should be selected
for their history of durability in a given region.

Installation—Bricks are laid in mortar that should be
tooled at the joints to compress it for increased resistance to the weather. Because both brick and mortar
are porous (increasingly so as they weather over the
years), they must be detailed to allow for ventilation
and drainage of the unexposed surface. A 1-in. air
space between the brick and the wood framing, with
weep holes located at the base of the wall, typically suf-
fices (see 117B). It is important to keep this space and
the weep holes clean and free of mortar droppings to
ensure proper drainage.

SHEATHING

AIR SPACE

BRICK

BACKER ROD

SEALANT

VERTICAL CASING OR
TRIM OF WOOD OR
OTHER MATERIAL

VERTICAL JOINTS SUCH AS WINDOW & DOOR
CASINGS AND AT TRANSITIONS TO OTHER MATERIALS
MUST BE CAREFULLY CAULKED TO SEAL AGAINST
THE WEATHER. BACKPRIME WOOD COVERED BY OR
IN CONTACT WITH BRICK.

Finish—A number of clear sealers and masonry
paints can be applied to the finished masonry to
improve weather resistance, but reapplication is
required every few years.

BOTH INSIDE & OUTSIDE
CORNERS CAN BE MADE
SIMPLY WITH THE BRICKS
THEMSELVES.

Brick Corner

SHEATHING

15-LB. FELT OVERLAPS
FLASHING.

1-IN. AIR SPACE

STEEL ANGLE LINTEL

HEAD FLASHING

CASING PREPRIMED
IF WOOD

Head Jamb

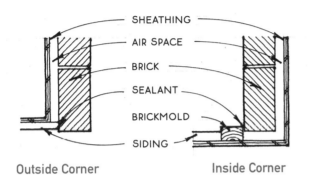

SHEATHING

AIR SPACE

BRICK

SEALANT

BRICKMOLD

SIDING

Outside Corner   Inside Corner

Brick and Siding Corners

SHEATHING

1-IN. AIR SPACE

SEALANT BETWEEN
CASING & BRICK VENEER

CAULK BETWEEN CASING
AND MOISTURE BARRIER.

CASING PREPRIMED
IF WOOD

Side Jamb

(A) BRICK VENEER
Corners

MASONRY TIES
AT 16 IN. O.C.
VERTICALLY &
HORIZONTALLY

1-IN. AIR SPACE
BETWEEN BRICK
& MOISTURE
BARRIER

SHEATHING

MUDSILL

15-LB. FELT
MOISTURE
BARRIER LAPS
FLASHING.

FLASHING
CONTINUOUS
UNDER BOTTOM
BRICK

FOUNDATION WALL
SEE 11C & D

ELIMINATE MORTAR
TO PROVIDE WEEP
HOLE AT HEAD
JOINTS EVERY 6 FT.

SILL PREPRIMED ON
UNDERSIDE IF WOOD

SEALANT BETWEEN SILL
AND BRICK.

ROWLOCK BRICK
SLOPED AT ANGLE
OF SILL

FLASHING CONTINUOUS
TO BACK OF SILL

SHEATHING

15-LB. FELT

1-IN. AIR SPACE

Sill

(B) BRICK VENEER
Wall Construction

(C) BRICK VENEER AT WINDOW/DOOR
Attachment to Casing & Sill

TRANSITION TO OTHER MATERIALS MADE WITH CASING BEAD AT TOP, SIDE, OR BOTTOM EDGES

INSIDE CORNERS ARE MADE WITH CONTINUOUS STUCCO   OR

TWO CASING BEADS USED TO MAKE AN EXPANSION JOINT

CASING BEAD AT TOP, SIDE, BOTTOM, OR RAKE EDGES. ALSO SEE INSIDE CORNERS.

CAULK

CASING BEAD AT TOP, SIDE, OR BOTTOM EDGES. ALSO SEE INSIDE CORNERS.

CONTROL JOINT ORIENTED HORIZONTALLY OR VERTICALLY & LOCATED OVER STRUCTURAL MEMBERS & DIAPHRAGMS BREAKS STUCCO PANELS INTO 18-FT. (MAX.) DIMENSIONS (OR LENGTH-TO-WIDTH RATION OF 2.5:1).

SELF-FURRING GALVANIZED 17-GAUGE 1½-IN. MESH STUCCO WIRE (SHOWN) OR GALVANIZED EXPANDED METAL LATH

15-LB. FELT BOND BREAK

MOISTURE BARRIER/DRAINAGE PLANE

SOLID SHEATHING STRONG ENOUGH TO RESIST PRESSURE OF STUCCO APPLICATION

AT OUTSIDE CORNERS, USE A CORNER BEAD WHERE A SCREED IS REQUIRED.   OR   WRAP WITH CONTINUOUS STUCCO.

WEEP SCREED AT BASE OF WALL LAPS OVER SHEATHING TO FORM DRIP   OR   STUCCO CONTINUES TO BELOW GRADE

Stucco is made of cement, sand, and lime. It is usually applied in three coats, building to a minimum thickness of ¾ in. Cost may be moderate in areas with high use, but high where skilled workers are few.

Materials—Reinforcing materials through which the plaster is forced are either stucco wire or metal lath. This reinforcing is fastened either to sheathing or directly to the framing (without sheathing). When sheathing is used, it must be rigid enough to remain stiff during the process of applying the stucco—⅝-in. plywood is typical.

A double-layer moisture barrier between the reinforcing and the framing is important because the stucco will bond with the outer layer of barrier, destroying its ability to repel water. The outer layer forms a bond break so that the inner layer will remain intact to protect the framing. The inner layer performs best if it is thick, with drainage channels.

Application—The first (scratch) coat has a raked finish, the second (brown) coat has a floated finish, and the final (color) coat may have a variety of finishes. Applying stucco takes skill, so stucco is the least appropriate of all the exterior wall finishes for owner-builders to attempt.

Finish—Textures ranging from smooth to rustic are achieved by troweling the final coat. Color may be integral in the final coat or may be painted on the surface. Stucco is not very moisture resistant and must be sealed or painted.

Ⓐ STUCCO WALL SYSTEM

TOP OR SIDE EDGES AT TRANSITION TO ADJACENT MATERIALS SEALED WITH BACKER ROD & SEALANT.

ADJACENT MATERIAL

BACKER ROD & SEALANT

EIFS WITH WRAPPED BASE COAT OR CASING BEAD

CASING BEAD AT TOP, SIDE, OR RAKE EDGES

OR

WRAPPED BASE COAT WITH FIBERGLASS MESH

FINISH COAT WITH INTEGRAL COLOR

BASE COAT WITH EMBEDDED FIBERGLASS MESH

RIGID INSULATION WITH GROOVED BACK

OR

STANDARD RIGID INSULATION ON PLASTIC LATH DRAINAGE MAT

MOISTURE BARRIER LAPPED TO DRAIN

STARTER TRACK WITH WEEPS

PLYWOOD OR OSB SHEATHING

BOTH OUTSIDE & INSIDE CORNERS ARE WRAPPED WITH CONTINUOUS STUCCO.

BUILT-UP PROFILES MADE WITH LAYERS OF INSULATION OR WIRE-CUT INSULATION.

NOTE
FOR BARRIER EIFS, STANDARD RIGID INSULATION IS GLUED DIRECTLY TO SHEATHING SO THERE IS NOT NEED FOR A MOISTURE BARRIER OR STARTER TRACK.

Synthetic stucco looks like traditional stucco but is really a flexible acrylic coating applied over rigid insulation. Called EIFS (Exterior Insulation and Finish Systems), synthetic stucco is more flexible than standard stucco and more moisture resistant. This moisture resistance, which certainly is a strength of the system, worked against early versions of its application when imperfect detailing led to moisture being trapped inside the wall behind the impermeable EIFS layer. With updated water-managed EIFS, it is now assumed that some moisture will penetrate the surface, and therefore a drainage path is provided for this moisture to escape.

Materials—There are several manufacturers of water-managed EIFS. Each starts with rigid insulation, fastened to the framing with nails fitted with large plastic washers designed to prevent crushing of the insulation. The insulation is protected from impact by a stucco base made of acrylic cement reinforced with fiberglass mesh. An acrylic finish coat with integral color provides moisture protection.

Application—All systems start with an effective moisture barrier applied to the wall sheathing. The next layer is a drainage plane that provides a clear path for moisture to escape. This drainage plane can be a separate plastic drainage mat or vertical grooves integrated into the back side of the rigid insulation, which is the following layer. The base coat of stucco is troweled directly onto the insulation, reinforced with mesh, and then another layer of base coat. The final coat is troweled over the hardened base coat.

Finish—There are a variety of common troweled finish textures. Color is integral in the final coat, so painting is unnecessary, but inspection and repair of sealant joints every few years is highly recommended.

Ⓐ **SYNTHETIC STUCCO (EIFS)**

INSULATED HEADERS
SEE 76

WALLS USED TO
VENT ROOFS
& DECKS
SEE 205

INSULATION &
CONTINUITY OF VAPOR
RETARDER & AIR
INFILTRATION BARRIER
AT FLOORS SEE 60-61

WALL INSULATION
AT FOUNDATION
SEE 62

FRAMING FOR
INSULATION
AT CORNERS
SEE 70,
71, 75

Wall insulation is typically provided by fiberglass batts. Building codes in most climates allow 2x4 walls with 3½ in. of insulation (R-11) or 2x6 walls with 5½ in. of insulation (R-19).

Vapor retarder—Vapor retarders are installed in conjunction with wall insulation. The purpose of a vapor retarder, a continuous membrane located on the warm side of the insulation, is to prevent vaporized (gaseous) moisture from entering the insulated wall cavity, where it can condense, leading to structural or other damage.

Common vapor retarders include 4- or 6-mil polyethylene film applied to the inside of framing or specially formulated paint or primer applied to the surface of drywall. Rigid insulation with taped joints may also be used.

VAPOR
MIGRATION

COOL

VAPOR
RETARDER

WARM

Various vapor retarder materials have different rates of permeability (see 88A), and, because moisture can enter a wall assembly from either side, it is wise to use the most permeable material proven to be effective in a given region so as not to trap moisture within the assembly.

The vapor retarder should always be located on the warm side of the insulation. In a cold, dry climate the

retarder goes on the inside of the wall. But in mixed climates the migration of vapor can reverse in the summer. For this reason, building scientists recommend against using low-permeability materials on the inside of air-conditioned walls.

The location of the vapor barrier may be adjusted in upgraded applications provided that two-thirds or more of the insulative value of the wall remains to the cold side of the barrier.

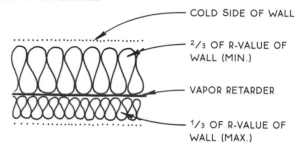

COLD SIDE OF WALL

²/₃ OF R-VALUE OF
WALL (MIN.)

VAPOR RETARDER

¹/₃ OF R-VALUE OF
WALL (MAX.)

Air barrier—An air barrier is intended to control the migration of air through the insulated envelope of a building. Standard construction practices allow voids and breaks in the building envelope that can leak up to two times the total air volume of the building per hour—accounting for up to 30% of the total heat loss (or gain) of the building. Upgrading the envelope can cut this air leakage to one-third of an air change per hour and can thus have significant consequences for energy bills in most climates.

An effective air barrier combines a continuous membrane with tight seals around openings such as windows where the membrane is penetrated. It may be made of a variety of materials and may be located either inside or outside of the insulation. When inside the insulation, the barrier may be drywall, rigid insulation, or the same film that forms a vapor retarder. Outside the insulation, building wrap, rigid insulation, or sheathing may be used. In each case, joints are taped or overlapped and caulked, and tight seals are made with floor and ceiling air barriers. Windows, doors, electrical, plumbing, and other services that penetrate the membrane are sealed with expansive foam, caulk, and/or special tape.

It is important to consider that the reduced ventilation rate due to control of air leakage can lower indoor air quality. The provision of controlled ventilation with simple energy-saving devices such as air-to-air heat exchangers can alleviate this problem.

(A) **INSULATION**
Standard Practice

Unfaced batts—The most common method of insulating walls is to use unfaced batts that are fitted between studs. A vapor retarder is applied to the warm side of the wall in the form of a vapor retarding paint or primer or a 4-mil polyethylene film. Properly detailed, this vapor retarder can serve as the air barrier.

COLD SIDE

CONTINUOUS VAPOR RETARDER

WARM SIDE

Faced batts—Batt insulation is often manufactured with a paper facing that, in cold climates, serves as both vapor retarder and means of attachment. For attachment, the facing material has tabs that are stapled in place between the studs.

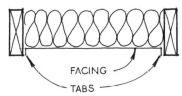

FACING

TABS

To use the facing as a vapor retarder, it is better to staple the tabs to the face of the studs to make a better seal. However, this interferes with the installation of interior finish materials because the tabs build up unevenly on the face of the studs.

Rigid insulation—In standard construction, rigid insulation is generally used only in extreme situations where wall depth is limited but a code-prescribed R-value is required. Examples of such situations include headers (see 76A & B) and locations where heat ducts, vents, or plumbing must be in exterior walls. In upgraded framing systems, however, rigid insulation is used extensively (see 122A).

Spray-foam insulation—It can cost many times as much as competing insulations, but spray-foam insulation can equal the R-value of the best rigid foam, double as a vapor retarder, and fully fill the most awkwardly shaped framing cavity. Except for its high cost, it is a nearly ideal insulating material for mixed climates where warm and cold sides of the envelope reverse during the year.

In climatic zones with extremely cold or hot weather (or high utility rates), there is special incentive to insulate buildings beyond code minimums. A decision to super-insulate affects the construction of walls more than floors or roofs because walls are generally thinner (being constructed of 2x4s or 2x6s rather than 2x10s or 2x12s). Walls are also in direct contact with the ambient air because they do not have a crawl space or attic to intervene as a buffer.

The most direct way to increase the insulative capacity of walls is to make them thicker. A 2x4 framed wall upgraded to 2x6, for example, will increase from a combined (batt plus framing) R-value of 9.0 to a value of R-15.1. But increasing wall thickness alone is only effective to a point because a significant part of the wall (about 9% of a wall framed at 24 in. o.c.) is composed of studs, plates, etc., which conduct heat at about three times the rate of insulative batts. When headers and other extra framing are considered, walls often have as much as 20% of their area devoted to framing. The conductance of heat through this framing is called thermal bridging.

There are two strategies for decreasing the effects of thermal bridging. The first is to reduce the quantity of framing members and is called advanced framing (see 74). The second strategy is to insulate the framing members that remain so that they do not "bridge" between the cold and warm sides of the wall. Several ways to insulate framing members are discussed on the following pages.

Rigid insulation—Rigid insulation added to the exterior or interior of a framed wall can typically add an R-value of 7 to 14 at the same time that it interrupts thermal bridging (see 122).

Strapping—Horizontal nailing strips are attached to the inside of a stud wall. Insulative values of R-25 are easily attainable (see 123).

Staggered-stud framing—A double offset stud wall framed on a single, wide plate. Combined insulative values of R-30 are common (see 124).

Double wall framing—A duplicate (redundant) wall system with R-values of up to 40 is easily reached (see 125).

Ⓐ INSULATION
Standard Practice

Ⓑ UPGRADED INSULATION

RIGID INSULATION

SHEATHING

2X6 STUD WALL AT 24 IN. O.C. WITH BATT INSULATION

VAPOR RETARDER

ROOF OR UPPER FLOOR STRUCTURE WITH INSULATION AND CONTINUOUS AIR/VAPOR BARRIER SEE 197 OR 63

RIGID INSULATION OVER SHEATHING OR OTHER LATERAL BRACING

BATT INSULATION IN 2X6 STUD WALL

FURRING SAME THICKNESS AS RIGID INSULATION AT WINDOW & DOOR OPENINGS AND AS REQUIRED FOR NAILING OF SIDING

VAPOR RETARDER LOCATED AT INTERIOR FACE OF 2X6 STUD WALL

FLOOR STRUCTURE WITH INSULATION AND CONTINUOUS AIR/VAPOR BARRIER SEE 61-62

RIGID INSULATION MAY BE CONTINUOUS OVER WALL OR FOUNDATION BELOW

Rigid insulation, with a potential R-value approximately double that of batt insulation, is a very attractive alternative for upgrading the thermal performance of walls. The material is easy to install in large lightweight sheets, has sufficient strength to support most siding and interior finish materials, and can double as an air/vapor barrier in some cases. Its disadvantages are high cost and potential for toxic offgassing in a fire.

Rigid insulation is most effective when used on the exterior of the building because it covers the entire skin of the building continuously without the interruption of floors or interior partitions. It can act as the backing for siding but does not provide the strength to act as structural sheathing. Alternative methods of bracing the building, such as structural sheathing (see 78A) or let-in bracing (see 77B & C), must therefore be used. Hybrid systems, in which structural sheathing is used only at necessary locations with rigid insulation elsewhere, can also provide cost effective insulation upgrades.

When applied to the exterior of buildings in cold climates, the low permeability of rigid insulation can trap vapor in the stud cavities, causing structural damage. The reverse can be true in warm climates. It is therefore advisable to carefully coordinate the use of rigid insulation with a high-permeability vapor retarder based on the specific climatic zone and to verify the practicality of specific types of insulation with local professionals.

Used on the interior of a building in a cold climate, rigid insulation can perform three functions at once: insulation, vapor retarder, and air barrier. To accomplish this, a foil-faced insulation board carefully taped at all seams and caulked and/or gasketed at top, bottom, and openings would be used.

The use of interior rigid insulation requires deep electrical boxes and the need for extra-wide backing at corners and at the top plate.

Ⓐ **RIGID INSULATION**

SHEATHING

2X6 STUD WALL WITH
BATT INSULATION

VAPOR RETARDER

HORIZONTAL 2X3
STRAPPING WITH
HORIZONTAL INSULATION

ROOF OR UPPER FLOOR
STRUCTURE WITH INSULATION
AND CONTINUOUS AIR/VAPOR
BARRIER SEE 197 OR 63

SINGLE 2X6 TOP PLATE

STRUCTURAL SHEATHING
OR OTHER BRACING

BATT INSULATION IN
2X6 STUD WALL

STRAPPING FOR NAILING
AROUND OPENINGS

HORIZONTAL 2X3 STRAPPING
AT 24 IN. O.C. NAILED TO
STUDS

HORIZONTAL BATT
INSULATION BETWEEN
STRAPPING

VAPOR RETARDER LOCATED
AT INTERIOR FACE OF
2X6 STUD WALL

WIRING AND PLUMBING
LOCATED WITHIN
STRAPPING LAYER

DOUBLE STRAPPING FOR
BASE TRIM NAILING

FLOOR STRUCTURE WITH
INSULATION AND
CONTINUOUS AIR/VAPOR
BARRIER SEE 61-62

Strapping consists of horizontal nailing strips attached to the inside of a stud wall. The strapping touches the studs only at the intersection between the two, so thermal bridging is virtually eliminated. Strapping is used extensively in energy-efficient buildings. With 2x6 studs and 2x3 strapping, an R-25 value can be achieved.

The advantages of the system are that it is simple and straightforward and uses a minimal amount of extra framing materials. With two-thirds of the insulative value in the (2x6) stud cavities, an air/vapor barrier can be located at the inside face of the framed wall, thus eliminating the need to puncture it with services. In addition, the plumbing and electrical work itself is simplified by the creation of horizontal chases on the walls.

Strapping must be fastened securely to the studs to prevent rotation, but interior finish panels will ultimately tie the strapping together to keep it in place.

Extra strapping is usually required for nailing at corners, at window and door openings, and at the base of the wall (see drawing above). In addition, vertical blocks are required for the attachment of electrical boxes.

Strapping may also be applied to the exterior of a building. In this case, the strapping is more easily installed, but the advantage of a horizontal chase interior of the vapor retarder is lost. Furthermore, the strapping insulation must be installed from the exterior, exposed to the weather.

Ⓐ **STRAPPING**

SHEATHING

2X4 STUDS AT
24 IN. O.C. WITH
BATT INSULATION
AND ALIGNED WITH
OUTER EDGE OF
PLATE

2X4 STUDS AT 24 IN. O.C.
WITH BATT INSULATION
ALIGNED WITH INNER
EDGE OF PLATE & OFFSET
FROM OUTER STUDS

VAPOR RETARDER

2X8 OR 2X10 PLATE

ROOF OR UPPER FLOOR
STRUCTURE WITH
INSULATION AND
CONTINUOUS AIR/VAPOR
BARRIER SEE 197 OR 63

SINGLE TOP 2X TOP PLATE

PLYWOOD GUSSET TIES
STUD WALLS AT OPENINGS

STAGGERED 2X4 STUD
WALLS FILLED WITH BATT
INSULATION

VAPOR RETARDER
LOCATED AT INTERIOR
FACE OF INNER FRAMED
WALL

SINGLE 2X SOLE PLATE

FLOOR STRUCTURE
WITH INSULATION AND
CONTINUOUS AIR/VAPOR
BARRIER SEE 61-62

Staggered-stud framing is essentially a double stud wall framed on a single wide plate with the studs offset from one another so that there is negligible thermal bridging. The system is appreciated by builders for its minimal deviation from standard frame construction. Staggered-stud framing is substantially the same as platform framing, and subcontractors are sequenced in the same order as standard construction. With this technique, insulative values of R-30 or more can be attained. A 2x8 or 2x10 plate with staggered 2x4 studs at 24 in. o.c. is most common.

Because there are effectively two separate walls, this system offers a special opportunity at windows and doors to splay the opening.

SHEATHING

PLYWOOD GUSSET
ON CHAMFERED
STUDS

FINISH WALL

WINDOW OR
DOOR WITH TRIM

By increasing the rough-opening size at the "inner wall," the opening will be more generous from the inside and reflect light better into the room.

The disadvantages of the system also stem from its similarity to standard platform frame construction. Unlike strapping systems or double wall systems, staggered-stud systems have the air/vapor barrier located on the inside (warm) face of the wall, with the attendant problems of sealing perforations of the barrier from plumbing and electrical services.

Ⓐ **STAGGERED STUD FRAMING**

SHEATHING

2X4 STUD WALL WITH BATT INSULATION

BATT INSULATION

VAPOR RETARDER

2X4 STUD WALL WITH BATT INSULATION

ROOF OR UPPER FLOOR STRUCTURE WITH INSULATION AND CONTINUOUS AIR/VAPOR BARRIER SEE 197 OR 63

SHIM SO THAT ROOF (OR UPPER FLOOR) STRUCTURE BEARS ON OUTER WALL.

PLYWOOD GUSSET ACTS AS FIRESTOP AND TIES WALLS AT TOP PLATE.

PLYWOOD GUSSET TIES STUD WALLS AT OPENINGS FOR ALTERNATIVE DETAIL SEE 124

CAVITY BETWEEN STUD WALLS FILLED WITH BATT INSULATION

VAPOR RETARDER LOCATED AT EXTERIOR OF INNER FRAMED WALL

WIRING AND PLUMBING LOCATED IN INNER STUD WALL

FLOOR STRUCTURE WITH INSULATION AND CONTINUOUS AIR/VAPOR BARRIER SEE 61-62

Double wall framing is capable of achieving the highest insulation values of all the upgraded framing techniques. Values of R-40 are common. Slightly more framing materials and considerably more labor (than strapping or staggered stud) are required for the increased performance.

The outer framed wall is most commonly used as the bearing wall. This strategy has two advantages: The insulation and the inner wall can be installed under the roof out of the weather, and the shear walls are most easily installed and logically located at this (outer wall) location. However, finish detailing at the wall/ceiling joint is complicated if the inner wall is nonstructural, and the continuity of the air/vapor barrier is somewhat difficult to achieve at the wall/floor intersection.

Less common (and not illustrated) is the use of the inner wall as the bearing wall. This system avoids the minor disadvantage of the outer bearing wall system, but has two major disadvantages: it requires support of the outer wall beyond the edge of the foundation and the outer wall and the extra insulation must be installed from the outside of the building, exposed to the weather.

The ability to locate an air/vapor barrier at the outside surface of the inner wall contributes significantly to its continuity because plumbing and electrical services can be located within the inner wall without having to penetrate the barrier. To get the air/vapor barrier into this position is simple with an interior bearing wall, but somewhat involved with an exterior bearing wall. It can be accomplished, however, by fastening the barrier to the (outer face of the) inner wall before it is tipped into place. The cavity can be filled with horizontal batts tied to the exterior wall before the inner wall is positioned or insulation can be blown in afterward through holes predrilled in the top plywood gusset.

(A) DOUBLE WALL FRAMING

ROOFS

The roof is the part of the wood-frame structure that varies most widely across the country. This is because the roof plays the most active role of all the parts of a building in protecting against the weather, and in the United States, variations in weather are extreme. Some roofs protect primarily against the heat of the sun; others must shelter the inhabitants under tons of snow.

SELECTION OF ROOF SLOPE

One of the most obvious variations of roof form has to do with the slope or pitch of the roof. The main factors affecting the slope of a roof are stylistic considerations, the type of roofing material to be used, and the space desired beneath the roof. The climate also has a strong influence on roof slope. Areas of significant rainfall have roofs pitched to shed the rain, while warm, arid climates tend to favor flatter roofs.

The slope or pitch of a roof is measured as a proportion of rise to run. A roof that rises 4 in. in 1 ft. (12 in.) is said to have a 4-in-12 pitch (or 4:12). The second number in the roof-pitch proportion is always 12.

THE SHAPE OF ROOFS

Roof shapes tend to have a regional character that reflects not only climatic variation, but also historical and material influences. All roof forms are derived from four basic roof shapes shown below: the flat roof, the shed roof, the gable roof, and the hip roof.

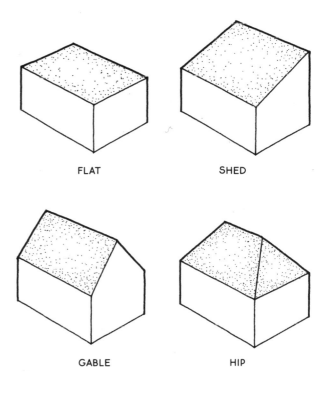

FLAT

SHED

GABLE

HIP

12 IN.

4 IN.

4-IN-12 PITCH

12 IN.

12 IN.

12-IN-12 PITCH

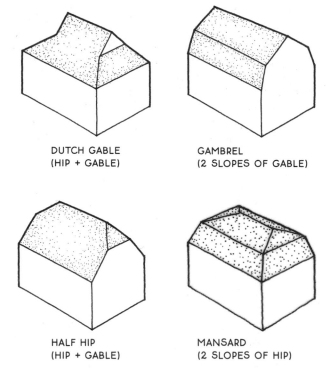

DUTCH GABLE
(HIP + GABLE)

GAMBREL
(2 SLOPES OF GABLE)

HALF HIP
(HIP + GABLE)

MANSARD
(2 SLOPES OF HIP)

Virtually any roof form may be made by combining the four basic shapes with the connections illustrated in this chapter. Some of these composite shapes are so common they have their own names. For example, the hip and gable shapes can combine to form a Dutch gable. Two different slopes of gable roof can combine to form a gambrel roof. A shed dormer may be added to a gable roof, and so forth. Four common combinations are shown above.

WHAT TYPE OF CONSTRUCTION SYSTEM?

Roofs are constructed either with rafters (stick-framed roofs) or with trusses. Stick-framed roofs are usually made with dimension lumber but may also use composite materials such as I-joist rafters (see 151-154).

Stick framing originated before the development of balloon-frame construction in the 19th century. Antecedents of the modern stick-framed roof can be seen on ancient roofs around the world, and modern stick-frame roofing remains popular because it is the most flexible roof-framing system and the materials are least expensive.

Trusses are made of a number of small members (usually 2x4s) joined in a factory or shop to make one long structural assembly. Only in very simple buildings does the labor savings of a truss system compete with stick framing.

Stick framing— One advantage of stick framing is that the space within the roof structure can become living space or storage. Vaulted (cathedral) ceilings, half-story living spaces on upper floors, and true storage attics are all examples. A second advantage is that complex roofs may be stick-framed more economically than truss-framed. For owner-builders who need not include the cost of labor, stick framing is especially attractive.

STICK-FRAMED
ROOF

Truss framing—Trusses can span much farther than stick-framed roofs, leaving large open areas below them or permitting partition walls to be relocated without consideration for the roof structure above. Trusses go up quickly, usually resulting in a cost saving over stick-framed roofs on simply shaped buildings. A big disadvantage of trusses is that the truss roof is almost impossible to remodel, since trusses should never be cut.

TRUSS ROOF

OTHER CONSIDERATIONS

In addition to the choices about pitch, shape, and structure discussed above, many other decisions contribute to the overall performance of the roof. These include selection of sheathing, underlayment, and roofing material; eave, rake, and flashing details; gutters and downspouts; and insulation and ventilation of the roof assembly. All of these issues are discussed in this chapter.

RIDGE
SEE 131B & C

VALLEYS
SEE 137

ROOF PITCH
CHANGE
SEE 133B

ROOF OPENINGS
SEE 135-136

RAKE OR FASCIA
DIES ON ROOF
SEE 149D

RAFTER DIES
ON ROOF
SEE 149B

COLLAR TIES
SEE 130

CEILING
JOISTS
SEE 132

HIPS
SEE 138

RAFTER/
EAVE-WALL
CONNECTION
SEE 133A, 150

ROOF ADJACENT
TO WALL SEE 134A

ABBREVIATED
EAVE SEE 141,
143A

OVERHANGING
EAVE SEE 141-
143, 159B

ABBREVIATED RAKE
SEE 141, 150A & B

EAVE/RAKE
INTERSECTION
SEE 140-141

ROOF ABUTTING
WALL STRUCTURE
SEE 134, 150C & D

OVERHANGING
RAKE SEE 141,
144-149

OVERHANGING
RAKE SEE 141,
144-149

PURLINS
SEE 130

FLAT ROOF
SEE 139

I-JOIST RAFTER
FRAMING
SEE 151-154

SHED ROOF
SEE 130, 134B

TRUSS ROOFS
SEE 155-159

ROOF SHEATHING
SEE 162-166

Rafter sizes are usually 2x6, 2x8, 2x10 or 2x12, and spacing is usually 16 in. or 24 in. o.c. Species of wood vary from region to region. Rafter sizing depends primarily on span, spacing, roof loads, and sometimes on required insulation depth.

For a rafter-span table, see 131A.

(A) ROOF FRAMING

Stick-framed rafters may be supported by the walls of the building, by a structural ridge beam, or by purlins.

Simple-span roof—The simplest sloped roof—the shed roof—has rafters that span from one wall to another, as shown at right. These rafters must be strong enough to carry the dead-load weight of the roof itself and subsequent layers of reroofing, plus the live-load weight of snow. The rafters must usually be deep enough to contain adequate insulation.

The total roof load is transferred to the ends of the rafters, where it is supported by the walls. In the simple example at right, each wall carries part of the roof load.

Triangulated roof—Common (full-length) rafters are paired and usually joined to a ridge board, as shown in the drawing at right. Each rafter spans only half the distance between the two walls (the gable roof, shown in the drawing at right, is the simplest version). Horizontal ties—either ceiling joists or collar ties—form a triangle with the rafters. Ceiling joists are generally located on the top plate of the walls but may also be located higher to form a partially vaulted ceiling. Collar ties are usually nailed near the top of the roof between opposing rafters and spaced at 4 ft. o.c. Collar ties are not sufficient by themselves to resist the outward thrust of the rafters.

Rafters in triangulated roofs are shallower than those in shed roofs of equal width because they span only half the distance of the shed rafters and because they do not usually contain insulation.

Structural ridge beam—The horizontal ties that are required in a triangulated roof may be avoided if the rafters are attached at the ridge to a structural ridge beam (or a wall), which effectively changes the triangulated roof into two simple-span roofs, as shown in the drawing below.

RAFTER SUPPORT AT
TOP OF RAFTER
SEE 131A & 143B

RAFTERS WITH INSULATION

RAFTER SUPPORT
AT EAVE
SEE 133A & 142

NONSTRUCTURAL RIDGE
BOARD SEE 133B

COLLAR TIE

RAFTER

RAFTER SUPPORT
AT EAVE SEE 131A

CEILING
JOIST WITH
INSULATION
SEE 132, 198-199

RAFTER SPAN | RAFTER SPAN

Purlin—A purlin is a horizontal member that supports several rafters—usually at midspan. Purlins were commonly used to help support the long slender rafters of pioneer houses and barns. Today they are also used occasionally to reduce the span of a set of rafters, but the purlins must themselves be supported by the frame of the structure, as shown in the drawing below.

STRUCTURAL
RIDGE BEAM
SEE 131C

RAFTER SUPPORT
AT EAVE
SEE 133A

RAFTERS WITH
INSULATION

RAFTER SPAN | RAFTER SPAN

RAFTERS

PURLINS

CEILING
JOIST

PURLIN
SUPPORT TO
STRUCTURE
BELOW

NOTE
THE NAME "PURLIN" IS ALSO GIVEN TO A MEMBER THAT SPANS
ACROSS RAFTERS TO SUPPORT ROOF DECKING. SEE 150C

Ⓐ STICK FRAMING
Terminology

ALLOWABLE RAFTER SPANS IN FEET			
Rafter size, species, and grade	Joist spacing (ft.)		
	12 in. o.c	16 in. o.c.	24 in. o.c.
2x6 spruce-pine-fir #2	12.1	11.0	9.0
2x6 Douglas fir #2	12.6	11.3	9.2
2x8 spruce-pine-fir #2	15.9	14.1	11.5
2x8 Douglas fir #2	16.5	14.3	11.6
2x10 spruce-pine-fir #2	19.9	17.2	14.0
2x10 Douglas fir #2	20.1	17.4	14.2
9.5 x 2.06-inch I-joist	21.4	19.4	16.8
2x12 spruce-pine-fir #2	23.0	19.9	16.3
2x12 Douglas fir #2	23.4	20.2	16.5
11.9 x 2.06-inch I-joist	25.5	23.1	19.0

This table compares two species of sawn lumber and one I-joist for use as rafters on a roof with a 30-psf live load. The table is for estimating purposes only. For a roof-sheathing span table, see 163.

ROOF SHEATHING

RAFTERS NAILED TO RIDGE BOARD WITH 16D NAILS

2X RIDGE BOARD DEEPER THAN PLUMB CUT OF RAFTERS

NOTE
RIP RIDGE BOARD IF INTERIOR FINISH MEETS AT RIDGE.

Common Rafters

RIDGE BOARD (BEYOND)

SLIGHTLY UNDERCUT THE PLUMB CUT ON BARGE OR VERGE RAFTERS IF LUMBER IS GREEN; THE BOARDS WILL SHRINK TO MEET AT CENTERLINE.

NAIL INTO RIDGE BOARD NEAR BOTTOM OF RAFTERS; UPPER NAILS MAY BE ADDED AFTER LUMBER DRIES.

Barge or Verge Rafters

(A) RAFTER-SPAN COMPARISON TABLE

(B) RAFTER/RIDGE
Nonstructural Ridge Board

ROOF SHEATHING

RAFTERS ATTACHED TO EACH OTHER WITH METAL STRAP AT TOP OR SIDES OF RAFTER OR WITH PLYWOOD GUSSETS

BIRD'S-MOUTH CUT IN RAFTERS, SEE 133A; RAFTERS NAILED OR BOLTED TO BEAM

ROOF SHEATHING

2X BLOCKING NAILED TO RIDGE BEAM BETWEEN RAFTERS

RAFTERS NAILED TO BEAM & TO BLOCKING

NOTE
AS AN ALTERNATIVE, USE METAL RIDGE HANGERS FOR SMALL RAFTERS UP TO 7-IN-12 PITCH.

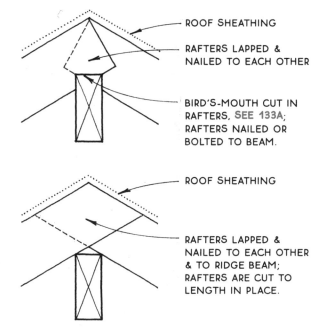

ROOF SHEATHING

RAFTERS LAPPED & NAILED TO EACH OTHER

BIRD'S-MOUTH CUT IN RAFTERS, SEE 133A; RAFTERS NAILED OR BOLTED TO BEAM.

ROOF SHEATHING

RAFTERS LAPPED & NAILED TO EACH OTHER & TO RIDGE BEAM; RAFTERS ARE CUT TO LENGTH IN PLACE.

NOTE
RAFTERS IN THESE DETAILS LAP AT RIDGE; SO AT THE END RAFTERS, FUR OUT INNER RAFTER TO ALIGN WITH OUTER RAFTER.

(C) RAFTER/RIDGE
Structural Ridge Beam: 4 Alternatives

Ceiling joists are very similar to floor joists. In fact, the second-floor joists of a two-story building act as the ceiling joists for the story below. Ceiling joists are distinguished from floor joists only when there is no floor (except an attic floor) above the joists.

Ceiling joists are sized like floor joists. The span of the joists depends on spacing and whether the attic above the joists will be used for storage.

RAFTER SYSTEM

CEILING-JOIST SYSTEM

JOIN JOISTS TO CONTINUE STRUCTURE TO OPPOSING WALL SEE 36A

SPAN OF CEILING JOISTS

BEARING WALL

BEARING WALL

Joist size, species, and grade	Joist spacing (ft.)		
	12 in. o.c	16 in. o.c.	24 in. o.c.
2x6 spruce-pine-fir #2	12.9	11.7	10.2
2x6 Douglas fir #2	13.5	12.2	10.7
2x8 spruce-pine-fir #2	17.0	15.4	13.5
2x8 Douglas fir #2	17.8	16.1	14.1
2x10 spruce-pine-fir #2	21.7	19.7	17.2
2x10 Douglas fir #2	22.7	20.6	18.0
9.5 x 2.06-inch I-joist	22.8	20.6	17.9
2x12 spruce-pine-fir #2	26.4	24.0	20.6
2x12 Douglas fir #2	27.6	25.1	20.8
11.9 x 2.06-inch I-joist	27.2	24.6	21.4

ALLOWABLE CEILING JOIST SPANS IN FEET

This table is based on a light attic load of 20 psf and a deflection of L/360. The table is for estimating purposes only.

The joists can function as ties to resist the lateral forces of rafters. For this purpose, it is important to attach the joists securely to the rafters.

RAFTER WITH BIRD'S-MOUTH CUT SEE 133A

CEILING JOISTS NAILED TO RAFTERS RESIST OUTWARD THRUST OF RAFTERS.

STUD WALL WITH SHEATHING

NOTE
CHECK CODES FOR NAILING REQUIREMENTS & ANGLE NAILS THROUGH JOISTS INTO RAFTERS TOWARD CENTER OF BUILDING.

The underside of ceiling joists is often furred down with a layer of 1x lumber to resist plaster or drywall cracking due to movement of the joists. The drawing below illustrates furring parallel to the joists to resist cracking along a beam that interrupts the continuity of the joists. Furring perpendicular to the joists, usually called strapping, is also common.

DISCONTINUOUS CEILING JOIST HUNG FROM STRUCTURAL BEAM FLUSH AT TOP FOR FLOOR ABOVE

FURRING ON BOTTOM OF JOIST TO FLUSH OUT WITH BOTTOM OF BEAM IF REQ'D

CONTINUOUS FURRING NAILED TO UNDERSIDE OF JOISTS LIMITS CRACKS ALONG BEAM IN FINISH CEILING

Ⓐ RAFTERS/CEILING JOISTS

At walls or beams that support them at the eave, rafters are cut at the point of support with a notch called a bird's mouth.

ROOFING & SHEATHING

RAFTER

FOR EAVE DETAILS SEE 142-143

BIRD'S MOUTH CUT

EAVE STUD WALL

The width of the bird's mouth is equal to the width of the sheathed stud wall (or unsheathed wall if sheathing is to be applied later). The underside of the rafters should meet the inside corner of the top of the wall. This is especially important if the ceiling is vaulted and a smooth transition between wall and ceiling is desired (see below).

BLOCKING PREVENTS ROTATION OF RAFTERS & ALLOWS VENTILATION OF ROOF.

RAFTER WITH BIRD'S MOUTH CUT

CEILING JOISTS SEE 132

STUD WALL WITH SHEATHING

Flat Ceiling

BLOCKING PREVENTS ROTATION OF RAFTERS & ALLOWS VENTILATION OF ROOF.

RAFTER WITH BIRD'S MOUTH CUT

SLOPE OF RAFTERS CREATES CEILING PLANE.

STUD WALL WITH SHEATHING

NOTE
FOR RAFTER SUPPORT AT RAKE WALL, SEE 134C.

Vaulted Ceiling

Wherever the pitch of a roof changes from shallow to steep (as in a gambrel roof) or from steep to shallow (as in a shed dormer) the two ends of the rafters must be supported. If the pitch change occurs over a wall, the wall itself will provide the support.

If the pitch change does not occur over a wall, the support will have to be provided by a purlin or a beam (header).

ROOFING & SHEATHING

LOW-PITCH & HIGH-PITCH RAFTERS LAP/ BOTH BEAR ON SUPPORT.

BEAM, PURLIN, OR WALL

ROOFING & SHEATHING

LOW-PITCH & HIGH-PITCH RAFTERS LAP; BOTH BEAR ON SUPPORT.

BEAM, PURLIN, OR WALL

Pitch Changes with Support Below

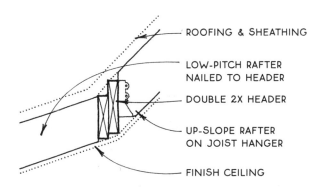

ROOFING & SHEATHING

LOW-PITCH RAFTER NAILED TO HEADER

DOUBLE 2X HEADER

UP-SLOPE RAFTER ON JOIST HANGER

FINISH CEILING

Pitch Changes without Support Below

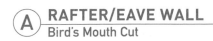
Ⓐ RAFTER/EAVE WALL
Bird's Mouth Cut

Ⓑ ROOF PITCH CHANGE

STUD WALL CONTINUOUS TO BELOW ROOF

SHEATHING

SIDING

BLOCKING FOLLOWS PITCH OF ROOF.

STEP OR SIDEWALL FLASHING **SEE 171**

ROOFING

ROOF SHEATHING

COMMON RAFTER

END RAFTER NAILED TO STUDS

(A) ROOF/WALL
Rafters Parallel to Wall

The end rafters of a gable or a shed roof are supported by the walls under them, called rake walls. The framing of the rake should be coordinated with the detailing of the rake. Of the three drawings below, the first example is the simplest method of support and is used with all types of rake, often in conjunction with an unfinished attic. The second example is best for supporting lookouts for an exposed or boxed-in rake. The third example provides nailing for a boxed-in rake or an exposed ceiling. Elements from the three examples may be combined differently for specific situations. For rake-wall framing, see 72A, B & C.

ROOFING

ROOF SHEATHING

RAKE TRIM **SEE 146-147**

END RAFTER

BALLOON OR PLATFORM-FRAMED RAKE WALL **SEE 72B**

ROOFING

ROOF SHEATHING

LOOKOUTS TO SUPPORT OVERHANG NOTCHED INTO RAFTER OR SET ON DOUBLE TOP PLATE **SEE 145A**

BALLOON-FRAMED RAKE WALL **SEE 72C**

ROOFING

ROOF SHEATHING

EXTERIOR RAFTER FOR BOXED-IN RAKE

BOXED-IN RAKE **SEE 147D**

INTERIOR RAFTER FOR INTERIOR FINISH

BALLOON OR PLATFORM-FRAMED RAKE WALL **SEE 72B & C**

WALL SHEATHING

FLASHING

NAILING BLOCK

ROOF SHEATHING

ROOFING

2X LEDGER NAILED TO STUDS

RAFTER

SAME AS ABOVE BUT WITH LEDGER LET INTO STUDS

RAFTER LAPS STUD.

NOTE FOR VENTILATION, SEE 150D.

(B) SHED ROOF/WALL
Rafters Perpendicular to Wall

(C) RAFTER/RAKE WALL
3 Alternatives

Framing the elements that project through the roof of a building—skylights, chimneys, and dormers—begins with a rectangular opening in the framing. For openings in a single roof plane framed entirely with common rafters, framing is relatively easy. An opening three rafter spaces wide or less can be made by heading off the interrupted rafters and doubling the side rafters, as shown below. Obviously, it is more efficient if the width and placement of the opening correspond to the rafter spacing. Larger openings should be engineered. Openings that straddle hips, valleys, or pitch changes must have special support, special framing, and special flashing.

RIDGE

DOUBLED COMMON RAFTER AT SIDES OF OPENING

TOP & BOTTOM RAFTER HEADER (OFTEN DOUBLED)

Headers for simple openings are, in most cases, either plumb or perpendicular to the rafters, as shown in the drawing below. Plumb openings require a header deeper than the rafters.

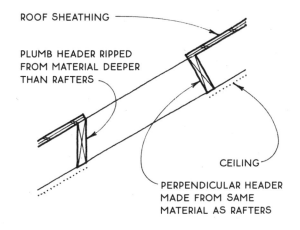

ROOF SHEATHING

PLUMB HEADER RIPPED FROM MATERIAL DEEPER THAN RAFTERS

CEILING

PERPENDICULAR HEADER MADE FROM SAME MATERIAL AS RAFTERS

FOR DORMER OPENINGS SEE 135B.
FOR SKYLIGHT OPENINGS SEE 136A & B.
FOR CHIMNEY OPENINGS SEE 136C.

 A **ROOF OPENINGS**
General

Dormers are often more than three rafter spaces wide so their structure cannot be calculated by rules of thumb. The opening in the roof may be structured to support all or part of the loads imposed by the dormer. The dormer walls and roof are framed like the walls and roof of the main building.

DETAILS BELOW

If the dormer walls do not extend below ceiling level, the roof structure at the edge of the opening must support the dormer.

DORMER WALL SUPPORTED ON ROOF FRAMING

ROOF SHEATHING

ENGINEERED RAFTERS AT SIDE OF DORMER OPENING

ROUGH OPENING

If the dormer has side walls that extend to the floor, the floor may be used to support the dormer, and the rafters at the side of the opening may be single.

ROOF SHEATHING
BLOCKING
RAFTER
ROUGH OPENING

FOR DETAILS SEE 134A.

DORMER WALL SUPPORTED ON SUBFLOOR

FLOOR SYSTEM SUPPORTING DORMER WALL

B **DORMER OPENING**

ROOFING

SHEATHING

RAFTER

2X HEADERS

SKYLIGHT
SEE 175B & C, 176

INSULATED
STUD WALL
BETWEEN ROOF
ROUGH
OPENING &
CEILING ROUGH
OPENING

CEILING JOIST

2X HEADERS

LINE OF FINISH
CEILING

RAFTER

2X HEADING

ROOF ROUGH
OPENING

2X HEADER

DOUBLED
RAFTER AT
SIDES OF
OPENING

DOUBLED
CEILING
JOIST AT
SIDES OF
OPENING

CEILING
ROUGH OPENING

Framing Isometric

A **SKYLIGHT OPENING**
Light Well

ROOFING

SHEATHING

RAFTER

SKYLIGHT
SEE 175B & C, 176

2X HEADER

Square

ROOFING

SHEATHING

RAFTER

SKYLIGHT
**SEE 175B & C,
176**

2X HEADER

Splayed

B **SKYLIGHT OPENINGS**
Vaulted Ceiling

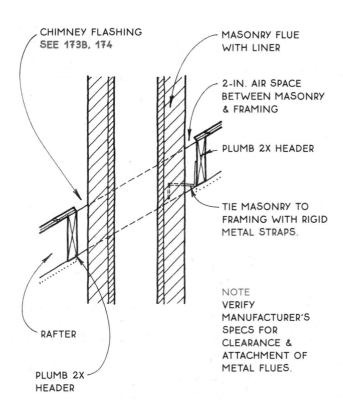

CHIMNEY FLASHING
SEE 173B, 174

MASONRY FLUE
WITH LINER

2-IN. AIR SPACE
BETWEEN MASONRY
& FRAMING

PLUMB 2X HEADER

TIE MASONRY TO
FRAMING WITH RIGID
METAL STRAPS.

NOTE
VERIFY
MANUFACTURER'S
SPECS FOR
CLEARANCE &
ATTACHMENT OF
METAL FLUES.

RAFTER

PLUMB 2X
HEADER

C **CHIMNEY OPENING**

The inside corner of two intersecting roof planes is called a valley. In most cases, valleys are supported by a valley rafter that extends from the outside wall of the building to the ridge or to a header. These valley rafters support large loads and should be engineered. Jack rafters support the area between the valley rafter and the ridge or header.

TOP EDGE OF JACK FAFTERS ALIGN WITH CENTER OF VALLEY RAFTER.

BOTTOM EDGE OF VALLEY RAFTER MUST BE FLUSH WITH BOTTOM OF JACK RAFTERS WHEN INTERIOR SURFACE IS TO BE FINISHED

OR

IT MAY PROJECT BELOW JACKS WHEN NO INTERIOR FINISH IS REQUIRED, OR IF JACK RAFTERS ARE FURRED.

RIDGE

RIDGE

JACK RAFTERS

VALLEY RAFTER

Valley Rafter Supported by Ridge

As shown at right, valley rafters can be supported at the top by a ridge or by a header. The ridge support system is more practical when the ridges of the intersecting roofs are close together; however, the header support system is better when the lower ridge intersects the main roof near or below the center of the rafter span.

RIDGE

DOUBLED HEADER

DOUBLED COMMON RAFTERS

VALLEY RAFTER

Valley Rafter Supported by Header

Where headroom is not required between intersecting roofs, a simpler "farmer's valley" or "California valley" may be constructed. This valley is made without a valley rafter. One roof is first built entirely of common rafters without any special valley framing. Then 2x sleepers are installed over the rafters or over the sheathing of the first roof, and jack rafters are attached to the sleepers.

JACK RAFTER

2X SLEEPER

JACK RAFTER

COMMON RAFTER

COMMON RAFTER

2X SLEEPER

Farmer's Valley

Ⓐ **VALLEY FRAMING**

HIP RAFTERS

RIDGE

DOUBLE TOP PLATE

BIRD'S MOUTH

COMMON RAFTERS

JACK RAFTERS

BIRD'S MOUTH IN HIP RAFTER

TYPICAL SECTIONS AT INTERSECTION OF HIP AND JACK RAFTERS, SEE BELOW.

A hip is the outside corner where two planes of a roof meet. It is composed of a hip rafter at the corner and jack rafters from the hip to the eave. The hip rafter is supported at its lower end by the wall at plate level (or by a post) and at its upper end by the ridge (or by a wall).

Most codes require that the hip rafter project below the bottom edge of the jack rafters (see the top drawing at right). This is not very logical because, unlike a valley rafter, a hip rafter does not support much roof load. The extra depth presents no problem in an attic space, but if the inside face of the roof is to be made into a finish ceiling, the hip rafter will have to be ripped to allow the planes of the finish ceiling to meet (middle drawing at right). If codes will not permit ripping the hip rafter, furring may be added to the underside of the jack and common rafters to allow the finish ceiling to clear the hip rafter.

The top ends of the jack rafters may be cut off to permit venting at the top of the hip roof (bottom drawing at right).

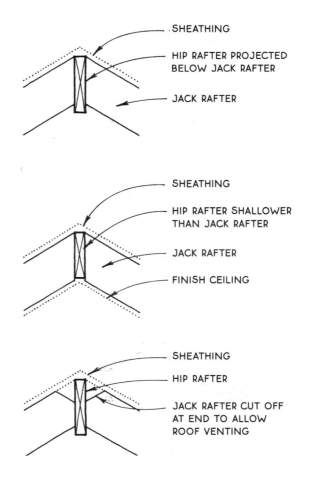

SHEATHING

HIP RAFTER PROJECTED BELOW JACK RAFTER

JACK RAFTER

SHEATHING

HIP RAFTER SHALLOWER THAN JACK RAFTER

JACK RAFTER

FINISH CEILING

SHEATHING

HIP RAFTER

JACK RAFTER CUT OFF AT END TO ALLOW ROOF VENTING

(A) **HIP FRAMING**

The framing of a flat roof is more like a floor than it is like a pitched roof. The joists are level or nearly level and support the ceiling below and the live loads above. Connections to walls are like those for floors (see 32), as are the framing details for openings (see 38B) and cantilevers (see 39A). As for floors, the structure of a flat roof may be a joist system (dimension lumber or I-joists), a girder system, or a truss system. Blocking and bridging (see 38A) must be considered at the appropriate locations.

Flat roofs are unlike floors, however, in that they are not really flat. They might be more properly called "low-slope" roofs because they must slope at least ¼ in. per ft. in order to eliminate standing water. This minimal slope may be achieved in several ways:

1. The joists themselves may slope if the ceiling below does not have to be level, or if the ceiling is furred to level.

2. Trusses may be manufactured with a built-in slope.

3. Shims may be added to the top of the joists.

4. Tapered rigid insulation may be added to the top of the sheathing.

5. The joists may be oversize and tapered on top.

6. Sloped rafters can be scabbed alongside level ceiling joists.

The easiest and most direct way to support an overhang at the corner of a flat roof is with a beam below the joists cantilevered from the top of a bearing wall, as shown in the drawing below.

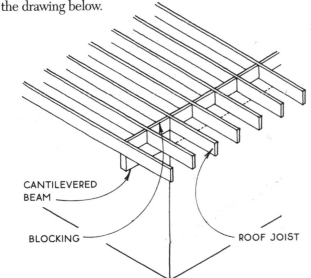

CANTILEVERED BEAM

BLOCKING

ROOF JOIST

A traditional framing method for a cantilevered corner without a beam is with joists that radiate from a doubled central diagonal joist, as shown below. A strong fascia board is advisable here, as with all framing using cantilevered joists.

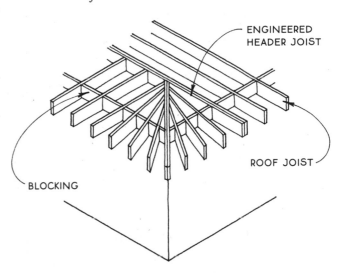

ENGINEERED HEADER JOIST

ROOF JOIST

BLOCKING

A third option for framing a cantilevered corner is shown below. All methods illustrated should be engineered by a professional.

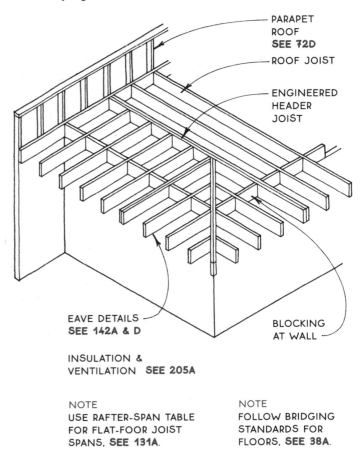

PARAPET ROOF **SEE 72D**

ROOF JOIST

ENGINEERED HEADER JOIST

EAVE DETAILS **SEE 142A & D**

BLOCKING AT WALL

INSULATION & VENTILATION **SEE 205A**

NOTE
USE RAFTER-SPAN TABLE FOR FLAT-FOOR JOIST SPANS, **SEE 131A.**

NOTE
FOLLOW BRIDGING STANDARDS FOR FLOORS, **SEE 38A.**

Ⓐ **FLAT-ROOF FRAMING**

Designing the basic shape of the roof and designing the configuration of eaves and rakes are the most critical tasks in roof design. Stylistically, the selection of eave and rake types should complement both the roof form and the roofing material.

Functionally, the eave and rake should help protect the building from the elements. The shape of the roof will suggest certain eave and/or rake shapes (see 140B), and certain eave types work best with particular rake types (see 141).

Eave—The eave is the level connection between the roof and the wall. Eaves are common to all sloped roofs and often to flat roofs. There are four basic types of eave (see 141). For eave details, see 142 and 143A & B.

Rake—The rake is the sloped connection between the roof and the wall. Only shed and gable roof types and their derivatives have a rake. There are three basic types of rake (see 141). For rake support and rake details, see 144–147. The way in which one edge of a

CONNECTION OF
EAVE TO RAKE
SEE 148

RAKE

EAVE

A **EAVES & RAKES**
Introduction

The basic shape and structure of a roof system need to be coordinated with the finish of the roof at the edges. The shape of the roof affects the treatment of the edges, and vice versa. A hip roof, for example, is easier to finish with a soffited eave than is a gable roof. The basic roof shapes are best suited for the following finish treatment at the edges:

HIP ROOFS HAVE ONLY EAVES, WHICH MAY BE ABBREVIATED, BOXED, SOFFITED, OR EXPOSED WITH ALMOST EQUAL EASE.

Hip Roof

SHED ROOFS HAVE BOTH A RAKE & AN EAVE. ALL EAVE TYPES EXCEPT FOR SOFFITS CAN BE COMBINED WITH ALL RAKE TYPES. A SPECIAL EAVE DETAIL IS REQUIRED FOR THE TOP EDGE. SEE 143B

Shed Roof

FLAT ROOFS HAVE NO RAKES. OVERHANGING EAVES CAN BE DETAILED WITH A SOFFIT OR WITH EXPOSED RAFTERS. WHEN THERE ARE 0 OVERHANGS, THERE IS AN ABBREVIATED EAVE OR A PARAPET. SEE 72D

Flat Roof

GABLE ROOFS, LIKE SHED ROOFS, HAVE BOTH EAVES & RAKES. EXCEPT FOR SOFFITED EEAVES, ALL EAVE & RAKE TYPES CAN BE COMBINED. A SPECIAL DETAIL IS REQUIRED AT THE RIDGE, WHERE THE TWO RAKES MEET. SEE 131B & 144C

Gable Roof

COMBINATION ROOF TYPES USUALLY HAVE BOTH RAKES & EAVES. THEY FOLLOW THE GUIDELINES OF THE INDIVIDUAL ROOF TYPES.

Combination Types

B **ROOF SHAPE & EAVE/RAKE SELECTION**

roof is finished affects the detailing of the other edges. For example, a soffited eave on a gable-roofed building is easier to build with an abbreviated rake than with an exposed rake. The designer should attempt to match the level edge of the roof (the eave) to the sloped edge (the rake).

In examining the details of the eave and rake, therefore, the two must be considered as a set. It is logical to start with the eave, because all sloped roof types have eaves, but not all have rakes.

There are four basic sloped-roof eave types. All four types are appropriate for hip roofs, and all but the soffited type can make a simple and elegant transition from eave to rake on gable and shed roofs. The eave types and their most appropriate companion rakes are diagrammed below.

EAVES \ RAKES	OVERHANGING RAKES SEE 141-147		
	Exposed Rake SEE 146, 147A, B, D; 148	Boxed-In Rake SEE 147D	Abbreviated Rake SEE 150
Overhanging Eaves SEE 142 **Exposed Eave** SEE 142A GOES WITH SHED, GABLE, HIP ROOFS EQUALLY WELL.	VERY COMMON; SIMPLE TO BUILD. SEE 146, 147A, B, C	AWKWARD TO DETAIL & BUILD.	NOT COMMON, BUT COULD BE BUILT WITH SIMPLE DETAILS.
Soffited Eave SEE 142B & C WORKS BEST ON HIP (OR FLAT) ROOFS WITH NO RAKE; OFTEN USED ON GABLE ROOFS AS WELL.	LESS COMMON; EASIER TO BUILD SEE 148 & SLIGHTLY LESS CLUNKY THAN SOFFITED EAVE WITH BOXED-IN RAKE.	COMMON & FAIRLY SIMPLE CONSTRUCTION, BUT NOT ELEGANT. SEE 148B	COMMON COMBINATION; CAN BE BUILT IN TWO BASIC WAYS. SEE 148A
Boxed-In Eave SEE 142D GOES WITH SHED, GABLE, HIP ROOFS EQUALLY WELL.	AWKWARD TO DETAIL & BUILD.	VERY COMMON FOR THIS TYPE OF EAVE; VERY SIMPLE CONSTRUCTION.	NOT COMMON, BUT COULD BE BUILT WITH SIMPLE DETAILS.
Abbreviated Eave SEE 143A GOES WITH SHED, GABLE, HIP ROOFS EQUALLY WELL.	AWKWARD TO DETAIL & BUILD.	AWKWARD TO DETAIL & BUILD.	VERY COMMON; SIMPLE CONSTRUCTION. SEE 150B

(A) **EAVE/RAKE COMBINATIONS**

ROOFING

ROOF SHEATHING

ALTERNATIVE FRIEZE BLOCK
WITH VENT LOCATION

FRIEZE BLOCK WITH
SCREENED VENT **SEE 202A**

GUTTER
SEE 193-196

CONTINUOUS
FASCIA

ALTERNATIVE FASCIA
PROFILE

SOLID T&G SHEATHING
OR EXTERIOR PLYWOOD AT
EXPOSED PORTION OF EAVE

EXPOSED RAFTER TAIL

TRIM

STUD WALL WITH
SHEATHING &
FINISH

(A) EXPOSED EAVE

ROOFING

ROOF SHEATHING

BLOCKING AS REQUIRED WITH
SPACE FOR VENTILATION

2X SOFFIT JOIST NAILED
TO RAFTERS

CONTINUOUS
SUBFASCIA

GUTTER
SEE 193-196

FINISH
FASCIA

CONTINUOUS SOFFIT OF
EXTERIOR PLYWOOD OR
OTHER EXTERIOR-RATED
FINISH

CONTINUOUS SCREENED
VENT **SEE 202B**

CONTINUOUS LEDGER
FOR SOFFIT JOISTS

STUD WALL WITH
SHEATHING & FINISH

(B) SOFFITED EAVE

ROOFING

ROOF SHEATHING

BLOCKING AS REQUIRED
WITH SPACE FOR VENT
IF NECESSARY

LEVEL-CUT RAFTER TAIL
WITH 2X4 BACKING

CONTINUOUS
SCREENED VENT
SEE 202B, C & 203A

1X4 OR 1X6

SOLID T&G SHEATHING OR
EXTERIOR PLYWOOD

STUD WALL WITH
SHEATHING & FINISH

NOTE
THIS DETAIL WORKS WELL ON STEEP ROOFS,
WHERE A FASCIA MAY APPEAR TOO BULKY.

(C) SOFFITED EAVE
Alternative Detail

ROOFING

ROOF SHEATHING

RAFTER

DOUBLE SUBFASCIA

FINISH
FASCIA

EXTERIOR PLYWOOD OR
OTHER EXTERIOR-GRADE
FINISH

CONTINUOUS SCREENED
VENT
SEE 202B, C & 203A

STUD WALL WITH
SHEATHING & FINISH

NOTE
NO GUTTER SHOWN. HANG GUTTER FROM STRAP
SEE 195C
OR USE VERTICAL FASCIA ON PLUMB-CUT RAFTERS
TO ACCOMMODATE STANDARD GUTTERS.

(D) BOXED-IN EAVE

ROOFING

ROOF SHEATHING

RAFTER

GUTTER
SEE 193-196

CONTINUOUS FASCIA

CONTINUOUS
SCREENED VENT
WITH TRIM
SEE 202B

STUD WALL WITH
SHEATHING & FINISH

ROOFING

ROOF SHEATHING

FLASHING WITH DRIP

TRIM

FASCIA

CONTINUOUS
SCREENED VENT

TRIM

BLOCKING AS REQUIRED
WITH SPACE FOR
VENTILATION

STUD WALL WITH
SHEATHING & FINISH

RAFTER WITH
INSULATION
SEE 197A

 A **ABBREVIATED EAVE**

B **SHED-ROOF EAVE**
Top of Rafter at Wall

NOTE
DUMMY RAFTERS ARE
RELATIVELY SHORT,
SO A HIGH GRADE OF
MATERIAL MAY BE USED.
CONSIDER USING THEM
IF THE EXPOSED PART OF
THE RAFTER IS TO BE A
DIFFERENT SIZE THAN
THE UNEXPOSED PART OF
THE RAFTER OR TRUSS;
OR IF EXPOSED RAFTERS
ARE DESIRED WHEN
PLYWOOD I-RAFTERS ARE
USED FOR THE ROOF
STRUCTURE, SEE 151-
153. FOR ABBREVIATED
EAVES, THE ENTIRE EAVE
ASSEMBLY MAY BE SHOP-
BUILT IN LENGTHS UP TO
ABOUT 16 FT.

ROOFING

RAFTER

ROOF SHEATHING
NAILED TO TOP OF
DUMMY RAFTER TAILS

2X DUMMY RAFTER
TAIL ALIGNED WITH
RAFTER

1X FASCIA

GUTTER
SEE 193-196

1X SOFFIT WITH
CONTINUOUS
SCREENED VENT

1X6 OR 1X8 BOARD
SCREWED TO DUMMY
TAILS & TOP PLATE

Abbreviated Eave

ROOFING

ROOF SHEATHING

RAFTER

BLOCKING

T&G SHEATHING OR
EXTERIOR PLYWOOD
AT EXPOSED EAVE

2X FASCIA

GUTTER
SEE 193-196

DUMMY RAFTER GLUED
& NAILED TO COMMON
OR JACK RAFTER; LAP
EQUALS 1½X OVERHANG

FRIEZE BLOCK WITH
SCREENED VENT SEE 202A

Exposed Eave

C **DUMMY RAFTER TAIL**

When an overhang is required at the rake, the overhang is made with barge rafters, which stand away from the building and need support. There are several ways to support barge rafters. The roof sheathing alone may be strong enough to support the barge rafters (see 144B), or the ridge board or beam can be designed to support the barge rafters at their upper ends (see 144C), and the fascia may be extended to support the barge rafters at their lower ends (see below). Lookouts or brackets may be also used to support an overhanging rake (see 145A & B).

The roof sheathing can assist in supporting the barge rafter along its length, as shown below.

SHEATHING CONTINUOUS TO COMMON RAFTER HELPS SUPPORT BARGE.

FIRST COMMON RAFTER

BARGE RAFTER

END RAFTER

(B) **OVERHANGING RAKE**
Supported by Sheathing

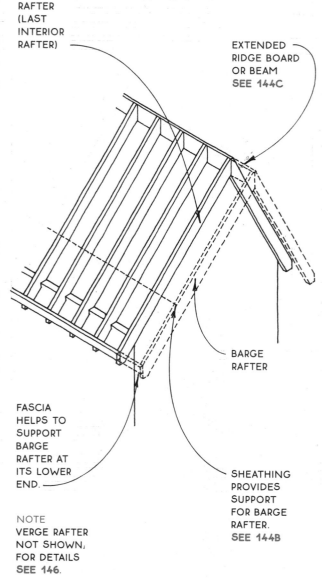

END RAFTER (LAST INTERIOR RAFTER)

EXTENDED RIDGE BOARD OR BEAM SEE 144C

BARGE RAFTER

FASCIA HELPS TO SUPPORT BARGE RAFTER AT ITS LOWER END.

NOTE VERGE RAFTER NOT SHOWN; FOR DETAILS SEE 146.

SHEATHING PROVIDES SUPPORT FOR BARGE RAFTER. SEE 144B

ALTERNATIVE CUT IN RIDGE BOARD ALLOWS FOR BOXED-IN OVERHANGING RAKE.

BARGE RAFTERS MEET AT CENTERLINE OF RIDGE.

COMMON RAFTER

RIDGE BOARD OR RIDGE BEAM SEE 131

STUD WALL UNDER END COMMON RAFTER

RIDGE BOARD MAY BE CUT AT ANY ANGLE OR SHAPE THAT ALLOWS FOR ATTACHMENT OF BARGE RAFTERS WITHOUT HAVING END EXPOSED BELOW THEM.

(A) **OVERHANGING RAKE**
Methods of Support

(C) **OVERHANGING RAKE**
Supported by Ridge Board or Beam

If the ridge, the fascia, and the sheathing together do not provide sufficient support for the barge, look-outs may be added. Lookouts extend from the barge rafter to the first common rafter (or truss) inside the wall. The lookouts are notched through the end rafter at the top of the wall or, alternatively, bear directly on the wall. The size and spacing of lookouts depend on rafter spacing and live loading.

Brackets attached to the face of the wall framing can support the barge rafter by means of triangulation.

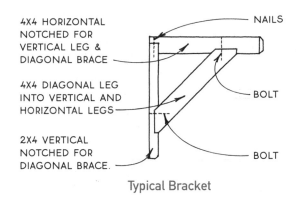

4X4 HORIZONTAL NOTCHED FOR VERTICAL LEG & DIAGONAL BRACE

NAILS

4X4 DIAGONAL LEG INTO VERTICAL AND HORIZONTAL LEGS

BOLT

2X4 VERTICAL NOTCHED FOR DIAGONAL BRACE.

BOLT

Typical Bracket

Attaching the bracket to the inside of the barge rafter avoids problems of weathering.

ROOFING

ROOF SHEATHING

BARGE RAFTER

SIDING

WALL SHEATHING

BLOCK FOR SUPPORT AT BASE OF BRACKET

The alternative bracket connection to the barge rafter shown below is common on Craftsman-style buildings. With this detail, moisture collects on top of the bracket, and this contributes to the decay of the bracket and the barge rafter.

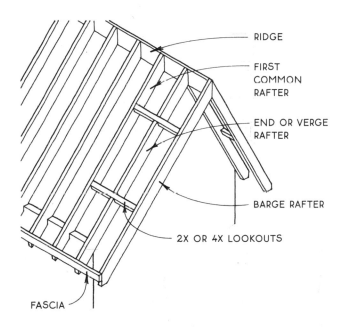

RIDGE

FIRST COMMON RAFTER

END OR VERGE RAFTER

BARGE RAFTER

2X OR 4X LOOKOUTS

FASCIA

FIRST COMMON RAFTER

BARGE RAFTER

A LADDER OF LOOKOUTS THE SAME DIMENSION AS RAFTERS & AT 16 IN. OR 24 IN. O.C. PROVIDES STRENGTH AND NAILING FOR BOXED-IN RAKE. SEE 147D

(A) **OVERHANGING RAKE**
Supported by Lookouts

(B) **OVERHANGING RAKE**
Supported by Brackets

NOTCH VERGE RAFTER;
IF LOOKOUTS ARE
REQUIRED, **SEE 145A.**

SECTION
SEE 146C

VERGE RAFTER APPLIED
OVER SHEATHING &
CONTINUOUS TO FASCIA

CORNER DETAIL
SEE 146B

NOTES
EXPOSED ROOF SHEATHING MUST BE EXTERIOR-RATED
PANEL OR SOLID (T&G) MATERIAL.
FOR ALTERNATIVE DETAIL WITH TRIM BOARD, **SEE 147A & B.**

(A) EXPOSED RAKE WITH VERGE RAFTER
Framing

COMMON
RAFTER

WALL
SHEATHING

END
RAFTER
CUT FLUSH
WITH FRIEZE
BLOCK

FRIEZE BLOCK
SEE 142A & B

FASCIA MAY BE SQUARE
CUT (AS SHOWN) AND
COVERED WITH BARGE TRIM
OR IT CAN BE MITERED

CORNER OF BUILDING

LOOKOUT
SEE 145A

VERGE
RAFTER

BARGE
RAFTER

(B) EXPOSED RAKE WITH VERGE RAFTER
Corner Framing

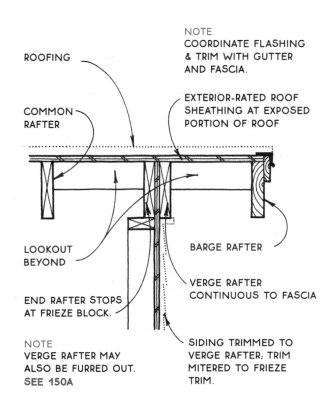

ROOFING

COMMON
RAFTER

NOTE
COORDINATE FLASHING
& TRIM WITH GUTTER
AND FASCIA.

EXTERIOR-RATED ROOF
SHEATHING AT EXPOSED
PORTION OF ROOF

LOOKOUT
BEYOND

END RAFTER STOPS
AT FRIEZE BLOCK.

NOTE
VERGE RAFTER MAY
ALSO BE FURRED OUT.
SEE 150A

BARGE RAFTER

VERGE RAFTER
CONTINUOUS TO FASCIA

SIDING TRIMMED TO
VERGE RAFTER; TRIM
MITERED TO FRIEZE
TRIM.

(C) EXPOSED RAKE WITH VERGE RAFTER
Section

ROOFING

END
RAFTER

NOTE
DUMMY RAKES, LIKE
DUMMY ABBREVIATED
EAVES, **SEE 143C,**
MAY BE SHOP-BUILT IN
LONG LENGTHS.

ROOF SHEATHING
FASTENED TO TOP
OF BLOCKING

FLASHING & TRIM
COORDINATED WITH
GUTTER & FASCIA

1X RAKE PROJECTS
BELOW BOXING
TO FORM DRIP.

1X OR WEATHER-
RATED COMPOSITE
BOXING

2X BLOCKING
AT 24 IN. O.C.

1X6 OR 1X8
BOARD SCREWED
TO BLOCKING &
TO END RAFTER

(D) DUMMY RAKE

COMMON RAFTER

END RAFTER SAME AS COMMON RAFTERS

WALL SHEATHING

FRIEZE BLOCK **SEE 142A & B**

LOOKOUT **SEE 145A**

TRIM BOARD (NOT SHOWN) **SEE 147C**

FASCIA SQUARE-CUT (AS SHOWN) & COVERED WITH BARGE TRIM, OR MITERED TO BARGE RAFTER

BARGE RAFTER

CORNER OF WALLS

Ⓐ EXPOSED RAKE WITH TRIM BOARD
Corner Framing

ROOFING

ROOF SHEATHING

FLASHING & TRIM COORDINATED WITH GUTTER & FASCIA

COMMON RAFTER

LOOKOUT BEYOND

BARGE RAFTER

TRIM BOARD RIPPED TO DEPTH OF RAFTERS EXTENDS FROM RIDGE TO CORNER BLOCK. **SEE 147C**

END RAFTER SAME AS COMMON RAFTERS

TRIM AT TOP OF SIDING MEETS TRIM BOARD.

Ⓑ EXPOSED RAKE WITH TRIM BOARD
Section

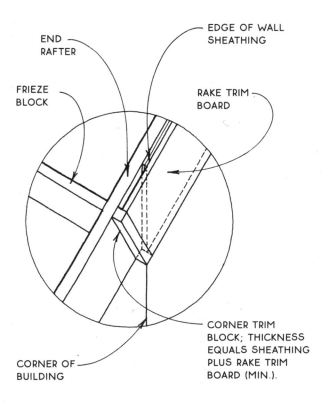

END RAFTER

EDGE OF WALL SHEATHING

FRIEZE BLOCK

RAKE TRIM BOARD

CORNER OF BUILDING

CORNER TRIM BLOCK; THICKNESS EQUALS SHEATHING PLUS RAKE TRIM BOARD (MIN.).

Ⓒ EXPOSED RAKE WITH TRIM BOARD
Detail at Eave

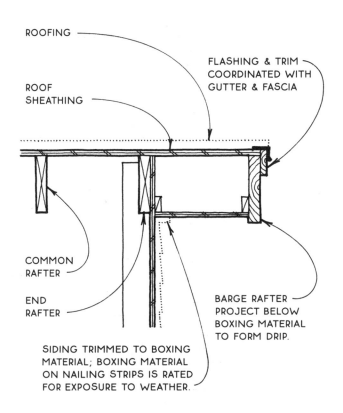

ROOFING

ROOF SHEATHING

FLASHING & TRIM COORDINATED WITH GUTTER & FASCIA

COMMON RAFTER

END RAFTER

SIDING TRIMMED TO BOXING MATERIAL; BOXING MATERIAL ON NAILING STRIPS IS RATED FOR EXPOSURE TO WEATHER.

BARGE RAFTER PROJECT BELOW BOXING MATERIAL TO FORM DRIP.

Ⓓ BOXED-IN RAKE

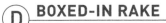

The transition from soffited eave to rake can demand some carpentry heroics. Only when the soffit is terminated at the plane of the end wall is the detailing reasonably direct, requiring only that the end of the soffit space be finished. This situation may occur with an abbreviated rake (see below) or with an overhanging rake (see below and 148B). As shown below, the end of the soffit space may be finished with a pork chop or with a layered gable—a continuation of the gable-wall finish over the end of the soffit.

When the soffit extends beyond the plane of the end wall, the rear side of the soffited space (opposite the fascia) must be finished as well as the end. As shown in the drawings below, this may be accomplished most elegantly with a Greek return, or with a simpler soffit return.

PORK CHOP WITH ABBREVIATED RAKE (ALSO USED WITH OVERHANGING RAKE); VERGE RAFTER OR TRIM BOARD LAPS PORK CHOP. CHOP COVERS END OF SOFFIT SPACE.

BARGE RAFTER DIES ON ROOF. SEE 149B

FRAMING DETAILS SEE 149A

GREEK RETURN EXTENDS SOFFIT AROUND CORNER OF BUILDING & COVERS IT WITH A SMALL HIP ROOF. FASCIA MITERED AT CORNERS FOLLOWS EDGE OF HIP ROOF & DIES INTO END WALL.

LAYERED GABLE WITH ABBREVIATED RAKE (ALSO USED WITH OVERHANGING RAKE); GABLE-WALL FINISH EXTENDS TO COVER END OF SOFFIT SPACE. VERGE RAFTER OR TRIM BOARD LAPS FINISH & FINISH MAY LAP SECOND WALL FINISH BELOW.

PORK CHOP AT END

SOFFIT MATERIAL COVERS REAR OF SOFFIT SPACE.

SOFFIT RETURN TAKES THE DIRECT APPROACH TO COVER BOTH THE END & REAR OF THE SOFFITED SPACE. THIS DETAIL MAY BE USED WITH BOXED-IN OR WITH EXPOSED RAKE.

FRAMING DETAILS SEE 149C

Ⓐ **SOFFITED EAVE/RAKE TRANSITION**
Abbreviated or Overhanging Rake

Ⓑ **SOFFITED EAVE/RAKE TRANSITION**
Overhanging Rake

BARGE RAFTER RESTS ON FINISHED ROOF. **SEE 149B**

FASCIA

END RAFTER

HIPS

WALL SHEATHING

SOFFIT JOIST

FASCIA

CORNER OF WALLS BELOW

FASCIA RETURNS TO WALL SHEATHING.

(A) GREEK RETURN
Framing

NOTE
THIS SITUATION USUALLY OCCURS WHEN A BARGE (OR VERGE) RAFTER DIES ON TOP OF A ROOF SURFACE.

BARGE RAFTER

ROOFING

BARGE TRIM

AIR SPACE TO PREVENT DECAY

Elevation

BARGE TRIM

VALLEY

BARGE RAFTER

CUT RAFTER ABOVE LEVEL OF ROOFING.

SHEATHING

ROOFING ON MAIN ROOF

SUPPORT RAFTER ON FLASHING SO THAT WATER MAY PASS UNDER IT.

Section

(B) RAFTER DIES ON ROOF

END RAFTER

DOUBLE TOP PLATE OF WALL

WALL SHEATHING

COMMON RAFTER

BARGE RAFTER

SOFFIT JOIST

PORK CHOP

FASCIA

EXTEND SOFFIT LEDGER PROVIDES SUPPORT TO RAKE.

(C) SOFFIT RETURN
Framing

ROOFING

SHEATHING

CUT ON FASCIA IS MADE AT PITCH OF ROOF & ABOVE LEVEL OF ROOFING; FASCIA IS SUPPORTED BY RAFTERS & SHEATHING.

ROOFING ON MAIN ROOF

SHEATHING

Elevation

AIR SPACE TO PREVENT DECAY

ROOFING

ROOFING ON MAIN ROOF

SHEATHING

SHEATHING

FASCIA

Section A-A

(D) FASCIA DIES ON ROOF

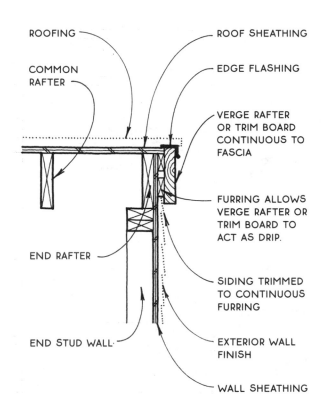

ROOFING

COMMON RAFTER

ROOF SHEATHING

EDGE FLASHING

VERGE RAFTER OR TRIM BOARD CONTINUOUS TO FASCIA

END RAFTER

FURRING ALLOWS VERGE RAFTER OR TRIM BOARD TO ACT AS DRIP.

SIDING TRIMMED TO CONTINUOUS FURRING

END STUD WALL

EXTERIOR WALL FINISH

WALL SHEATHING

Ⓐ ABBREVIATED RAKE

END RAFTER

COMMON RAFTER

WALL SHEATHING

FURRING CONTINUOUS BEHIND VERGE RAFTER **SEE 150A**

VERGE RAFTER OR TRIM BOARD

CORNER OF WALLS BELOW

DOUBLE TOP PLATE

FASCIA SHOWN MITERED TO VERGE; IT MAY ALSO BE SQUARE-CUT & COVERED WITH TRIM OR GUTTER.

Ⓑ ABBREVIATED RAKE/EAVE
Corner Framing

SIDING

WALL SHEATHING

FLASHING

NAILING BLOCK

ROOF SHEATHING

ROOFING

2X LEDGER NAILED TO STUDS

2X PURLINS PERPENDICULAR TO RAFTERS PROVIDE 1½-IN. AIR SPACE FOR LATERAL AIR MOVEMENT. PROVIDE INTAKE & EXHAUST VENTS. **SEE 201**

NOTE
FOR INSULATION & ROOF VENTILATION, **SEE 197-205.**

Ⓒ TOP OF RAFTER/WALL
Shed Roof with Purlins

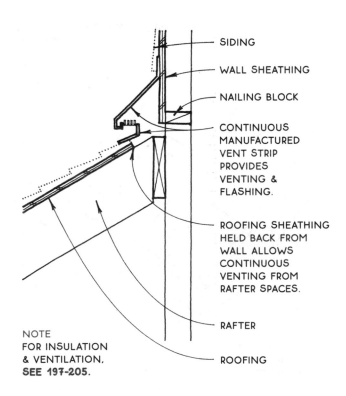

SIDING

WALL SHEATHING

NAILING BLOCK

CONTINUOUS MANUFACTURED VENT STRIP PROVIDES VENTING & FLASHING.

ROOFING SHEATHING HELD BACK FROM WALL ALLOWS CONTINUOUS VENTING FROM RAFTER SPACES.

RAFTER

ROOFING

NOTE
FOR INSULATION & VENTILATION, **SEE 197-205.**

Ⓓ TOP OF RAFTER/WALL
Shed Roof with Continuous Vent Strip

I-JOIST
RAFTER HIPS
SEE 153D

ENGINEERED LUMBER
RAFTERS & HEADERS
SEE 153C

I-JOIST RAFTER
VALLEYS
SEE 153C

I-JOIST RAFTER
RIDGES
SEE 153A & B

I-JOIST RAFTER
AT CEILING JOIST
SEE 152D

FOR OTHER
COMMON I-JOIST
CONNECTIONS
SEE 43B & 44D.

I-JOIST RAFTER
EAVE DETAILS
SEE 154C

I-JOIST RAFTER
AT EAVE
SEE 152A, B & C

The strength, precision manufacturing, and long lengths that make engineered lumber appropriate for floor framing (see 43A) also indicate its use for roof framing. I-joists used as rafters constitute the bulk of engineered lumber used for roof framing; and they are stiffer, stronger, and lighter than their solid-sawn counterparts, but they also cost more, and their appearance is not generally satisfactory if exposed.

Despite the many advantages, engineered lumber as roof framing has not seen the explosive growth that has been the case with floor framing. Part of the reason is that roof framing with engineered lumber is hardware intensive. Virtually every connection must be made with a metal connector, and most also require the addition of two web stiffeners, one on each side of the I-joist rafters. This adds considerable time and labor cost to the task of roof framing.

Another difference between framing roofs with solid-sawn or engineered lumber is that engineered lumber almost always requires a structural ridge beam.

This means that roof loads must usually be carried down to the foundation through the core of the building.

The cost/benefit ratio for framing roofs with engineered lumber favors its use only for simple gable or shed roof forms. However, many builders have found ways to combine the advantages of both solid-sawn and engineered lumber on the same building. In these hybrid roofs, engineered lumber is used for the basic forms, and solid-sawn lumber is employed for the smaller-scale parts and the more complicated forms. This mixing of materials is practical for roof construction where differential shrinkage is not usually a significant problem.

The general framing principles that apply to roof framing with solid-sawn lumber also hold true for engineered lumber. To perform as designed, however, engineered lumber roof components must be installed completely in accordance with the individual manufacturer's instructions. The drawings in this section therefore emphasize roof framing conditions that are specific to engineered lumber.

Ⓐ I-JOIST RAFTERS
Introduction

I-JOIST RAFTER

WEB STIFFENER AT EACH SIDE PER MANUFACTURER'S SPECS FOR DEEP RAFTERS

NOTE
BLOCK ALL I-RAFTERS WITH I-JOIST OR LSL FRIEZE BLOCK.

DOUBLE TOP PLATE OF STUD WALL

BEVELED BEARING PLATE ELIMINATES NEED FOR BIRD'S MOUTH AND IS PREFERRED CONNECTION FOR HEAVY LOADS.

(A) I-JOIST RAFTER AT EAVE
With Beveled Bearing Plate

I-JOIST RAFTER

WEB STIFFENER AT EACH SIDE PER MANUFACTURER'S SPECS FOR DEEP RAFTERS

DOUBLE TOP PLATE OF STUD WALL

VARIABLE-SLOPE METAL CONNECTOR ELIMINATES NEED FOR BIRD'S MOUTH ON RAFTERS UP TO 12:12 SLOPE.

NOTE
BLOCK ALL RAFTERS WITH I-JOIST OR LSL FRIEZE BLOCKING.

(B) I-JOIST RAFTER AT EAVE
With Metal Connector

I-JOIST RAFTER

WEB STIFFENER AT EACH SIDE REQUIRED OVER BIRD'S MOUTH

NOTE
BLOCK ALL RAFTERS WITH I-JOIST OR LSL FRIEZE BLOCK.

NOTE
EXTEND WEB STIFFENERS INTO EAVE AS REQUIRED FOR STRUCTURE

DOUBLE TOP PLATE OF STUD WALL

BIRD'S MOUTH IN LOWER CHORD OF RAFTER MUST BEAR ENTIRELY ON TOP PLATE.

(C) I-JOIST RAFTER AT EAVE
With Bird's Mouth

CEILING JOIST RESISTS OUTWARD THRUST OF RAFTERS. SEE 130

WEB STIFFENER AT RAFTER PROVIDES NAILING SURFACE FOR CEILING JOISTS.

DOUBLE TOP PLATE OF STUD WALL

I-JOIST RAFTER

NOTE
MOST I-JOIST MANUFACTURERS DO NOT SUPPORT THIS DETAIL.

NOTE
BLOCK ALL RAFTERS WITH I-JOIST OR LSL FRIEZE BLOCK. EXTEND WEB STIFFENERS INTO EAVE AS REQUIRED FOR STRUCTURE.

(D) I-JOIST RAFTER/CEILING JOIST

ROOF SHEATHING

RAFTERS ATTACHED TO EACH OTHER WITH 3/4-IN. PLYWOOD GUSSETS ON BOTH SIDES.

DOUBLE-BEVELED WOOD FILLER PLATE

STRUCTURAL RIDGE BEAM

ROOF SHEATHING

METAL STRAP

I-JOIST RAFTER

WEB STIFFENER

METAL RAFTER HANGER

STRUCTURAL RIDGE BEAM

STRUCTURAL RIDGE BEAM METAL STRAP CONTINUOUS ACROSS TOP OF RAFTERS & TOP OF RIDGE BOARD

I-JOIST RAFTER

WEB STIFFENER

METAL RAFTER HANGER

(A) I-JOIST RAFTER/STRUCTURAL RIDGE BEAM

STRUCTURAL RAFTER OF LVL, LSL, OR DOUBLE I-JOISTS @ SIDE OF DORMER, SKYLIGHT, OR OTHER ROOF OPENING

PERPENDICULAR LSL HEADER ON METAL HANGERS

PLUMB LSL HEADER ON METAL HANGERS

COMMON I-JOIST RAFTER

(B) STRUCTURAL RAFTER/HEADER

SOLID-SAWN JACK RAFTER FOR SHORT SPANS

SKEWABLE METAL HANGER ACCOMMODATES A RANGE OF SLOPES

I-JOIST JACK RAFTER

NOTE
FOR POSITION OF JACK RAFTERS RELATIVE TO VALLEY OR HIP RAFTERS, SEE 137 & 138.

VALLEY (OR HIP) RAFTER OF LVL OR LSL

(C) LVL OR LSL VALLEY/HIP

I-JOIST RAFTER

WEB STIFFENERS AT BOTH SIDES PER MANUFACTURER'S SPECS

ROOFING

ROOF SHEATHING

LSL RIM OR BLOCKING

BIRD'S-MOUTH CUT AT LOWER FLANGE OF RAFTER MUST HAVE FULL BEARING ON PLATE.

EXTERIOR FINISH WALL WITH TRIM

CEILING JOIST **SEE 132**

DOUBLE TOP PLATE OF STUD WALL

WALL SHEATHING

Ⓐ I-JOIST RAFTER
Abbreviated Eave

I-JOIST RAFTER

WEB STIFFENER AT BOTH SIDES PER MANUFACTURER'S SPECS FOR DEEP RAFTERS

ROOFING

ROOF SHEATHING

NAILING BLOCK FOR SUBFASCIA

FASCIA & SUBFASCIA

BIRD'S-MOUTH CUT AT LOWER FLANGE OF RAFTER MUST HAVE FULL BEARING ON PLATE.

CEILING JOIST **SEE 132**

DOUBLE TOP PLATE OF STUD WALL

VENTED SOFFIT **SEE 202B, C & 203A**

EXTERIOR WALL FINISH

WALL SHEATHING

NOTE
BLOCK ALL RAFTERS WITH I-JOIST OR LSL FRIEZE BLOCK.

Ⓑ I-JOIST RAFTER
Soffited Eave

ROOFING

ROOF SHEATHING

DUMMY RAFTER NAILED TO WEB STIFFENERS

I-JOIST RAFTER

WEB STIFFENER

BIRD'S-MOUTH CUT AT LOWER FLANGE OF RAFTER MUST HAVE FULL BEARING ON PLATE.

DOUBLE TOP PLATE OF STUD WALL

NOTE
DUMMY RAFTER LAPS I-JOIST RAFTER 1½ X DISTANCE OF OVERHANG.

(VENTED) FRIEZE BLOCK **SEE 202A**

DUMMY RAFTER

EXTERIOR WALL FINISH

WALL SHEATHING

Ⓒ I-JOIST RAFTER AT EXPOSED EAVE
Exposed Dummy Rafter

ALIGN TOP OF DUMMY RAFTER AND TOP OF I-JOIST RAFTER.

ROOFING

ROOF SHEATHING

I-JOIST RAFTER

WEB STIFFENER

DOUBLE TOP PLATE OF STUD WALL

DUMMY RAFTER NAILED TO WEB STIFFENERS

SUPPORT BLOCK UNDER DUMMY RAFTER IF RAFTER DOES NOT BEAR ON DOUBLE TOP PLATE

Section Parallel to Eave

TRUSS HIPS
SEE 157A

TRUSS VALLEYS
SEE 157B

TRUSS EAVES
SEE 159

GABLE-END
TRUSSES
SEE 156

OPENINGS IN
TRUSS ROOFS
SEE 158

TRUSS/WALL
CONNECTION
SEE 159

Roof trusses, like floor trusses, are a framework of small members (usually 2x4s) that are connected so that they act like a single large member. They are always engineered by the manufacturer.

Engineered roof trusses can span much greater distances than the stick-framed rafter-and-tie system. Long spans (over 40 ft.) are possible with simple trusses so that large open rooms may be designed with roof loads bearing only on the perimeter walls. Interior walls may simply be partition walls and may be repositioned without compromising the roof structure.

A second advantage of roof trusses is the reduction in roof framing labor. Trusses are typically set in place by the delivery truck and may be positioned and fastened in a fraction of the time it would take to frame with rafters and ties.

One major disadvantage of roof trusses is the difficulty of adapting them to complex roof forms. Roofs with numerous hips, valleys, or dormers are usually less expensive to build if they are framed with rafters.

Another disadvantage of roof trusses is that the webs of the truss occupy space that could be available for storage or as a full-size attic. Furthermore, these webs cannot be cut for any future remodeling purposes.

Five common roof truss types are shown in the drawings below.

King-Post Truss

THE SIMPLEST TRUSS IS A KING-POST TRUSS, WHICH CAN SPAN ABOUT 25 FT.

Mono-Pitch Truss

A MONO-PITCH TRUSS, FOR SHED ROOF BUILDINGS, SPANS ABOUT 25 FT.

Fink Truss

FINK TRUSSES SPAN OVER 40 FT.

Parallel-Chord Truss

PARALLEL-CHORD TRUSSES ARE FOR FLAT ROOFS; STANDARD SPANS ARE AVAILABLE UP TO 30 FT.

Attic Truss

PROVIDES USEABLE SPACE WITHIN THE TRUSS WITH SPANS TO OVER 30 FT.

Scissors Truss

THE SLOPING BOTTOM CHORDS OF SCISSORS TRUSSES CAN INCREASE INTERIOR VOLUME. SPANS UP TO 40 FT. ARE POSSIBLE.

A ROOF TRUSSES
Introduction

A gable-end truss transfers the load of the roof to the wall on which it bears through 2x4 struts at 24 in. o.c. The standard gable-end truss is the same size as a standard truss. A gable-end truss can be used with a rake overhang of 12 in. or less when the barge rafter is supported by the roof sheathing. It can also be used with flat 2x4 lookouts let into the truss above the struts. A dropped gable-end truss (see 156B) is shorter than a standard truss by the depth of the lookouts.

STANDARD TRUSSES

DOUBLE TOP PLATE OF WALL

GABLE-END TRUSS

EDGE OF ROOF

ROOFING

ROOF SHEATHING

TOP CHORD OR GABLE-END TRUSS

EXTERIOR WALL FINISH

WALL SHEATHING

BOTTOM CHORD OF GABLE-END TRUSS

CEILING NAILER

INTERIOR FINISH

DOUBLE TOP PLATE

Truss/Gable-End Wall

(A) STANDARD GABLE-END TRUSS

NOTE
A DROPPED GABLE-END TRUSS IS SHORTER THAN A STANDARD TRUSS BY THE DEPTH OF THE LOOKOUTS.

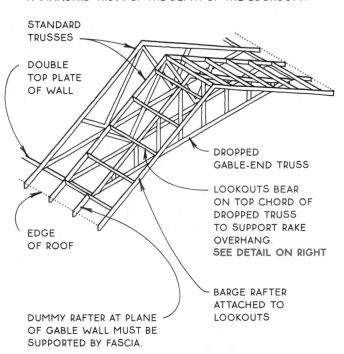

STANDARD TRUSSES

DOUBLE TOP PLATE OF WALL

DROPPED GABLE-END TRUSS

LOOKOUTS BEAR ON TOP CHORD OF DROPPED TRUSS TO SUPPORT RAKE OVERHANG. **SEE DETAIL ON RIGHT**

EDGE OF ROOF

BARGE RAFTER ATTACHED TO LOOKOUTS

DUMMY RAFTER AT PLANE OF GABLE WALL MUST BE SUPPORTED BY FASCIA.

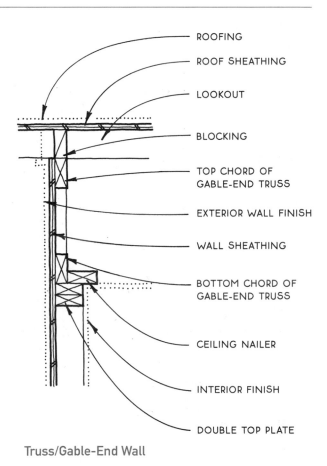

ROOFING

ROOF SHEATHING

LOOKOUT

BLOCKING

TOP CHORD OF GABLE-END TRUSS

EXTERIOR WALL FINISH

WALL SHEATHING

BOTTOM CHORD OF GABLE-END TRUSS

CEILING NAILER

INTERIOR FINISH

DOUBLE TOP PLATE

Truss/Gable-End Wall

(B) DROPPED GABLE-END TRUSS

There are several ways to frame a hip roof using trusses. None is simple, so many builders elect to frame hips (even on a truss roof) with rafters (see 138).

The most common method of framing a hip with trusses is called the step-down system. A series of progressively shallower trusses with flat tops is used to create the end roof pitch of the hip roof. The last of these trusses is the girder truss, which carries the weight of short jack trusses or rafters that complete the roof.

COMMON TRUSS

STEP-DOWN TRUSS

GIRDER TRUSS

JACK TRUSS

DOUBLE TOP PLATE OF WALL

FRAME CORNERS WITH LUMBER HIP & RAFTERS
SEE 138

LINE OF FASCIA

(A) HIP FRAMING WITH TRUSSES
Step-Down System

Framing a valley with trusses is a simple matter of attaching a series of progressively smaller trusses to the top chords of the trusses of the main roof. The main-roof trusses do not have to be oversize since the only extra weight they will carry is the dead weight of the jack trusses themselves. Simple as this system is, many builders still prefer to frame these roof intersections as a farmer's valley (see 137) with solid-sawn lumber.

VALLEY JACK TRUSS MANUFACTURED WITH BOTTOM CHORD RIPPED TO SLOP OF MAIN-ROOF PITCH

LINE OF VALLEY

LINE OF RIDGE

COMMON TRUSSES

INTERSECTING TRUSS WITHOUT OVERHANG BEARS ON DOUBLE TOP PLATE.

DOUBLE TOP PLATES OF WALLS

(B) VALLEY FRAMING WITH TRUSSES
Valley Jack Trusses

Rectangular openings for skylights or chimneys may be constructed in a truss roof. Small openings less than one truss space wide may be simply framed between trusses as they would be in a rafter-framed roof (see 135–136). Openings up to three truss spaces wide are made by doubling the trusses to either side of the opening and attaching header and mono or other special trusses to the doubled trusses. Larger openings (more than three truss spaces wide) require specially engineered trusses in place of the doubled trusses. Obviously, it is most efficient if the width and placement of the opening correspond to truss spacing.

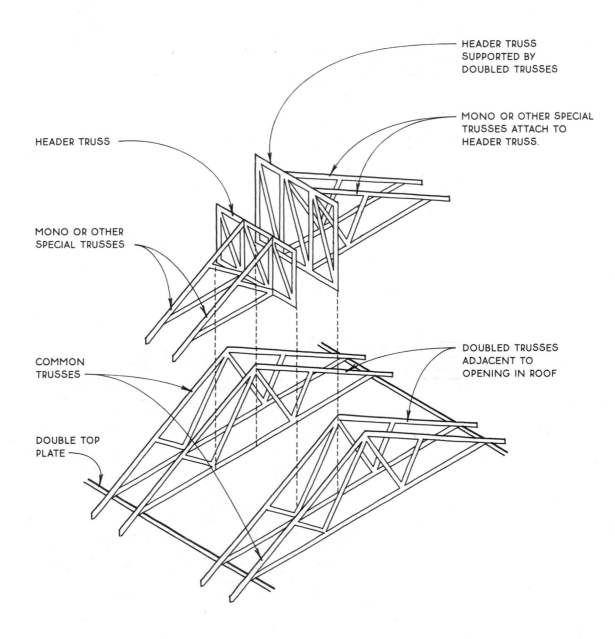

HEADER TRUSS SUPPORTED BY DOUBLED TRUSSES

MONO OR OTHER SPECIAL TRUSSES ATTACH TO HEADER TRUSS.

HEADER TRUSS

MONO OR OTHER SPECIAL TRUSSES

DOUBLED TRUSSES ADJACENT TO OPENING IN ROOF

COMMON TRUSSES

DOUBLE TOP PLATE

(A) OPENINGS IN TRUSS ROOF
Headers between Double Trusses

ROOFING

ROOF SHEATHING

TOP CHORD OF TRUSS

VENTILATION CHANNEL
AS REQUIRED
SEE 201

BLOCKING ALLOWS FOR
VENTILATION.

CONTINUOUS FASCIA
OR TRIM WITH VENTS
SEE 203B

SIDING

FRAMED WALL
WITH SHEATHING

(A) TRUSS WITH ABBREVIATED EAVE

ROOFING

ROOF SHEATHING

VENTILATION CHANNEL
AS REQUIRED
SEE 201

TOP CHORD
OVERHANG

CONTINUOUS
FASCIA

VENTED FRIEZE
BLOCK BETWEEN
TRUSSES **SEE 202A**

FRAMED WALL
WITH SHEATHING

(B) TRUSS WITH OVERHANGING EAVE
Exposed or Boxed-In Eave

ENGINEERED HEEL TIED TO WEB SYSTEM OF
TRUSS ALLOWS DEEP CEILING INSULATION
SEE 198-199

ROOFING

ROOF SHEATHING

TOP CHORD

CONTINUOUS
FASCIA

VENTED SOFFIT
SEE 202B & C, 203A

FRAMED WALL
WITH SHEATHING

(C) TRUSS WITH SOFFITED EAVE
Cantilevered Truss

ROOFING

ROOF SHEATHING

VENTILATION CHANNEL
AS REQUIRED
SEE 201

TOP CHORD
OVERHANG

FASCIA AND
SUBFASCIA

VENTED SOFFIT
SEE 202B & C & 203A

FRAMED WALL
WITH SHEATHING

(D) TRUSS WITH SOFFITED EAVE
Overhanging Truss

Because roofs are the highest part of a building and are the least weighted down by other parts of the building, they are the most vulnerable to the effects of wind. In areas prone to high winds, the design and detailing of roofs is one of the most critical concerns for the longevity of a building. The bracing of buildings to resist lateral wind forces is discussed in Chapter 3 (see 77 & 82).

Wind generally moves horizontally to impose lateral forces on buildings, much as earthquakes do. But wind flows in complex shifting patterns around a building, creating pressures on some surfaces and suction on others. Thus it can create vertical forces that actually lift the roof off a building.

These vertical forces can be created in three ways. First, they may be produced as a negative pressure (suction) if developed on the leeward side of a building. In the case of a pitched roof, this condition theoretically occurs whenever the pitch of the roof is 7-in-12 or more.

A second way for wind to exert a vertical force on a roof is for the wind to catch a protrusion such as an eave or rake overhang. In this case, the force of the wind is localized at the edge of the roof.

Finally, wind can lift the roof structure from the inside of the building. This generally occurs as a weak point in the shell of the building such as a window or garage door giving way to the pressure of the wind. The wind suddenly enters the structure, pressurizing it and forcing the roof up.

To resist the force of high winds on roofs, several strategies may be employed. Some involve design decisions to minimize the impact of high winds in the first place, others involve strengthening what is built to minimize damage.

Design strategies—One basic strategy to increase a roof's chance of survival in high winds is to keep the roof pitch low. High-pitch roofs extend higher into the sky, where wind velocity is greater, and present a greater surface area than do low-pitched roofs. Pitches between 2:12 and 7:12 are recommended for high-wind areas.

The shape of the roof also has a large impact on its durability in a windstorm. Generally, hip roofs fare the best because their geometry makes them self-bracing, and they have low eaves with no tall walls. Gable roofs present a weak point at the gable end itself, which is a tall vertical surface.

The width of overhangs at both eave and rake are important considerations for high-wind zones. Many buildings have been destroyed by winds that catch the underside of the eave and lift it off the building. Eaves of 8 in. or less are recommended for high-wind areas unless special measures are taken to anchor them.

Anchoring strategies—Assuming the building is shaped appropriately to withstand the force of high wind, it is still necessary to reinforce it beyond typical code standards. Framing members must be anchored to resist uplift and overturning, sheathing must be stronger, and fasteners must be increased. These measures are illustrated on the following page.

NOTE
AREAS WITHIN 4 FT. OF ROOF EDGES
REQUIRE MORE NAILS IN HIGH-WIND ZONES.

 ROOF FRAMING FOR HIGH WIND

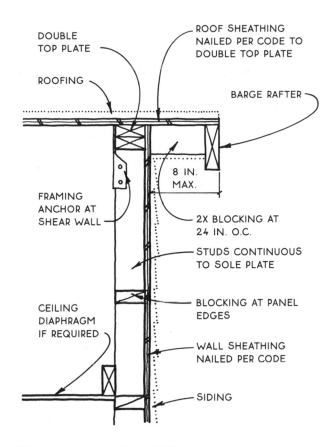

DOUBLE
TOP PLATE

ROOF SHEATHING
NAILED PER CODE TO
DOUBLE TOP PLATE

ROOFING

BARGE RAFTER

8 IN.
MAX.

FRAMING
ANCHOR AT
SHEAR WALL

2X BLOCKING AT
24 IN. O.C.

STUDS CONTINUOUS
TO SOLE PLATE

CEILING
DIAPHRAGM
IF REQUIRED

BLOCKING AT PANEL
EDGES

WALL SHEATHING
NAILED PER CODE

SIDING

Ⓐ HIGH-WIND RAKE
Balloon Frame to Sheathing

FRAMING ANCHOR
AT EACH LOOKOUT

2X6 BLOCKING
BETWEEN LOOKOUTS

2X6 LOOKOUTS
AT 24 IN. O.C.

ROOFING

SHEATHING
NAILED PER
CODE TO
LOOKOUTS

24 IN. MAX.

BARGE RAFTER

BLOCKING AT PANEL
EDGES

DOUBLE TOP
PLATE

STUDS CONTINUOUS
TO SOLE PLATE

CEILING
DIAPHRAGM
IF REQUIRED

WALL SHEATHING
NAILED PER CODE

SIDING

Ⓑ HIGH-WIND RAKE
Balloon Frame with Lookouts

ROOFING

ROOF SHEATHING
NAILED PER CODE
TO TRUSSES

TOP CHORD OF
ENGINEERED
TRUSS

BARGE RAFTER

8 FT. 2X4 AT APPROXIMATELY
5 FT. O.C. NAILED TO TOP
OF BOTTOM CHORD

8 IN.
MAX.

2X BLOCKING
24 IN. O.C.

BOTTOM CHORD OF
ENGINEERED TRUSS

ENGINEERED
METAL STRAP
TIES TRUSSES TO
WALL BELOW

BLOCKING
BELOW STRAP

WALL SHEATHING
NAILED PER CODE

DOUBLE
TOP PLATE

SIDING

Ⓒ HIGH-WIND RAKE
Platform Frame

ROOFING

ROOF SHEATHING

ENGINEERED ROOF
TRUSS OR RAFTER WITH
COLLAR TIES

FRIEZE BLOCK WITH
SCREENED VENT

FRAMING ANCHOR TIES ROOF
FRAMING TO WALL SHEATHING
TO PREVENT UPLIFT

3 FT. TOTAL EAVE
WIDTH MAX

NOTE
TOENAILING (OR MORE FRAMING
ANCHORS) TIE ROOF FRAMING TO
DOUBLE TOP PLATE TO RESIST SHEAR
FORCES PARALLEL AND PERPENDICULAR
TO WALL.

STUD WALL
WITH SHEATHING
AND FINISH

Ⓓ HIGH-WIND EAVE

Roof sheathing attaches to the surface of the rafters or trusses to form the structural skin of the roof. It spans the rafters to support the roofing and, in the case of panel sheathing such as plywood or OSB, it acts with the walls to resist horizontal loads. Roof-sheathing material must be coordinated with the roofing itself, since each type of roofing has special requirements.

At exposed roof overhangs, the sheathing must be rated for exposure to the weather. The everyday sheathing used on the body of a roof is not rated for weather exposure, so when exposed eaves and/or rakes occur at the perimeter, a different (more expensive) weather-rated grade of plywood or OSB must be used. Solid board sheathing may also be used at these exposed locations.

SHEATHING MUST BE WEATHER RATED IF EXPOSED AT EAVE, RAKE, PORCH, ETC.

The two basic types of sheathing are solid sheathing and open sheathing.

Solid sheathing—Solid sheathing provides a continuous surface at the plane of the roof. This type of sheathing is necessary for composition roofing and built-up roofing, which have no structural capacity themselves. Metal, tile, and shingle roofing may also be applied to solid sheathing. For economic and structural (lateral-load) reasons, solid sheathing is almost always plywood, OSB, or other structural panels (see 163). The structural panels act as a diaphragm to transfer lateral loads at the plane of the roof to the walls. When an exposed ceiling is desired, solid sheathing may

also be constructed of solid-wood tongue-and-groove boards. Tongue-and-groove sheathing, however, does not act as a diaphragm, so other methods of providing lateral-load stability, such as diagonal bracing, must be employed.

Open sheathing—Open sheathing, also called skip sheathing, is composed of boards spaced apart (see 166). This type of roof sheathing is used under wood shingles and shakes, which usually require ventilation on both sides of the roofing material. Open sheathing may also be chosen for economic reasons, but only if used with roofing systems such as metal or tile, which have the structural capacity to span between sheathing boards. Alternative methods of providing a roof diaphragm, such as diagonal bracing, must be used with open sheathing.

Combinations, of course, are also possible and often appropriate. For example, solid sheathing at exposed overhangs is often combined with open sheathing on the rest of the roof.

Recommendations—Sheathing recommendations for roofs by roofing types are as follows:

Composition and built-up roofing must be applied to solid sheathing because these roofing materials do not have the structural capacity to span between the boards of open sheathing.

Wood shingle and shake roofing is best applied over open sheathing because the spacing between the open sheathing allows the roofing to breathe from both sides, prolonging its life. Shingle and shake roofs may also be applied to solid sheathing at exposed eaves and rakes and similar locations. In some regions, the common practice is to place a moisture barrier over open sheathing to keep out wind-driven rain. In very windy areas, solid sheathing is often used. Consult with local codes and builders for the accepted practice.

Metal and tile roofing may be applied to either solid or open sheathing. Both roofing materials have the strength to span across open sheathing, but there is no advantage for either in having them breathe from both sides.

Ⓐ **ROOF SHEATHING**
Introduction

APA-RATING
SHEATING-GRADE
PANELS (UNSANDED)

LONG PANEL DIMENSION
PERPENDICULAR TO SUPPORTS.

PROTCT EDGES OF PANELS
AGAINST EXPOSURE TO
WEATHER.
SEE 169C

STAGGER
END JOINTS
OF ALL ROOF
SHEATHING
PANELS.

PANEL EDGE CLIPS
BETWEEN RAFTERS
PROVIDE EDGE
SUPPORT, OR USE
T&G PANELS OR
BLOCKING.
SEE BELOW

NOTE
MOST MANUFACTURERS
SPECIFY A 1/8-IN. SPACE
BETWEEN THE EDGES OF
PANELS TO ALLOW FOR
EXPANSION. PANELS SIZED
FOR THIS SPACING ARE
AVAILABLE. THE GAP MAY
BE OMITTED IN VERY DRY
CLIMATES; CHECK WITH
LOCAL CODES & BUILDERS
FOR ACCEPTED PRACTICE IN
YOUR AREA.

LOWER EDGE OR PANELS BEAR
ON FASCIA. SOME MAY REQUIRE
NAILING AT FASCIA. SEE 142 & 164

NOTE
USE APA EXTERIOR OR EXPOSURE AT GRADE PANEL FOR EXPOSED EAVE,
RAKE, OR SOFFIT. FOR APA RATING STAMP, SEE 48.

Panel installation—Low cost and ease of installation make plywood or OSB panels the sheathing of choice for most modern roofs. The system provides a structural diaphragm and is appropriate for all but wood shingle or shake roofing, which requires ventilation. The standard panel size is 4 ft. by 8 ft., so rafter or truss spacing that falls on these modules is most practical. Care must be taken to protect panel edges from the weather by the use of trim or edge flashing (see 169C). Sheathing at exposed overhangs must be exterior or exposure 1–rated and must be thick enough to hold a nail or other roof fastener without penetration of the exposed underside.

Recommended fastening—Recommended fastening is 6 in. o.c. at edges and 12 in. o.c. in the field (6 in. in the field for supports at 48 in. o.c.). For sheathing spans greater than 24 in., tongue-and-groove edges, lumber blocking, or panel edge clips are required at edges between supports. Use two clips for spans of 48 in.

ROOF-SHEATHING SPANS		
APA rating	Thickness	Maximum span
12 / 0	5/16 in.	12 in.
16 / 0	5/16 in. to 3/8 in.	16 in.
24 / 0	3/8 in. to 1/2 in.	24 in.
32 / 16	15/32 in. to 5/8 in.	32 in.
48 / 24	23/32 in. to 7/8 in.	48 in.

Notes—Values in the table above are based on APA-rated panels continuous over two or more spans with the long dimension of the panel perpendicular to supports. Verify span with panel rating. (For the APA rating stamp, see 48.)

Spans are based on a 30-lb. live load and 10-lb. dead load, the minimum rated by the APA—The Engineered Wood Association. Check local codes and with design professionals for higher loading such as greater snow loads or higher dead loads of concrete tiles or other heavy roofing. These ratings are minimum. For a more solid roof, reduce spans or increase thickness.

Ⓐ **SOLID ROOF SHEATHING**
Plywood & Non-Veneered Panels

NOTE
JOINTS MAY BE MADE AT MID-SPAN FOR SOME END-MATCHED DECKING. VERIFY NAILING WITH MANUFACTURER'S SPECS. TOENAILING AT MID-SPAN IS REQUIRED FOR LONGER SPANS. VERIFY WITH MANUFACTURER.

TWO NAILS (MIN.) PER SUPPORT

STAGGER JOINTS OVER SUPPORTS.

LOCATE JOINTS OVER SUPPORTS FOR APPEARANCE.

EXPOSED DECKING AT EAVE SEE 165

NOTE
WIRING MUST BE RUN EXPOSED ON THE SURFACE OF THE CEILING, IN A CONDUIT THROUGH THE INSULATION ABOVE THE DECKING, OR IN A CHANNEL IN A RAFTER.

T&G sheathing (decking) is most often used for exposed ceiling applications. It can also be used selectively at exposed eaves or overhanging rakes. Rafters are spaced at wide centers since the decking will span more than 24 in. in most cases (see the table at right). Because this sheathing material does not provide a diaphragm at the plane of the roof, other means of bracing the roof against horizontal loads must usually be employed. For example, the roof may be braced with metal straps applied to the top of the sheathing or with a layer of plywood or OSB over the decking.

Insulation for an exposed ceiling must be located above the sheathing. Insulation will vary with climate and with roofing material. Rigid insulation is usually the most practical because of its thin profile, but it is more expensive than batt insulation. Batts are often chosen for colder climates, where the thickness of either type

of insulation (rigid or batts) requires adding a second level of structure above the decking to support the roof.

This table assumes a 30-lb. live load for Douglas-fir or southern pine species. The table is for comparison and approximating purposes only. The actual span capacity depends on roof pitch, species, live-load values, and end-joint pattern.

EXPOSED T&G DECKING SPANS	
Nominal thickness	Approximate span
2 in.	6.0 ft.
3 in.	10.5 ft.
4 in.	13.5 ft.
5 in.	17.0 ft.

A SOLID ROOF SHEATHING
Exposed T&G Decking

ROOFING

RIGID INSULATION OVER
TEMPERATURE-CONTROLLED SPACE

T&G EXPOSED DECKING

VAPOR BARRIER BETWEEN
INSULATION & DECKING
CONTINUOUS TO INSIDE OF
WALL & CAULKED AROUND
RAFTERS.

FURRING STRIPS
AND/OR PLYWOOD
SHEATHING OVER
EXPOSED EAVE

FRIEZE BLOCK

T&G DECKING
EXPOSED AT EAVE

INSULATION

NAILING BLOCK
FOR FINISH WALL

ROOFING

FURRING OVER RIGID INSULATION
NAILED TO DECKING

RIGID INSULATION OVER
TEMPERATURE-CONTROLLED SPACE

T&G EXPOSED DECKING

VAPOR BARRIER BETWEEN
INSULATION & DECKING
CONTINUOUS TO INSIDE OF
WALL & CAULKED AROUND
RAFTERS.

FURRING STRIPS
OVER EAVE AT
SAME SPACING
AS FURRING OVER
INSULATION

T&G DECKING
EXPOSED AT EAVE

INSULATION

FRIEZE BLOCK

NAILING BLOCK FOR FINISH WALL

Metal or composition roofing may be applied directly over rigid insulation on T&G sheathing. For this construction, fasteners must be sized to penetrate through the insulation but not through the decking.

Preformed metal roofing—Preformed metal roofing may be applied directly to the insulation over a layer of 15-lb. or 30-lb. felt. If the insulation is more than 3½ in. thick, wooden nailers equal to the thickness of the insulation and parallel to the decking are recommended to provide a stable surface for roof fasteners. Nailers should be located 3 ft. to 5 ft. o.c., depending on the profile of the metal roofing.

Composition roofing—Composition roofing may also be applied directly if the insulation board is strong enough to withstand the rigors of the roofing process. Most asphalt-shingle manufacturers, however, will not honor their warranty unless the shingles are applied to a ventilated roof. Unventilated shingles can get too hot and deteriorate prematurely. The addition of vertical furring strips and sheathing over the insulation with vents at the top and bottom of the assembly will satisfy the requirement for ventilation.

Wood or tile roofing requires another layer of material over the insulation. In some cases, it may be more economical to substitute nonrigid insulation.

Wood shingles or shakes—Wood shingles and shakes last longer if they are allowed to breathe from both sides, so they should be raised on furring strips above the level of the insulation. The furring strips may be nailed through the rigid insulation to the decking, or they may be attached directly to the decking between rows of insulation. The spaces and cracks between the shakes or shingles will usually provide adequate ventilation.

Despite the advantages of breathing, shingles should be installed over solid sheathing and underlayment in areas with extreme wind-driven rain or snow or if the roof pitch is as low as 3-in-12 or 3½-in-12.

Ceramic or concrete tiles—Ceramic and concrete tiles, like shingles, commonly require furring strips. The furring strips should be spaced according to the length of the tiles (see 187B, 188, and 189).

A EXPOSED T&G DECKING AT EAVE
Metal or Composition Roof

B EXPOSED T&G DECKING EAVE
Wood or Tile Roof

STAGGERED JOINTS
OVER SUPPORTS

RAFTER OR TRUSS SPACING
UP TO 24 IN. FOR MOST
1X4 OR 1X6 SHEATHING

DIAGONAL BRACING
ENGINEERED IN SEISMIC
OR HIGH-WIND ZONES
(SEE BELOW).

NOTE
ALL BOARDS MUST BE
CONTINUOUS THROUGH
TWO OR MORE SPANS.

TWO NAILS (MIN.)
PER BOARD AT
EACH SUPPORT

SPACING BETWEEN
SHEATHING BOARDS
DEPENDS ON TYPE OF
ROOFING (SEE BELOW).

NOTE
MANY ROOFERS PREFER THREE
OR FOUR ROWS OF SOLID
SHEATHING AT THE EAVES
FOR STARTER COURSES.

Open, or skip, sheathing is usually made with 1x4 or 1x6 boards nailed horizontally to the rafters with a space between the boards. Since this sheathing material does not provide a diaphragm at the plane of the roof, other means of bracing the roof against horizontal loads must be employed. Let-in wooden bracing or metal strap bracing applied to the top or bottom surface of the rafters will suffice in most cases. This bracing must be engineered in seismic or high-wind zones or for very large roofs. Bracing may sometimes be omitted on hip roofs because the shape of the roof provides the bracing.

Spacing for open sheathing depends on the type of roofing. The ability of the sheathing to span between

supports depends on the spacing and on the type of roofing applied over it. Check with local codes and with roofers for accepted local practices.

Wood shingles or shakes require spacing equal to the exposure of the shingles or shakes—usually about 5 in. for shingles to 10 in. for shakes. The sheathing is usually 1x4.

Concrete tiles, depending on the type, may be installed on open sheathing spaced in the 12-in. to 14-in. range. The roofing material is heavy, so 1x6 or 1x8 or 2x4 sheathing is practical.

Preformed metal roofing is lightweight and runs continuously in the direction of the rafters. In most cases, 1x6 sheathing at 24 in. o.c. is adequate.

Ⓐ OPEN ROOF SHEATHING

VALLEY FLASHING
SEE 170

RIDGE FLASHING
SEE 203C & D

CHIMNEY FLASHING
SEE 173B & 174

PITCH-CHANGE FLASHING
SEE 173A

SKYLIGHT FLASHING
SEE 175B & C, 176

SIDEWALL & STEP
FLASHING
SEE 171

ROOF JACKS
& VENTS
SEE 175A

LEVEL-WALL/
ROOF FLASHING
SEE 169D

EAVE FLASHING
& ICE-DAM
CONTROL
SEE 169A & B

RAKE
FLASHING
SEE 169C

INSIDE CORNER
FLASHING
SEE 172B

OUTSIDE CORNER
FLASHING
SEE 172A

HEMMED EDGES &
FASTENERS
SEE 168

Flashing is a necessary component of most roofing systems. Flashing makes the roof watertight at edges, openings, and bends in the roof where the roofing material cannot perform the job alone.

Flashing materials and details must be coordinated with the roofing material to make a durable and waterproof roof. Although design principles are transferable from one type of roofing to another, proportions of materials may vary. For example, the details drawn in this section show a thin-profile roofing material such as asphalt or wood shingles, but flashing for thicker roofing materials such as tile or shake will have different proportions. Some of these special flashings can be found with the details for the particular roofing type.

You may want to use different flashing materials for roofs than for walls, because roofs are constantly exposed to the weather and, in most cases, are replaced much more frequently than walls. (For a discussion of wall flashing materials, see 102.) Moreover, roof flashing itself is not always replaced at the same time as the roof. Chimney or wall flashing may not be easily changed when the building is reroofed, so it should be made of materials like copper or stainless steel, which can last as long as the building. Valley or pitch-change

flashing will be easy to replace at the time of reroofing if the original roof is removed. This flashing may be made of material with a life span equivalent to the roof itself.

The flashing and its fasteners must be compatible with each other and with the roofing material itself. For example, flashing and fasteners for metal roofs must be compatible with the roofing metal to avoid galvanic corrosion. Flashing may be isolated from other materials with 30-lb. felt or bituminous paint.

The basic principle of roof flashing is to have the roofing, the flashing, and other materials overlap one another like shingles. Water running down the surface of the roof should always be directed by the flashing across the surface of the roof. Gravity will then work to direct water down the roof, away from the gaps covered by the flashing. This way, only wind-driven rain can force water through the roofing to the waterproof underlayment (see 177), which acts as a second line of defense. Each detail may have local variations to account for such weather-related factors. All flashing materials, therefore, should be discussed with local sheet-metal contractors or roofers.

Ⓐ **ROOF FLASHING**
Introduction

Hemmed edges—One very important detail for roof flashing is the hemmed edge, which folds back on itself about ½ in.

This fold makes the flashing thicker at the edge, which, aside from forming a stronger and neater edge when exposed, helps control the flow of water on roofs, as shown in the drawings on this page. Tucked under roofing, the turned-up hemmed edge creates an air gap that prevents moisture from migrating between the roofing and flashing by capillary action.

FLASHING WITH HEMMED EDGE

ROOFING

1/8-IN. (APPROX.) AIR GAP

ROOF SHEATHING & UNDERLAYMENT

A hemmed edge also works when it is horizontal, as in sidewall flashing (see 171A & B), where the hemmed edge not only resists capillary action but also forms a barrier to water running down the flashing and thus keeps it from running onto the roof sheathing.

WALL SHEATHING

SIDING & MOISTURE BARRIER LAP FLASHING.

ROOFING

FLASHING WITH HEMMED EDGE

8/16-IN. (APPROX.) AIR GAP

ROOF SHEATHING & UNDERLAYMENT

Turned down and lapped over roofing, the hemmed edge creates an air gap under the flashing that discourages capillary action. The hemmed edge can also form a seal on smooth surfaces such as skylight glass, which is only made more complete by the presence of water adhering by surface tension to the two surfaces.

FLASHING WITH HEMMED EDGE

1/8-IN. (APPROX.) AIR GAP

ROOFING

ROOF SHEATHING & UNDERLAYMENT

Fasteners—Flashing is usually nailed to the structure. Nails are located at the edge of the flashing to avoid punctures in the flashing where it is designed to keep moisture from entering. Care must be taken to select nails that will not cause galvanic corrosion.

Another method of attaching flashing is the cleat, a small metal clip usually made of the same material as the flashing itself. Cleats fasten flashing to the roof without puncturing the flashing and allow for expansion and contraction of flashing metal without dislodging of fasteners. Cleats may also be used to make concealed connections of flashing.

FLASHING

CLEAT AT BOTTOM EDGE OF FLASHING

NAIL

CLEAT AT TOP EDGE OF FLASHING

CONCEALED CLEAT AT BOTTOM EDGE OF FLASHING

(A) ROOF FLASHING
Hemmed Edges & Fasteners

ROOFING

FELT UNDERLAYMENT LAPS OVER METAL EAVE FLASHING.

SHEATHING

METAL EAVE FLASHING WITH DRIP LAPS FASCIA (& GUTTER).

GUTTER **SEE 196**

FASCIA

RAFTER

TYPICAL EAVE FLASHING PROFILES WITH DRIP EDGE

A **EAVE FLASHING**
Standard

CONTINUOUS BITUMINOUS WATERPROOFING MEMBRANE EXTENDS 1/4 IN. PAST METAL EDGE.

STANDARD METAL EAVE FLASHING

CONTINUOUS MEMBRANE EXTENDS 24 IN. (MIN.) BEYOND INNER FACE OF INSULATED WALL (36 IN. FOR 3:12 TO 4:12 ROOFS).

NOTE
THIS EAVE FLASHING IS REQUIRED BY CODE IN MANY AREAS WITH COLD WINTERS, BUT SHOULD BE CONSIDERED A BACKUP STRATEGY BECAUSE ICE DAMS CAN BE PREVENTED WITH ADEQUATE INSULATION AND VENTILATION. **SEE 197 & 200**

B **EAVE FLASHING**
Cold Climate

SHEATHING

FELT UNDERLAYMENT

ROOFING

RAKE FLASHING LAPS OVER BARGE RAFTER & UNDERLAYMENT.

ROOFING LAPS FLASHING

BARGE RAFTER

TYPICAL RAKE FLASHING PROFILES WITH DRIP EDGE

NOTE
METAL & TILE ROOFS HAVE SPECIAL RAKE FLASHINGS. **SEE 189B & C OR 191C**

C **RAKE FLASHING**

WALL SHEATHING

FLASHING NAILED TO WALL TO 3 IN. (MIN.) ABOVE LEVEL OF WALL FINISH

EXTERIOR WALL FINISH HELD 1 IN. (MIN.) ABOVE BEND IN FLASHING.

FLASHING EXTENDS 4 IN. (MIN.) ONTO ROOF, DEPENDING ON ROOF MATERIAL & PITCH.

HEMMED EDGE TURNED DOWN FOR BEST SEAL. **SEE 168**

ROOFING

ROOF SHEATHING

NOTE
THIS FLASHING IS USED AT THE TOP OF A ROOF WHERE THE ROOF ABUTS A VERTICAL WALL.

D **LEVEL WALL FLASHING**

Valleys on roofs, like valleys in the landscape, collect the runoff of all the slopes above them. To handle such a concentration of water, valleys must be carefully flashed. Except when using roofing materials that can bend, such as asphalt shingles or roll roofing, valleys are usually flashed with metal flashing.

Open valley flashing is the most common and may be used with virtually all roofing materials. An open valley allows the runoff water to flow within the confines of the exposed metal flashing rather than over the roofing material itself.

Cleats at 2 ft. o.c. fasten valley flashing to the roof without puncturing the flashing and allow for expansion and contraction of flashing metal without dislodging fasteners (see 168). Without cleats, flashing is wider and is nailed at the outer edges.

NOTE
BITUMINOUS SHEET WATERPROOFING LAPS VALLEY FLASHING IN LOCATIONS WITH SEVERE WEATHER. **SEE SECTION A-A AT LOWER RIGHT.**

VALLEY FLASHING EXTENDS FULL LENGTH OF VALLEY.

UNDERLAYMENT

ROOFING

VALLEY BETWEEN ROOFING IS WIDER AT EAVE THAN AT TOP, ESPECIALLY IN AREAS OF EXTREME COLD. TYPICAL VALLEY IS 5 IN. TO 6 IN. WIDE AT TOP AND INCREASED AT 1/8 IN. PER LINEAR FOOT OF VALLEY.

NOTES
FOR VALLEY FLASHING OF ASPHALT SHINGLES, **SEE 183B & C.**
FOR ROLL ROOFING WITHOUT FLASHING, **SEE 181B.**

ROOFING

VALLEY FLASHING WITH HEMMED EDGE

SHEATHING

CLEAT

ROOFING OVERLAPS FLASHING 4 IN. (MIN.)

VALLEY RAFTER

UNDERLAYMENT CONTINUOUS UNDER FLASHING IF REQUIRED FOR ROOFING

IN LOCATIONS WITH SEVERE WEATHER, BITUMINOUS SHEET WATERPROOFING IS LAPPED OVER VALLEY FLASHING AT BOTH SIDES FOR LENGTH OF VALLEY.

5-IN. CLEARANCE BETWEEN ROOFING

1-IN. CRIMP IN FLASHING IF ROOF PLANES DISCHARGE UNEQUAL AMOUNTS OF RAINWATER DUE TO UNEQUAL PITCHES OR UNEQUAL AREAS OF WATERSHED.

ROOFING

ROOF SHEATHING

VALLEY RAFTER

Section A-A

(A) VALLEY FLASHING

Sidewall flashing is a single-piece flashing installed before the roofing to create a flashing channel against the wall (see 171B). This type of flashing is adequate for most situations and allows easy reroofing.

Step flashing is a multiple-piece flashing that is woven in with the courses of roofing material (see 171C). This flashing is best for severe weather conditions. It may present some reroofing difficulties, especially if the type of roofing material is changed.

WALL SHEATHING

FLASHING

FINISH WALL AND MOISTURE BARRIER LAP FLASHING AT WALL.

MAINTAIN GAP BETWEEN SIDING AND ROOFING TO AVOID SOAKING SIDING.

KEEP ROOFING NAILS OUT OF FLASHING.

ROOFING

HEMMED EDGE FORMS CHANNEL.

FLASHING (SHOWN WITHOUT WALL FINISH)

ROOFING

SIDEWALL OR STEP FLASHING

Ⓐ SIDEWALL & STEP FLASHING
Introduction

Ⓑ SIDEWALL FLASHING

WALL SHEATHING

FLASHING

FINISH WALL AND MOISTURE BARRIER LAP FLASHING AT WALL.

KEEP SIDING NAILS OUT OF FLASHING TO ALLOW VERTICAL ADJUSTMENT WHEN REROOFING.

ROOFING

FLASHING

ROOFING

SHEATHING

FLASHING LAPS 2 IN. (MIN.) AT SIDEWALLS.

FLASHING EXTENDS 3 IN. (MIN.) UP WALL AND 4 IN. (MIN.) ONTO ROOF.

STEP FLASHING (BEFORE IT IS COVERED BY NEXT COURSE OF ROOFING)

NAIL NEAR TOP EDGE ABOVE PREVIOUS FLASHING.

ROOF COURSES LAID OVER EACH COURSE OF STEP FLASHING

NOTES
STEP-FLASHING PIECES ARE 2 IN. LONGER THAN ROOF COURSING EXPOSURE AND ARE INSTALLED WITH THE ROOFING MATERIAL, ONE COURSE AT A TIME. EXTERIOR WALL FINISH AND MOISTURE BARRIER WILL LAP STEP FLASHING. FLASHING DIMENSIONS DEPEND ON ROOFING MATERIAL AND PITCH.

Ⓒ STEP FLASHING

LAP FLASHING WITH MOISTURE BARRIER AND WALL FINISH (NOT SHOWN).

LEVEL WALL FLASHING, **SEE 169D**, NOTCHED FOR STEP OR SIDEWALL FLASHING

NOTE ROOFING (NOT SHOWN) LAPS SIDEWALL OR STEP FLASHING.

SLOPE OF ROOF

BOTTOM EDGES OF FLASHINGS LAP ROOFING.

STEP OR SIDEWALL FLASHING LAPS WALL FLASHING.

VERTICAL LEG OF STEP OR SIDEWALL FLASHING EXTENDS BELOW CORNER, AS ALLOWED BY SIDING.

Lapped Flashing for Moderate Weather

SOLDERED CORNER FLASHING WRAPS LEVEL WALL FLASHING.

LAP FLASHING WITH MOISTURE BARRIER AND WALL FINISH (NOT SHOWN).

SIDEWALL OF STEP FLASHING LAPS SOLDERED CORNER FLASHING.

SLOPE OF ROOF

BOTTOM EDGES OF SOLDERED CORNER FLASHING AND LEVEL WALL FLASHING LAP ROOFING.

NOTE ROOFING (NOT SHOWN) LAPS SIDEWALL OR STEP FLASHING AND SOLDERED CORNER FLASHING.

Soldered Flashing for Extreme Weather

LAP FLASHING WITH MOISTURE BARRIER AND WALL FINISH (NOT SHOWN).

SITE-BENT TOP EDGES OF STEP OR SIDEWALL FLASHING LAP ONTO TOP WALL.

NOTE: ROOFING (NOT SHOWN) LAPS SIDEWALL OR STEP FLASHING.

SLOPE OF ROOF

LEVEL WALL FLASHING LAPS ROOFING AND STEP OR SIDEWALL FLASHING.

Lapped Flashing for Moderate Weather

LAP FLASHING WITH MOISTURE BARRIER AND WALL FINISH (NOT SHOWN).

SOLDERED CORNER FLASHING LAPS SIDEWALL OR STEP FLASHING, WALL FLASHING, AND ROOFING.

SIDEWALL OR STEP FLASHING **SEE 171**

SLOPE OF ROOF

LEVEL WALL FLASHING **SEE 169D**

NOTE ROOFING (NOT SHOWN) LAPS SIDEWALL OR STEP FLASHING.

Soldered Flashing for Extreme Weather

(A) OUTSIDE CORNER FLASHING
Lapped Flashing for Moderate Weather

(B) INSIDE CORNER FLASHING
Lapped Flashing for Moderate Weather

LOCATE FLASHING FASTENERS AT UPPER EDGE OF FLASHING.

LOCATE ROOFING FASTENERS ABOVE FLASHING.

ROOFING STOPS ABOVE BREAK IN FLASHING.

ATTACH LOWER EDGE OF FLASHING WITH CLEATS TO AVOID PUNCTURING FLASHING.

ROOFING

SHEATHING

PITCH-CHANGE FRAMING SEE 133B

LENGTH OF UPPER LEG OF FLASHING DEPENDS ON ROOFING MATERIAL & SLOPE.

The flashing detail at left applies to both reduced pitch (shown) and increased pitch. Reduced pitch-change flashing can be avoided in favor of a cleaner detail by bending asphalt shingles or by soaking or steaming and bending wood shingles. The pitch change can also be made gradual by adding a strip of sheathing at the bend in the roof (see below) so that stiffer roofing materials such as wood shingles and shakes, tiles and slates can make the transition without flashing.

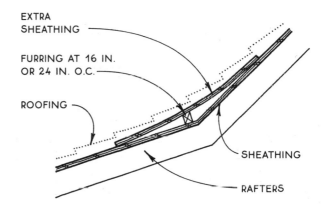

EXTRA SHEATHING

FURRING AT 16 IN. OR 24 IN. O.C.

ROOFING

SHEATHING

RAFTERS

(A) PITCH-CHANGE FLASHING

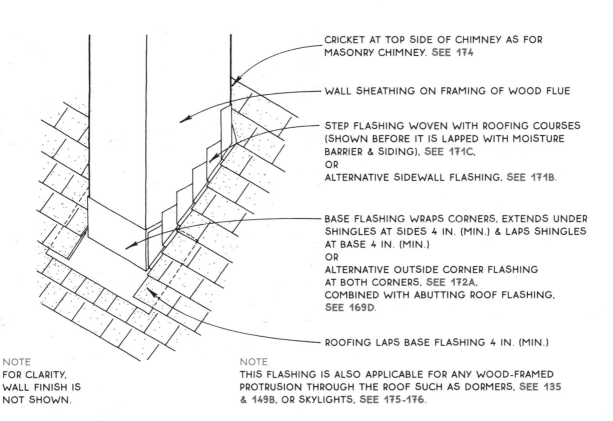

CRICKET AT TOP SIDE OF CHIMNEY AS FOR MASONRY CHIMNEY. SEE 174

WALL SHEATHING ON FRAMING OF WOOD FLUE

STEP FLASHING WOVEN WITH ROOFING COURSES (SHOWN BEFORE IT IS LAPPED WITH MOISTURE BARRIER & SIDING), SEE 171C, OR ALTERNATIVE SIDEWALL FLASHING, SEE 171B.

BASE FLASHING WRAPS CORNERS, EXTENDS UNDER SHINGLES AT SIDES 4 IN. (MIN.) & LAPS SHINGLES AT BASE 4 IN. (MIN.) OR ALTERNATIVE OUTSIDE CORNER FLASHING AT BOTH CORNERS, SEE 172A, COMBINED WITH ABUTTING ROOF FLASHING, SEE 169D.

ROOFING LAPS BASE FLASHING 4 IN. (MIN.)

NOTE FOR CLARITY, WALL FINISH IS NOT SHOWN.

NOTE THIS FLASHING IS ALSO APPLICABLE FOR ANY WOOD-FRAMED PROTRUSION THROUGH THE ROOF SUCH AS DORMERS, SEE 135 & 149B, OR SKYLIGHTS, SEE 175-176.

(B) CHIMNEY FLASHING
Wood-Framed Flue

The flashing for a masonry chimney is best made of permanent materials such as copper or stainless steel. The flashing fits to the roof using the same principles as flashing for wood-framed flues (see 173B). The top edge of this flashing is then lapped with a counterflashing that is set into the mortar joints between masonry units. Because of the complex shapes, many of the pieces in chimney flashing cannot be folded but must be soldered or welded.

A chimney located in the slope of the roof will require a cricket (also called a saddle), a ridged connection between chimney and roof that directs water away from the chimney. Most crickets may be formed with exterior-grade plywood; larger crickets may need to be framed like a typical roof. The entire surface of the cricket is flashed, as shown in the drawing below.

STEP FLASHING WOVEN WITH ROOFING COURSES **SEE 171C**

COUNTERFLASHING SET IN MORTAR 1 IN. (MIN.) AT TOP EDGE, LAPS ITSELF 2 IN. (MIN.) & LAPS STEP OR OTHER SIDE OF FLASHING 4 IN. (MIN.).

SOLDERED BASE FLASHING WRAPS CORNERS, IS SET IN MORTAR 2 IN. (MIN.) AT TOP EDGE, EXTENDS UNDER SHINGLES AT SIDES 4 IN. (MIN.) AND LAPS SHINGLES AT BASE 4 IN. (MIN.). THIS CAN ALSO BE MADE WITH TWO PIECES—A BASE FLASHING WITH COUNTERFLASHING SET IN MORTAR.

ROOFING LAPS BASE FLASHING 4 IN. (MIN.).

Side & Base

COUNTERFLASHING SET IN MORTAR & CUT TO SLOPE OF CRICKET

SOLDERED COUNTERFLASHING CONTINUOUS AROUND CORNER LAPS CRICKET.

STEP FLASHING (NOT VISIBLE) WOVEN WITH ROOFING COURSES. **SEE 171C**

SOLDERED CRICKET WRAPS CORNERS, EXTENDS UNDER ROOFING 6 IN. (MIN.) AND TURNS UP AGAINST CHIMNEY 4 IN. (MIN.).

Side & Cricket

In severe climates, a through-pan flashing that extends continuously through the chimney should be considered. Through-pan flashing prevents water from migrating through the masonry to a level below the flashing. It is made of lead or copper and is penetrated only by the flue. It is wrapped down at the edges, where it acts as counterflashing. The continuous flashing through the chimney does weaken the masonry bond, so this flashing should not be used in earthquake or hurricane zones.

FLUE

CHIMNEY

FLASHING

Through-Pan Flashing

(A) CHIMNEY FLASHING
Masonry

NEOPRENE
GASKET

ROOF JACK

ROOFING LAPS
FLASHING AT
SIDES & TOP.

FLASHING LAPS
ROOFING AT
BOTTOM.

Most skylights are manufactured with a complete flashing package and instructions for installation

in a rough opening in the roof framing. Some are available with a kit to adapt the flashing to unusual roofing materials or pitches. Skylights are available in fixed or operable types with screens and/or sun-shade devices. Rough-opening sizes are specified and usually correspond with standard rafter spacing.

Many fixed skylights require a flashed curb to which the manufactured skylight is attached. With these sky-lights, the curb must be flashed like any other large penetration of the roofing surface, such as a dormer or a chimney (see 174 and 175C). Site-built curbless sky-lights are fixed and appear flush with the roof (see 176). Some codes prohibit these skylights because of the requirement for a curb.

For skylight framing, see 136A & B.

Modern roof jacks are typically fitted with neoprene gaskets sized to seal plumbing vents and other roof penetrations. Jacks are woven in with roofing materials where possible. Jacks for metal roofs pose special problems.

Ⓐ ROOF JACKS AND VENTS

Ⓑ SKYLIGHT FLASHING
Notes

SOLDERED TOP FLASHING WRAPS CORNERS, EXTENDS UNDER ROOFING AT TOP EDGE 6 IN. (MIN.) & SIDE EDGES 4 IN. (MIN.) & TURNS UP AGAINST CURB.

RAFTER FORMS SIDE OF ROUGH OPENING.

2X CURB FRAMED ON TOP OF ROOF SHEATHING & PERPENDICULAR TO THE ROOF

SMOOTH SURFACE WOOD CURB SEALED & READY FOR APPLICATION OF SKYLIGHT

STEP FLASHING WOVEN WITH ROOFING COURSES
SEE 171C

SOLDERED (OR FOLDED) BASE FLASHING WRAPS CORNERS, EXTENDS UNDER SHINGLES AT SIDES 4 IN. (MIN.) & LAPS SHINGLES AT BASE 4 IN. (MIN.).

Ⓒ SKYLIGHT CURB FLASHING
For Use with Manufactured Skylight

NOTCH SIDE FLASHING HERE TO ALLOW ROOFING TO OVERLAP; CAULK OR SOLDER EDGE OR NOTCH.

ROOFING & TOP FLASHING LAP GLASS & SIDE FLASHING 3 IN. (MIN.).

TOP

SIDE

BOTTOM

GLASS & FLASHING LAP ROOFING 3 IN. (MIN.) AT BASE.

SIDE FLASHING & GLASS SUPPORTED BY LEDGER THAT SLOPES LESS THAN ROOF.

CLIPS HOLD GLASS AT BASE.

ROOFING

ROOF SHEATHING

TOP FLASHING LAPS GLAZING 3 IN. (MIN.).

SKYLIGHT GLAZING

2X LEDGER

ROUGH-OPENING FRAMING

Top

ROOFING

STEP FLASHING (SHOWN) OR SIDEWALL FLASHING

SPRING-FIT SIDE TRIM FLASHING

SKYLIGHT GLAZING

SIDE FLASHING WITH HEMMED EDGE FORMING GUTTER

1X LEDGER

ROOF SHEATHING

RAFTER

Side

TRIM FLASHING HOOKS ONTO CLIPS & PROTECTS GLASS EDGE.

SKYLIGHT GLAZING

CLIPS (SHOWN DASHED) SCREWED TO FRAMING & WITH CUSHIONS AT GLASS EDGE

HEMMED BOTTOM FLASHING NOTCHED FOR CLIPS

ROOFING

ROOF SHEATHING

ROUGH-OPENING FRAMING

Bottom

A site-built curbless skylight is woven in with the roofing. Its bottom edge laps the roofing, and its top edge is lapped by roofing. This means that the skylight itself must be at a slightly lower pitch than the roof. Ledgers at the sides of the rough opening provide the support at this lower pitch. If built properly, there is no need for any caulking of these skylights except at the notch at the top of the side flashing. Insulated glass should limit condensation on the glazing, but any condensation that does form can weep out through the clip notches in the bottom flashing. In extremely cold climates, the side flashing should be thermally isolated from the other flashing to prevent condensation on the flashing itself.

Curbless skylights are especially practical at the eave edge of a roof, where the lower edge of the skylight does not have to lap the roofing. This condition, often found in attached greenhouses, will simplify the details on this page because the slope of the skylight can be the same as the roof. The top and side details above right are suitable in such a case. Codes that require curbs preclude the use of these skylights.

Ⓐ **CURBLESS SKYLIGHT**

With the exception of wood roofs, which are now made with lower-grade material than in the past, today's roofing materials will last longer than ever before, and can be installed with less labor. Composite materials now take the place of most natural roofing materials, including wood shingle and slate.

The selection of a roofing material must be carefully coordinated with the design and construction of the roof itself. Some factors to consider are the type of roof sheathing (see 162–166), insulation (see 197–205), and flashing (see 167–176). For example, some roofing materials perform best on open sheathing, but others require solid sheathing. Some roofing materials may be applied over rigid insulation; others may not.

Many roofing materials require a waterproof underlayment to be installed over solid sheathing before roofing is applied. Underlayment, usually 15-lb. felt, which can be applied quickly, is often used to keep the building dry until the permanent roofing is applied. In the case of wood shakes, the underlayment layer is woven in with the roofing courses and is called interlayment (see 186).

Other considerations for selecting a roofing material include cost, durability, fire resistance, local climatic conditions, and the slope (pitch) of the roof.

Cost—Considering both labor and materials, the least expensive roofing is roll roofing (see 180–181). Next in the order of expense are asphalt shingles (see 182–183), followed by preformed metal (see 190), wood shingles (see 184–185), shakes (see 186–187A), and tile (see 187B–189). Extremely expensive roofs such as slate and standing-seam metal are not discussed in depth in this book.

Durability—As would be expected, the materials that cost the most also last the longest. Concrete-tile roofs typically have a 50-year warranty. Shake and shingle roofs can last as long under proper conditions but are never put under warranty. Preformed metal and asphalt shingles are usually under a warranty in the 15-year to 30-year range.

Fire resistance—Tile and metal are the most resistant to fire, but fiberglass-based asphalt shingles and roll roofing can also be rated in the highest class for fire resistance. Wood shakes and shingles can be chemically treated to resist fire, but are not as resistant as other types of roofing.

Slope—The slope of a roof is measured as a proportion of rise to run of the roof. A 4-in-12 roof slope, for example, rises 4 in. for every 12 in. of run.

There are wide variations among roofing manufacturers, but in general, the slope of a roof can be matched to the type of roofing. Flat roofs (⅛-in-12 to ¼-in-12) are roofed with a built-up coating or with a single ply membrane (see 178–179). Shallow-slope roofs (1-in-12 to 4-in-12) are often roofed with roll roofing. Special measures may be taken to allow asphalt shingles on a 2-in-12 slope and wood shingles or shakes on a 3-in-12 slope, and some metal roofs may be applied to 1-in-12 slopes. Normal-slope roofs (4-in-12 to 12-in-12) are the slopes required for most roofing materials. Some materials such as built-up roofing are designed for lower slopes and may not be applied to normal slopes.

12 IN.

4 IN.

4:12 SLOPE ROOF

Flat roofs aren't actually flat, but must slope to drain water or manufacturers will not guarantee their products. The actual slope depends on the application, but most manufacturers recommend 1/4 in. per ft. The slope may be achieved with the framing of the roof (see 139) or with tapered insulation. Water is usually contained at the edges of a flat roof with a curb or a wall and directed to a central drain (see 179B) or scupper at the edge of the roof (see 57D). A continuous gutter at the edge of a flat roof can also collect the water.

The selection of an appropriate roofing system for a flat roof can be complicated. As with all roofs, climate is one factor. But the fact that a flat roof is covered with a large continuous waterproof membrane presents some special technical problems, such as expansion and contraction. If the roof is going to be used for a terrace or walkway, the effects of foot traffic must also be considered (see 56 and 57). For these reasons, a flat roof is best selected by a design professional and constructed by a reputable roofing contractor.

There are several application methods for flat roofs:

Built-up roof—A built-up roof is composed of several layers of asphalt-impregnated felt interspersed with coats of hot tar (bitumen) and capped with gravel. This traditional and effective method is in widespread use. The application is technical and should be performed by professional roofers. Warranties range from one to five years.

Single-ply roof—A more recent development in roofing, the single-ply roof is less labor intensive and more elastic than the built-up roof. The single-ply roof is applied as a membrane and glued, weighted with gravel ballast, or mechanically fastened to the roof. Seams are glued with adhesive or heat sealed. Single-ply roofs are usually applied to large areas, but, like the built-up roof, can also cover small areas. Application is technical; warranties start at five years.

Liquid-applied roof—Liquid-applied roofing polymerizes from chemicals suspended in volatile solvents to form a watertight elastomeric membrane that adheres to the sheathing. Application is usually in several coats, using brush, roller, or spray. Liquid-applied roofs are practical for small areas, where they may be applied by an untrained person without specialized tools; their flexibility allows them to be applied without the cant strips required of built-up roofs (see 178B & C).

ROOF SLOPE ←

WOODEN CURB WITH CANT (SLOPE) TO PREVENT RIGHT ANGLES IN ROOFING MATERIAL

METAL FLASHING CONTINUOUS OVER CURB AND WITH DRIP AT WALL SIDE

ROOFING MATERIAL CONTINUOUS OVER TOP OF CURB

ROOF SHEATHING

SHEATHING & WALL FINISH

RAFTER

NOTE
THIS CURB IS GENERALLY USED IN CONJUNCTION WITH A SCUPPER WHEN THE ROOF SLOPES TOWARD THE OUTSIDE EDGE OF THE BUILDING. FOR SCUPPER, **SEE 57D.**

(B) FLAT ROOF EDGE WITH CURB

NOTE
WALL FRAMING & SHEATHING NOT SHOWN.

EXTERIOR WALL FINISH LAPS METAL FLASHING.

METAL FLASHING WITH DROP LAPS ROOFING MATERIAL.

CONTINUOUS WOODEN CANT STRIP PREVENTS RIGHT ANGLES IN ROOFING MATERIAL.

ROOFING MATERIAL CONTINUOUS TO ABOVE CANT STRIP.

ROOF SHEATHING

RAFTER

(A) FLAT ROOFING

Introduction

(C) FLAT ROOF EDGE AT WALL

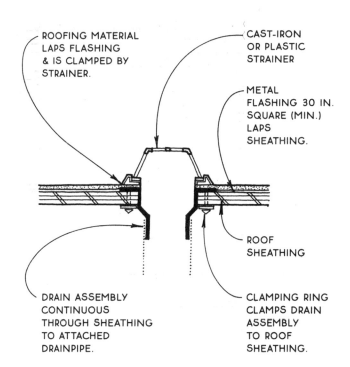

METAL GRAVEL-STOP
FLASHING SEALED TO
ROOFING MATERIAL

ROOF SLOPE

ROOFING MATERIAL
CONTINUOUS TO
GRAVEL STOP

ROOF SHEATHING

EXTERIOR WALL
SHEATHING & FINISH

ROOF JOIST

ROOFING MATERIAL
LAPS FLASHING
& IS CLAMPED BY
STRAINER.

CAST-IRON
OR PLASTIC
STRAINER

METAL
FLASHING 30 IN.
SQUARE (MIN.)
LAPS
SHEATHING.

ROOF
SHEATHING

DRAIN ASSEMBLY
CONTINUOUS
THROUGH SHEATHING
TO ATTACHED
DRAINPIPE.

CLAMPING RING
CLAMPS DRAIN
ASSEMBLY
TO ROOF
SHEATHING.

NOTE
THIS DETAIL IS GENERALLY USED WHEN THE ROOF
SLOPES AWAY FROM THE EDGE TOWARD A CENTRAL
DRAIN. **SEE 179B**

 FLAT ROOF EDGE WITH GRAVEL STOP

 FLAT ROOF DRAIN

Roll roofing is an inexpensive roofing for shallow-pitch roofs (1-in-12 to 4-in-12). The 36-in. wide by 36-ft. long rolls are made with a fiberglass or organic felt base that is impregnated with asphalt and covered on the surface with mineral granules similar to asphalt shingles. Several colors are available. Roll roofing weighs 55 lb. to 90 lb. per square (100 sq. ft.). The average life expectancy for roll roofing ranges from 10 to 15 years; fiberglass-base roofing is the longest lasting. Fiberglass-base rolls are also more resistant to fire. A disadvantage of all roll roofing is that it can bubble upward when hot because, unlike asphalt shingles, it cannot adjust to dimensional change.

Roll roofing must be applied over solid sheathing and does not require underlayment. It is easily nailed in place without using any specialized equipment.

There are two basic types of roll roofing, single coverage and double coverage.

Single coverage—Single-coverage roofing rolls are uniformly surfaced with mineral granules and are applied directly to the roof sheathing with only a 2-in.

to 4-in. lap, which is sealed with roofing adhesive. The rolls may be parallel to the eaves or to the rake. The roofing may be applied using the concealed-nail method (see 180B) or the exposed-nail method (not shown). A minimum pitch of 2-in-12 is required for the exposed-nail method. Single coverage is the least expensive and the least durable of the roll-roofing methods.

Double coverage—Double-coverage rolls are half surfaced with mineral granules and half smooth. The smooth part of the roll is called the selvage. The rolls are lapped over each other so that the surfaced portion of each roll laps over the smooth portion of the previous course. Each course of roofing is sealed to the previous course with either cold asphalt adhesive or hot asphalt. In this fashion, the roof is covered with a double layer of felt. The double layer of felt weighs 110 lb. to 140 lb. per square. Double-coverage roofing is more expensive than single-coverage roofing, but it makes a more durable roof. Double-coverage roll roofing may be applied with the courses parallel to the eave or to the rake (see 181A).

Ⓐ ROLL ROOFING
Introduction

TOP EDGE NAILING VARIES WITH MANUFACTURER.

SOLID ROOF SHEATHING **SEE 163 & 164**

COLD-SET ASPHALT ADHESIVE SEALS ROOFING TO ROOFING & TOP LAP.

12-IN. STARTER STRIP AT ALL EDGES NAILED AT 4 IN. O.C. & COVERED WITH ADHESIVE

12-IN. STARTER STRIP WITH ADHESIVE

3-IN. LAP

36-IN. ROLL

33-IN. EXPOSURE

1/4-IN. TO 3/8-IN. PROJECTION AT EAVE & RAKE

EAVE FLASHING **SEE 169A & B**

FASCIA

NOTE
LAP ALL END JOINTS 6 IN. (MIN.).

RAKE FLASHING **SEE 169C**

NOTE
ROOFING MAY ALSO BE INSTALLED WITH ROLLS PARALLEL TO RAKE OR WITH EXPOSED NAILING.

Ⓑ SINGLE-COVERAGE ROLL ROOFING
Conceded-Nail Method

NAILS IN SELVAGE PORTION OR ROLL PER MANUFACTURER'S INSTRUCTIONS

SOLID ROOF SHEATHING
SEE 163

COLD-SET ASPHALT ADHESIVE BETWEEN SELVAGE & MINERAL SURFACE PORTION OF EACH COURSE

19-IN. SELVAGE STARTER STRIP CUT FROM TOP OF ROLL & NAILED TO SHEATHING PER MANUFACTURER'S INSTRUCTIONS

LAP ALL END JOINTS 6 IN. (MIN.).

1/4-IN. TO 3/8-IN. PROJECTION AT EAVE & RAKE

EAVE FLASHING
SEE 169A & B

FASCIA

RAKE FLASHING
SEE 169C

19-IN. SELVAGE

17-IN. MINERAL SURFACE

36-IN. ROLL

16-IN. EXPOSURE

NOTE
ROOFING MAY ALSO BE INSTALLED WITH ROLLS PARALLEL TO RAKE.

(A) **DOUBLE-COVERAGE ROLL ROOFING**

18-IN. STRIP WITH MINERAL FACE DOWN EXTENDS ENTIRE LENGTH OF VALLEY.

36-IN. ROLL WITH MINERAL FACE UP EXTENDS ENTIRE LENGTH OF VALLEY; NAIL SPARSELY AT EDGES.

LAP ROLL ROOFING TO 3 IN. FROM CENTERLINE OF VALLEY; FASTEN EDGE WITH ROOFING ADHESIVE.

EAVE FLASHING
SEE 169A & B

FASCIA

ROOFING TRIMMED TO BUTT AT CENTERLINE OF HIP (SHOWN) OR RIDGE

12-IN. X 36-IN. STRIP CUT FROM DOUBLE-COVERAGE ROOFING MATERIAL; MINERAL-SURFACE PORTION LAPS ONTO SELVAGE PORTION NAILED PER MANUFACTURER'S DIRECTIONS AND COATED WITH ASPHALT ADHESIVE AS FOR DOUBLE-COVERAGE ROOF.

SINGLE (SHOWN) OR DOUBLE-COVERAGE ROLL ROOFING

NOTE
RIDGE DETAIL IS SIMILAR TO HIP DETAIL.

(B) **ROLL-ROOFING VALLEY & HIP (OR RIDGE)**
Double or Single Coverage

Composite asphalt shingles are almost the perfect roofing material. They are inexpensive, waterproof, lightweight, and easily cut and bent. That is why asphalt shingles are so popular nationwide. They are available in a wide range of colors and textures, some with extra thickness to imitate shakes, slate, or other uneven materials. There is also a range of quality, with warranties from 15 to 30 years.

Asphalt shingles have a fiberglass or organic-felt base that is impregnated with asphalt and covered on the surface with granulated stone or ceramic material, which gives them color. Shingles made with fiberglass are more durable and more resistant to fire than those of organic felt.

Asphalt shingles must be applied over a solid sheathing covered with 15-lb. felt underlayment. They are easily nailed in place, using no specialized equipment. Many roofing contractors, however, use air-driven staples.

STANDARD FIELD SHINGLES HAVE 3 TAPS & WEIGH 235 LB. PER SQUARE (100 SQ. FT.).

STANDARD FIELD SHINGLES MAY BE CUT INTO 3 PIECES TO MAKE HIP OR RIDGE SHINGLES.

SELF-SEALING ADHESIVE AVAILABLE ON TOP SIDE OF SHINGLES TO PROTECT AGAINST WIND.

ALTERNATIVE PATTERNS AVAILABLE WITH SOME THICKER TABS TO RESEMBLE MORE NATURAL ROOFS.

Common Shingle Patterns

OTHER LESS COMMON PATTERNS ARE ALSO AVAILABLE.

ALTERNATIVE STARTING PATTERN (SEE BELOW FOR SIMPLER SHINGLE PATTERN) REMOVES 4 IN. FROM SECOND COURSE & 8 IN. FROM THIRD COURSE. FOURTH COURSE STARTS WITH FULL SHINGLE MINUS ONE FULL TAB.

4 NAILS PER SHINGLE LOCATED ABOVE SLOTS & INDENTATIONS

DRIP EDGE LAPS UNDERLAYMENT AT RAKE.

RAKE FLASHING SEE 169C

THIRD COURSE STARTS WITH FULL SHINGLE MINUS ONE TAB.

SECOND COURSE STARTS WITH FULL SHINGLE MINUS 1/2 TAB.

FIRST COURSE STARTS WITH FULL SHINGLE.

SOLID ROOF SHEATHING SEE 163-165

CODES IN COLD CLIMATES OFTEN REQUIRE A 36-IN. STARTER STRIP OF BITUMINOUS WATERPROOFING. SEE 169B

15-LB. FELT UNDERLAYMENT LAPPED OVER EAVE FLASHING SEE 169A

STARTER COURSE WITH TABS CUT OFF TO BE OFFSET 3 IN.

EAVE FLASHING SEE 169A & B

FOR HIP, VALLEY & RIDGE DETAILS, SEE 183.

(A) **ASPHALT-SHINGLE ROOFING**

TRIM FIELD SHINGLES TO CENTERLINE OF HIP.

36-IN. ROLL ROOFING (MIN. 55 LB.) CENTERED ON HIP

EAVE FLASHING

FASCIA

DOUBLE FIRST COURSE OF HIP SHINGLES.

HIP SHINGLE MADE FROM 1/3 OF FIELD SHINGLE FOLDED OVER HIP & EXPOSED 5 IN. OR SAME AS FIELD SHINGLES.

(A) ASPHALT-SHINGLE HIP

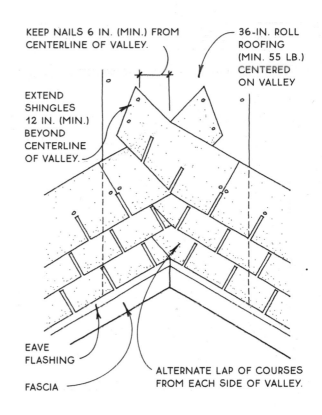

KEEP NAILS 6 IN. (MIN.) FROM CENTERLINE OF VALLEY.

36-IN. ROLL ROOFING (MIN. 55 LB.) CENTERED ON VALLEY

EXTEND SHINGLES 12 IN. (MIN.) BEYOND CENTERLINE OF VALLEY.

EAVE FLASHING

FASCIA

ALTERNATE LAP OF COURSES FROM EACH SIDE OF VALLEY.

(B) ASPHALT-SHINGLE VALLEY

EXTEND EACH SHINGLE 12 IN. (MIN.) BEYOND CENTERLINE OF VALLEY.

36-IN. ROLL ROOFING (MIN. 55 LB.) CENTERED ON VALLEY

EXTRA NAIL

EAVE FLASHING

APPLY ROOFING CEMENT UNDER EDGE OF SHINGLE TRIMMED 2 IN. FROM CENTER OF VALLEY.

FASCIA

(C) CLOSED-CUT VALLEY

RIDGE SHINGLES MADE FROM 1/3 OF FIELD SHINGLE FOLDED OVER RIDGE & EXPOSED 5 IN. OR SAME AS FIELD SHINGLES.

EXTEND FIELD SHINGLES TO RIDGE.

DIRECTION OF PREVAILING WIND

DOUBLE STARTER SHINGLES

WRAP UNDERLAYMENT OVER RIDGE.

(D) ASPHALT-SHINGLE RIDGE

For centuries, wood shingles have been used extensively for roofing, and they continue to be very popular. However, with the advent of the asphalt shingle, they have recently lost their dominance as a roofing material. Furthermore, their use continues to decline because of cost increases and a drop in the quality of the raw materials.

Roof shingles are made predominantly from clear western red cedar, but are also available in redwood and cypress. They are sawn on both sides to a taper, and have a uniform butt thickness. Standard shingles are 16 in. long; 18-in. and 24-in. lengths are also available. Widths are random, usually in the 3-in. to 10-in. range. There are several grades of wood shingles; only the highest grade should be used for roofing.

In most cases, wood shingles will last longer if applied over open sheathing (see 166) because they will be able to breathe and dry out from both sides and therefore be less susceptible to rot and other moisture-related damage. Use solid sheathing and underlayment, however, for low pitch (3-in-12 and 3½-in-12) and in areas of severe wind-driven snow.

Chemically treated fire-rated shingles are available. They must be installed over solid sheathing that is covered with a plastic-coated steel foil.

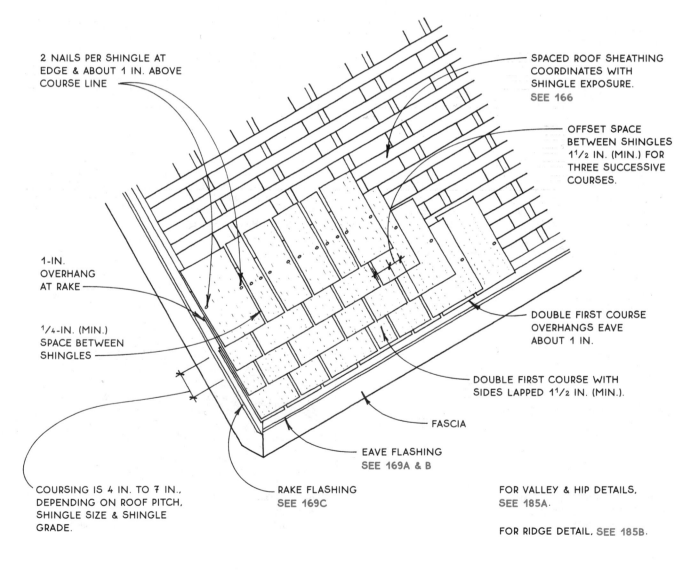

2 NAILS PER SHINGLE AT EDGE & ABOUT 1 IN. ABOVE COURSE LINE

SPACED ROOF SHEATHING COORDINATES WITH SHINGLE EXPOSURE. SEE 166

OFFSET SPACE BETWEEN SHINGLES 1½ IN. (MIN.) FOR THREE SUCCESSIVE COURSES.

1-IN. OVERHANG AT RAKE

¼-IN. (MIN.) SPACE BETWEEN SHINGLES

DOUBLE FIRST COURSE OVERHANGS EAVE ABOUT 1 IN.

DOUBLE FIRST COURSE WITH SIDES LAPPED 1½ IN. (MIN.).

FASCIA

EAVE FLASHING SEE 169A & B

COURSING IS 4 IN. TO 7 IN., DEPENDING ON ROOF PITCH, SHINGLE SIZE & SHINGLE GRADE.

RAKE FLASHING SEE 169C

FOR VALLEY & HIP DETAILS, SEE 185A.

FOR RIDGE DETAIL, SEE 185B.

A WOOD-SHINGLE ROOFING

MAINTAIN 6 IN. (MIN.) CLEARANCE BETWEEN SHINGLES.

METAL VALLEY FLASHING **SEE 170**

TRIM SHINGLES PARALLEL TO VALLEY.

SHINGLES LAP VALLEY FLASHING 6 IN. (MIN.).

SELECT WIDEST SHINGLES FOR VALLEY EDGES.

TRIM FIELD SHINGLES TO CENTERLINE OF RIDGE.

ALTERNATE LAP DIRECTION OF MANUFACTURED HIP SHINGLES.

TRIM DOUBLE FIRST COURSE OF HIP SHINGLES TO LINE OF EAVE.

EAVE FLASHING **SEE 169A & B**

FASCIA

(A) WOOD-SHINGLE VALLEY & HIP

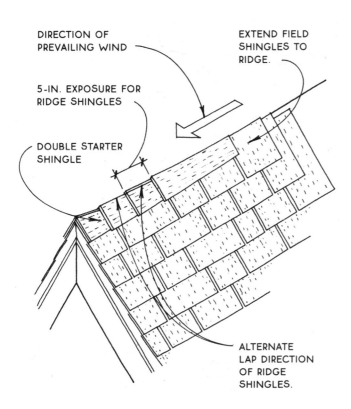

DIRECTION OF PREVAILING WIND

5-IN. EXPOSURE FOR RIDGE SHINGLES

DOUBLE STARTER SHINGLE

EXTEND FIELD SHINGLES TO RIDGE.

ALTERNATE LAP DIRECTION OF RIDGE SHINGLES.

(B) WOOD-SHINGLE RIDGE

Wood shakes are popular for their rustic look and their durability. They are made from the same materials as wood shingles, but they are split to achieve a taper instead of being sawn. Shakes may have split faces and sawn backs or be taper-split with both sides having a split surface. In either case, the split side is exposed to the weather because it has small smooth grooves parallel to the grain that channel rainwater down the surface of the shake. Because the weather side of the shake is split, not sawn, and because they are considerably thicker, shakes will last a great deal longer than wood shingles made of the same material.

Standard shakes are 18 in. or 24 in. long and come in heavy or medium thickness. Wood shakes may be applied over open sheathing (see 166) or solid sheathing (see 163). The courses of shakes are usually alternated with an interlayment of 30-lb. felt that retards the penetration of moisture through the relatively large gaps between shakes. Solid sheathing and cold-climate eave flashing (see 169B) are recommended in areas that have wind-driven snow.

SPACED ROOF SHEATHING AT SPACING EQUAL TO COURSE SPACING OF SHAKES SEE 166

INTERLAYMENT OF 18-IN. WIDE 30-LB. FELT

OFFSET SPACE BETWEEN SHAKES 1½ IN. (MIN.) FOR THREE SUCCESSIVE COURSES.

2 NAILS PER SHAKE AT EDGE & ABOUT 2 IN. ABOVE COURSE LINE

INTERLAYMENT SPACING EQUALS COURSE SPACING.

18-IN. INTERLAYMENT BETWEEN LAYERS OF DOUBLE FIRST COURSE

2-IN. (MIN.) OVERHANG AT EAVE

¼-IN. (MIN.) SPACE BETWEEN SHAKES

18-IN. INTERLAYMENT UNDER DOUBLE FIRST COURSE

FASCIA

EAVE FLASHING SEE 169A & B

DOUBLE FIRST COURSE OVERHANGS EAVE ABOUT 2 IN. (¾ IN. WITH GUTTER).

COURSE SPACING IS 7½ IN. TO 10 IN., DEPENDING ON ROOF PITCH, SHAKE SIZE & GRADE.

RAKE FLASHING SEE 169C

FOR SHAKE VALLEY & HIP (RIDGE) DETAIL, SEE 187A.

Ⓐ **WOOD-SHAKE ROOFING**

30-LB. FELT UNDER HIP OR RIDGE SHAKES

REGULAR COURSING SHAKES TRIMMED TO CENTERLINE OF HIP OR RIDGE

ALTERNATE LAP DIRECTION OF MANUFACTURED HIP (SHOWN) OR RIDGE SHINGLES.

DOUBLE FIRST COURSE WITH ALTERNATE LAPS.

TRIM DOUBLE FIRST COURSE TO LINE OF EAVE.

FASCIA

EAVE FLASHING SEE 169A & B

30-LB. FELT INTERLAYMENT LAPS VALLEY FLASHING.

METAL VALLEY FLASHING 12 IN. TO EACH SIDE OF CENTERLINE OF VALLEY. SEE 170

ALLOW 3 IN. CLEARANCE TO CENTERLINE OF VALLEY.

NOTE
WOOD-SHAKE RIDGE IS SIMILAR TO HIP.

(A) WOOD-SHAKE VALLEY & HIP

Clay tiles have been used in warm climates for centuries. Their use is still common in the southern extremes of this country, but they have recently been superseded by concrete tiles, which cost less and have better quality control.

Concrete tiles are made from high-density concrete coated with a waterproof resin. They are available in a variety of shapes and colors. Most tile patterns fall in the range of 16 in. to 18 in. long and 9 in. to 13 in. wide. Tiles weigh from 6 lb. to 10½ lb. per square foot (psf), which is about 2½ to 5 times the weight of asphalt shingles. This extra weight may require that the roof structure be bolstered in some situations.

The cost of concrete tiles themselves is high compared to other common roofing materials, but most concrete tile-roof systems have a 50-year warranty.

Most manufacturers recommend installing the tiles on solid sheathing with 30-lb. felt underlayment and pressure-treated nailing battens under each course. Course spacing is usually about 13 in., and can be adjusted to make courses equal on each slope of roof.

FIELD TILE

TYPICAL FIELD TILE PROFILES

RAKE TILE

HIP OR RIDGE TILE

(B) CONCRETE-TILE ROOFING
Introduction & Types of Tile

2 NONCORROSIVE NAILS AT TOP OF EACH TILE

1X2 PRESSURE-TREATED OR CEDAR BATTENS NAILED TO FACE OF UNDERLAYMENT

30-LB. FELT UNDERLAYMENT OVER SOLID SHEATHING; FELT LAPPED 2½ IN. AT HORIZONTAL JOINTS, 6 IN. AT JOINTS PARALLEL TO SLOPE.

NOTE
ADJUST TILE COURSE EXPOSURE AT EACH ROOF SLOPE TO MAKE COURSES EQUAL.

BARGE RAFTER

TILE COURSES LAP ABOUT 3 IN.

TOP OF RAKE TILES BUTT TO BOTTOM OF FIELD TILES.

RAKE TILES LAP FIELD TILES. SEE 189B

FOR METAL-TRIMMED RAKE DETAIL, SEE 189C.

STAGGER JOINTS BETWEEN TILES ON ALTERNATE COURSES.

NAIL RAKE TILES AT SIDE.

FIRST COURSE OF TILES WITH LOWER EDGE ELEVATED BY STARTER TILE, METAL CLOSURE STRIP, OR FASCIA. SEE 189A

TRIM HEAD OF BOTTOM RAKE TILE SO THAT TILE IS FLUSH WITH EAVE.

EAVE DETAIL SEE 189A

(A) CONCRETE-TILE ROOFING

CUT CONCRETE TILES PARALLEL TO VALLEY.

BUTT HIP TILES TO BOTTOM OF EACH COURSE OF FIELD TILES; NAIL EACH HIP TILE AT TOP.

MANUFACTURED HIP TILES CONFORM TO SLOPE OF ROOF.

HIP TILES LAP EACH OTHER BY SAME AMOUNT AS FIELD TILES.

VALLEY FLASHING SEE 170

CUT FIRST HIP OF TILE TO LINE OF EAVE.

NOTE
RIDGE TILES ARE SIMILAR TO HIP TILES, BUT ANGLE DIFFERS FOR STEEP PITCHES.

EAVE DETAIL SEE 189A

(B) CONCRETE-TILE VALLEY & HIP

30-LB. FELT (MIN.) UNDERLAYMENT

SOLID ROOF SHEATHING SEE 163-164

3-IN (MIN.) HEAD LAP

CONCRETE ROOF TILE

1X2 CEDAR OR PRESSURE-TREATED BATTEN AT CENTERS EQUAL TO EXPOSURE OF TILE COURSES.

RAFTER OR TRUSS

FLASH OVER FASCIA; LAP FLASHING WITH UNDERLAYMENT.

FASCIA ELEVATED TO MAINTAIN PITCH OF FIRST TILE COURSE.

(A) CONCRETE-TILE EAVE

RAKE TILE INTEGRATED WITH COURSING OF FIELD TILES & NAILED TO FURRING

2X2 (APPROX.) FURRING LEVEL WITH TOP EDGES OF FIELD TILES

FLASHING WITH EDGE TURNED UP FORMS CHANNEL UNDER EDGE OF FIELD TILES.

FIELD TILES

1X2 PRESSURE-TREATED OR CEDAR BATTEN

30-LB. FELT UNDERLAYMENT

ROOF SHEATHING

BARGE RAFTER OR TRIM BOARD

(B) CONCRETE-TILE RAKE
Tile Rake

FLASHING WITH EDGE TURNED UP FORMS CHANNEL UNDER EDGE OF FIELD TILES & WITH DRIP AT BARGE RAFTER.

FIELD TILES

1X2 PRESSURE-TREATED OR CEDAR BATTEN

30-LB. FELT UNDERLAYMENT

ROOF SHEATHING

BARGE RAFTER OR TRIM BOARD

(C) CONCRETE-TILE RAKE
Metal Rake

Low-cost metal roofs of aluminum or galvanized steel have been used for some time on agricultural and industrial buildings. The rolled metal panels are lightweight, long-lasting, and extremely simple to install. New panel patterns and new finishes have made metal roofing popular for residential and commercial buildings. A baked-on or porcelain enamel finish is often warranteed for 20 years, and the galvanized steel or aluminum over which it is applied will last for another 20 years in most climates.

Rolled-metal sheets are typically 2 ft. to 3 ft. wide and are factory-cut to the full length of the roof from eave to ridge. Because of the difficulty of field cutting at angles, metal roofs are best suited to simple shed or gable roofs without extensive valleys and hips. Small openings such as vents should be kept to a minimum and collected wherever possible into single openings. (Vents are best located at the ridge, where they are most easily flashed with the ridge flashing.)

The width of the roof itself should be carefully coordinated with the width of roofing panels so that rake trim, dormers, skylights, and other interruptions of the simple system will be located at an uncut factory edge.

Because the metal roofing has structural capacity, it is possible to install the roofing over purlins, which are 2x's spaced 2 ft. to 4 ft. apart. Most metal roofing panels will span 4 ft. or more, so the load on each purlin is great, and the design of the purlins that support the roofing is a critical factor.

A wide range of finish colors is available with coordinated flashing and trim metal. Translucent fiberglass or plastic panels that match the profile of some metal roofing patterns are also available as skylights.

Choose fasteners and flashing that are compatible with the roofing in order to avoid corrosive galvanic action. Care must also be taken to avoid condensation, which can occur on metal roofs. In cold climates, where proper ventilation of the roofing system does not suffice, a fiberboard backing covered with 30-lb. felt (installed parallel to the roofing panels) will insulate the roofing from moisture-laden air and also provide protection from what little condensation does occur.

RIDGE DETAIL
SEE 192B

PURLIN

OR

OPEN (SKIP) ROOF
SHEATHING
SEE 166

OR

SOLID SHEATHING
WITH UNDERLAYMENT
SEE 163-164

SPACING BETWEEN
SHEATHING BOARDS
DEPENDS ON ROOF
PITCH, SNOW LOADS &
TYPE OF ROOFING.

METAL ROOFING
FACTORY-CUT FULL LENGTH
FROM EAVE TO RIDGE

RAKE DETAIL
SEE 191C

VALLEY (& HIP) DETAILS
SEE 192A

EAVE DETAIL
SEE 191B

PITCH CHANGE
SEE 192C

Ⓐ PREFORMED METAL ROOFING

Ribbed Roofing

SCREW (OR NAIL) WITH NEOPRENE
WASHER LOCATED IN FLAT (VALLEY)
PART OF ROOFING PROMOTES TIGHT
SEAL OF WASHER.

Snap-Together Roofing

SUBSEQUENT PIECE SNAP-FASTENS
TO EDGE OF PIECE PREVIOUSLY NAILED.
FLAT-HEAD NAIL IS COVERED SO
NEOPRENE WASHER IS UNNECESSARY.
SECTIONS ARE NARROWER FOR
THIS TYPE.

Corrugated Roofing

SCREW (OR NAIL) WITH NEOPRENE
WASHER IS LOCATED ON RIDGE OF
CORRUGATION BECAUSE VALLEYS
ARE NOT WIDE OR FLAT ENOUGH.
IT'S DIFFICULT TO ADJUST
TENSION OF NAIL OR SCREW.

NOTE
SOME MANUFACTURERS RECOMMEND
NEOPRENE TAPE AT JOINTS.

(A) METAL ROOFING TYPES
Profiles

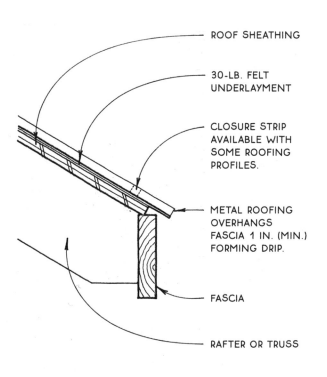

ROOF SHEATHING

30-LB. FELT
UNDERLAYMENT

CLOSURE STRIP
AVAILABLE WITH
SOME ROOFING
PROFILES.

METAL ROOFING
OVERHANGS
FASCIA 1 IN. (MIN.)
FORMING DRIP.

FASCIA

RAFTER OR TRUSS

(B) METAL-ROOF EAVE

ROOF SHEATHING

30-LB. FELT
UNDERLAYMENT

METAL ROOFING

RAKE FLASHING
LAPS HIGH POINT
OF ROOFING
METAL & LAPS
BARGE WITH DRIP;
ATTACH WITH
SCREWS OR NAILS
WITH NEOPRENE
WASHERS.

BARGE RAFTER
OR VERGE
RAFTER OR RAKE
TRIM

(C) METAL-ROOF RAKE

TYPICAL VALLEY
FLASHING
SEE 170

METAL
ROOFING

HIP FLASHING LAPS 6 IN.
(MIN.) TO EACH SIDE OF
CENTERLINE OF HIP; ATTACH
WITH SCREWS OR NAILS WITH
NEOPRENE WASHERS.

FASCIA

TRIM FLASHING TO
LINE OF EAVE.

Ⓐ METAL-ROOF VALLEY & HIP

FLASHING LAPS
ROOFING 6 IN. (MIN.)

METAL RIDGE
FLASHING MADE FROM
SAME MATERIAL AS
ROOFING

CLOSURE FLASHING
AT TOP OF METAL
ROOFING KEEPS
OUT INSECTS &
WIND-DRIVEN RAIN;
FLASHING LAPS 30-LB.
FELT UNDERLAYMENT.

METAL
ROOFING

ROOF
SHEATHING

RAFTER OR
TRUSS

RIDGE BOARD OR BEAM (OR
BLOCKING BETWEEN TRUSSES)

Ⓑ METAL-ROOF RIDGE FLASHING

30-LB. FELT UNDERLAYMENT
EDXTENDS UP BEYOND END
OF LOWER ROOFING PANEL.

BEAD OF CAULKING OR
SEALANT AT TOP EDGE OF
LOWER ROOFING PANEL
FORMS A DAM AGAINST
WIND-DRIVEN RAIN.

TOP ROOFING PANEL NESTS
AGAINST LOWER PANEL,
FORMING TIGHT SEAL.

SHEATHING

LOWER ROOFING PANEL
EXTENDS 3 IN. (MIN.)
BEYOND INTERSECTION
WITH TOP PANEL.

PITCH-CHANGE
FRAMING SEE 133B

Ⓒ METAL-ROOF PITCH CHANGE

SNOW GUARDS
SEE 196B

GUTTER
HANGER TYPES
SEE 195C

GUTTER SHAPES
SEE 195A & B

CONNECT DOWN-
SPOUT TO DRAIN PIPE
OR TO SPLASH BLOCK.
SEE 194

DOWNSPOUT FOR EVERY
40 FT. OF GUTTER

SPLASH PAN PROTECTS ROOFING
WHERE DOWNSPOUT EMPTIES ON ROOF.

NOTE
SIZE GUTTER AND DOWNSPOUT
ACCORDING TO RAINFALL INTENSITY
& AREA OF ROOF. CONSULT
LOCAL SHEET-METAL SHOP FOR
RULES OF THUMB IN YOUR AREA.

DIVERTER AVOIDS
SHORT GUTTER
WITH SEPARATE
DOWNSPOUT AT
SHORT EAVE.

NOTE
ALTHOUGH
GUTTERS ARE
CLOSE TO LEVEL
FOR APPEARANCE;
A SLOPE OF $1/16$ IN.
PER FT. IS PREFERRED
FOR DRAINAGE.

The collection of rainwater by gutters at the eave of a roof prevents it from falling to the ground, where it can splash back onto the building and cause discoloration and decay, or where it can seep into the ground, causing settling or undermining of the foundation. Gutters also protect people passing under the eaves from a cascade of rainwater. In areas of light rainfall, gutters may be eliminated if adequate overhangs are designed and a rock bed is placed below the eaves to control the water and prevent splashback.

Most wood-framed buildings are fitted with site-formed aluminum or galvanized steel gutters with a baked-enamel finish. Continuous straight sections of site-formed gutters are limited only by the need for expansion joints (see 194) and by the ability of workers to carry the sections without buckling them. Very long sections can be manufactured without joints, the most common location of gutter failures.

Vinyl gutters, although more expensive, are popular with owner-builders because they are more durable and can be installed without specialized equipment.

Downspouts conduct the water from the gutter to the ground, where it should be collected in a storm drain and carried away from the building to be dispersed on the surface, deposited in a dry well, or directed to a storm sewer system.

The problem of water freezing in gutters and downspouts may be solved with heat tapes.

Snow sliding off a roof can cause real problems—especially over porches, decks, and garages. The problem of sliding snow may be solved by keeping the snow on the roof with a low-pitched roof or with snow guards that project from the roofing surface to hold the snow mechanically in place (see 196B).

(A) **GUTTERS & DOWNSPOUTS**
Introduction

WIRE MESH
KEEPS LEAVES
OUT OF GUTTER.

END CAP

OUTLET (DROP)

ELBOWS AVAILABLE
IN 45°, 60°, 75°, OR 90°.

MITERED INTERIOR
CORNER

STRAINER KEEPS DEBRIS
OUT OF DOWNSPOUT.

HANGER TYPES
SEE 195C

GUTTER WITH EXPANSION
JOINT EVERY 40 FT. OF
STRAIGHT RUN

STRAPS AT TOP & BOTTOM
OF DOWNSPOUT
AND AT JOINTS IN
DOWNSPOUT

DOWNSPOUT FOR EVERY
40 LINEAR FEET OF
GUTTER (APPROX.)

SHOE (SHOWN) AT PAVED
SURFACES OR SPLASH
OR PLASTIC GUARD CAP
(NOT SHOWN)
AT CONNECTION
TO DRAIN PIPE

SPLASH BLOCK AT
LOCATIONS WHERE
DOWNSPOUT IS NOT
CONNECTED TO DRAIN
PIPE. BEFORE RELYING
ON A SPLASH BLOCK,
VERIFY LACK OF NEED TO
CARRY WATER TO STORM
SEWER OR DRY WELL.

NOTE
ALUMINUM GUTTER WILL
EXPAND 1/8 IN. OR MORE
IN A 40-FT. RUN &
GALVANIZED GUTTER
WILL EXPAND 1/16 IN.
OR MORE IN A 40-FT.
RUN WITH A 100°F
TEMPERATURE CHANGE.

Ⓐ **PARTS OF A GUTTER SYSTEM**

"K" or Ogee

OGEE IS THE MOST COMMON GUTTER SHAPE. AVAILABLE IN SITE-FORMED ALUMINUM OR GALVANIZED IN A VARIETY OF SIZES, IT IS ALSO MADE IN UNPAINTED GALVANIZED STEEL OR COPPER.

Beveled

SAME AS OGEE, EXCEPT NOT SO COMMON

Half-Round

HALF-ROUND GUTTER CANNOT BE SITE-FORMED; IT IS AVAILABLE IN VINYL OR UNPAINTED GALVANIZED STEEL OR COPPER.

Wooden Gutter

WOODEN GUTTERS ARE USED EXTENSIVELY IN THE NORTHEAST. THEY ARE DIFFICULT TO JOIN AT CORNERS OR FOR LONG LENGTHS & ARE PRONE TO DECAY.

Concealed Gutter

CONCEALED GUTTERS OF VARIABLE SHAPES & SIZES MAY BE DESIGNED TO FIT BEHIND THE FASCIA OR WITHIN THE SLOPE OF A ROOF. THESE ARE ALWAYS CUSTOM MADE & ARE THEREFORE EXPENSIVE. UPPER EDGE OF GUTTER IS TYPICALLY LAPPED BY ROOFING; LOWER EDGE CAPS FASCIA.

(A) GUTTER SHAPES

(B) SPECIAL GUTTERS

Bracket

Spike & Ferrule

Strap

BRACKET HANGERS ARE AVAILABLE FOR ALL TYPES OF GUTTER; SCREW TO FASCIA OR (WITH LONGER SCREWS) TO RAFTER TAILS.

SPIKE & FERRULE HANGERS ARE USED WITH BEVELED OR OGEE GUTTERS; SPIKE TO FASCIA OR TO RAFTER TAILS. THE NEED FOR EXPANSION JOINTS IS GREATEST WITH THIS TYPE OF CONNECTOR (MAXIMUM RUN WITHOUT JOINT IS 40 FT.).

STRAP HANGERS ARE USED WITH METAL HALF-ROUND GUTTERS; NAIL OR SCREW TO ROOF SHEATHING OR THROUGH SHEATHING TO TOP OF RAFTER. UNCOMMON, ARCHAIC.

(C) GUTTER HANGERS

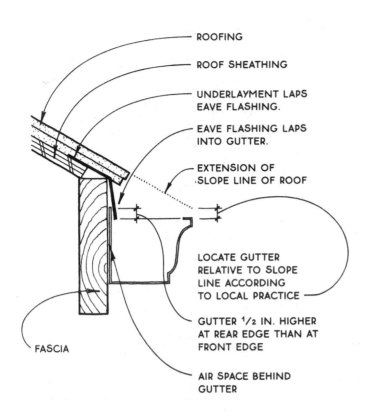

ROOFING

ROOF SHEATHING

UNDERLAYMENT LAPS
EAVE FLASHING.

EAVE FLASHING LAPS
INTO GUTTER.

EXTENSION OF
SLOPE LINE OF ROOF

LOCATE GUTTER
RELATIVE TO SLOPE
LINE ACCORDING
TO LOCAL PRACTICE

GUTTER ½ IN. HIGHER
AT REAR EDGE THAN AT
FRONT EDGE

AIR SPACE BEHIND
GUTTER

FASCIA

NOTES

FASCIA IS SHOWN PLUMB FOR EASE OF
INSTALLATION OF COMMON GUTTERS.
SQUARE-CUT RAFTER TAILS WORK WHERE THERE
ARE NO GUTTERS OR WHERE HALF-ROUND
GUTTERS ARE HUNG FROM STRAP HANGERS.
SEE 195C

FASCIA IS GENERALLY 2X MATERIAL FOR EASE
OF INSTALLATION OF COMMON GUTTERS.
IN SOME AREAS, THE 2X IS USED AS A SUB-FASCIA
AND COVERED WITH A HIGHER GRADE 1X FASCIA.
GUTTERS MAY BE HUNG FROM A SINGLE
1X FASCIA, BUT SPIKES MUST BE LOCATED
AT RAFTERS & FASCIA PREDRILLED TO PREVENT
SPLITTING. BRACKETS SHOULD BE LOCATED
NEAR RAFTERS.

 A GUTTER/EAVE

Snow guards, or snow clips, are metal protrusions that are integrated with the roofing to prevent snow from sliding off the roof. They are either clipped to the top edge of the roofing material (tiles and slate) or are nailed integral with it (shakes and shingles). Snow guards are used at the rate of 10 to 30 guards per square, depending on roof steepness.

SNOW GUARD
PROJECTS FROM
SPACE BETWEEN
ROOFING MATERIALS.

ROOFING LAPS
ATTACHMENT
OF SNOW GUARD
TO ROOF.

B SNOW GUARDS

CEILING
INSULATION
SEE BELOW

ROOF
INSULATION
**SEE DETAILS
AT RIGHT**

VAPOR BARRIER
& INFILTRATION
BARRIER AT
WALL/ROOF
SEE 88

WALL
INSULATION
SEE 120-125

FLOOR
INSULATION
SEE 61-63

EXTERIOR RIGID
INSULATION
SEE 121-122

FOR VENTING FLAT ROOFS
SEE 205A

Roof insulation—Roof insulation may be fiberglass batts or rigid insulation. If the rafters are deep enough, batts are the most economical. When the rafters do not have adequate depth for batts, rigid insulation must be fit between the rafters. In both cases, a 1-in. air space must be provided above the insulation for ventilating the roof.

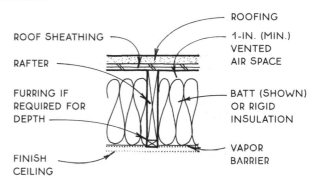

ROOF SHEATHING

RAFTER

FURRING IF
REQUIRED FOR
DEPTH

FINISH
CEILING

ROOFING

1-IN. (MIN.)
VENTED
AIR SPACE

BATT (SHOWN)
OR RIGID
INSULATION

VAPOR
BARRIER

When the rafters are exposed to the living space below, the roof must be insulated from above. Rigid insulation is typically used because of its compactness and/or its structural value. Some roofing materials may be applied directly to the rigid insulation (e.g., membrane roofing on flat roofs); others require additional structure and/or an air space for ventilation.

Most heat is potentially lost or gained through the roof, so ceilings and roofs are generally more heavily insulated than floors or walls. Building codes in most climates require R-30 in roofs. The temperature difference between the two sides of a roof or ceiling can cause condensation when warm, moist interior air hits cold surfaces in the roof assembly. It is therefore important to place a vapor barrier on the warm side of the insulation (see the drawing above right) and, in most cases, to ventilate the roof (see 200).

Ceiling insulation—Ceiling insulation consists typically of either fiberglass batts placed between ceiling joists before the ceiling is applied or loose-fill insulation blown (or poured) into place in the completed attic space. The loose-fill type has the advantage of filling tightly around trusses and other interruptions of the attic space and of being able to fill to any depth. With either type, the vapor barrier should be located on the warm side of the insulation.

When trusses or shallow rafters restrict the depth of insulation at the edges of the ceiling, ventilation channels may be needed (see 201). Baffles may also be required to keep insulation from obstructing roof intake vents or from being blown out of place.

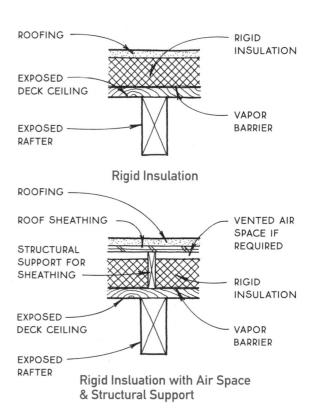

ROOFING

EXPOSED
DECK CEILING

EXPOSED
RAFTER

RIGID
INSULATION

VAPOR
BARRIER

Rigid Insulation

ROOFING

ROOF SHEATHING

STRUCTURAL
SUPPORT FOR
SHEATHING

EXPOSED
DECK CEILING

EXPOSED
RAFTER

VENTED AIR
SPACE IF
REQUIRED

RIGID
INSULATION

VAPOR
BARRIER

**Rigid Insulation with Air Space
& Structural Support**

Ⓐ **CEILING & ROOF INSULATION**

Compared to walls and floors, it is usually relatively simple to add insulation to the ceiling of a building. Insulation thickness can generally be increased without adding structure or other complications. Gravity holds the insulation in place, and the only disadvantage is a loss of attic space. In addition, the ceiling is where most of the heat is gained or lost from an insulated space, so the addition of insulation is especially effective.

INSULATION THICKNESS LIMITED HERE DUE TO ROOF PLANE

The only complication occurs at the edge of the building where roof structure typically restricts the potential for insulation thickness. In standard construction, it is common to compress the insulation in this area and allow for ventilation using vent channels made especially for this purpose (see 201). But for superinsulated buildings, the compression of insulation in this area is not acceptable.

THICKNESS OF R-38 BATT

REDUCTION OF R-VALUE IN BATT
INSULATION DUE TO COMPRESSION

To overcome the problem, several strategies have been developed:

Rigid insulation—Because rigid insulation can have R-values approximately double that of batt insulation, it may provide thermal protection at the edge of the ceiling without any adjustments to the framing (see 199A). This strategy may not be feasible when the roof pitch is very low, when rafter depth is shallow, or when the ceiling insulation value is very high.

Raised-heel truss—It is quite common when ordering trusses to specify a truss that has extra depth at the ends to accommodate extra insulation. This is called a raised-heel truss. Raised-heel trusses require blocking to prevent rotation, but otherwise are installed just the same as standard trusses (see 199B).

Dropped ceiling—Full insulation thickness at the edge of the building can also be accommodated by dropping the ceiling below the top plate. To maintain a given ceiling height, this strategy would require extra-length studs, extra siding, extra framing material for the ceiling, and extra labor. When using rafters (not trusses), a balloon-framed ceiling/wall connection (see 41A & B) would allow ceiling joists to act as ties and not be redundant (see 199C).

Raised plate—Raising the rafters to the top of the ceiling joists can increase the insulation thickness by the depth of the joists. The depth of the joists and rafters combined can be sufficient for superinsulation.

The extra cost of this strategy would include an extra rim joist, an extra plate, extra siding, and labor. The rafters need to be tied directly to the joists to counteract the thrust of the rafters (see 199D).

Vaulted ceilings—Vaulted ceilings do not restrict insulation thickness at the edge of the building because the insulation follows the pitch of the roof. The insulation value of vaulted roofs is limited only by the thickness of the roof itself (see 204A & B).

Ⓐ **SUPERINSULATED CEILINGS**

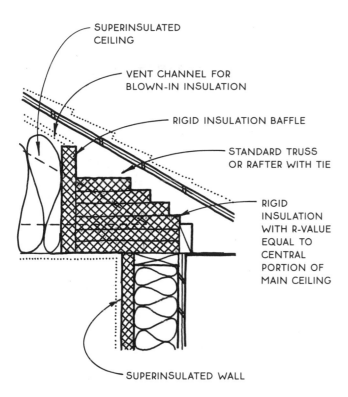

SUPERINSULATED CEILING

VENT CHANNEL FOR BLOWN-IN INSULATION

RIGID INSULATION BAFFLE

STANDARD TRUSS OR RAFTER WITH TIE

RIGID INSULATION WITH R-VALUE EQUAL TO CENTRAL PORTION OF MAIN CEILING

SUPERINSULATED WALL

A **SUPERINSULATED CEILING**
Rigid Insulation

SUPERINSULATED CEILING

VENT CHANNEL FOR BLOWN-IN INSULATION

RAISED-HEEL TRUSS
SEE 198

BLOCKING BETWEEN TRUSSES TO PREVENT ROTATION

SUPERINSULATED WALL

B **SUPERINSULATED CEILING**
Raised-Heel Truss

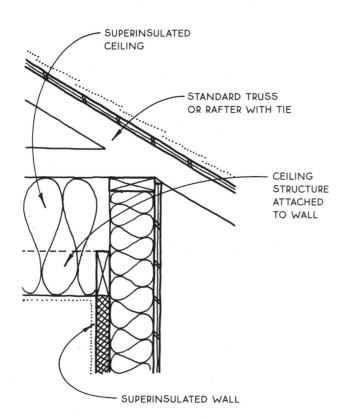

SUPERINSULATED CEILING

STANDARD TRUSS OR RAFTER WITH TIE

CEILING STRUCTURE ATTACHED TO WALL

SUPERINSULATED WALL

C **SUPERINSULATED CEILING**
Dropped Ceiling

SUPERINSULATED CEILING

RAFTER

VENT CHANNEL FOR BLOWN-IN INSULATION

GUSSET TIES RAFTER TO CEILING JOIST

PLATE AT TOP OF CEILING JOISTS

CONTINUOUS RIM OR BLOCKING

CEILING JOIST

SUPERINSULATED WALL

D **SUPERINSULATED CEILING**
Raised Plate

VENTING HIPS
SEE 138

THROUGH-ROOF VENTS
SEE 201

RIDGE VENTS
SEE 203C & D

FASCIA
VENTS
SEE 203B

GABLE VENTS
SEE 201

VENTIING AN
ABUTTING ROOF
SEE 150D, 204

SOFFIT VENTS
SEE 202B & C, 203A

FRIEZE VENTS
SEE 202A

Roofs and attics must be vented to prevent heat buildup in summer and to help minimize condensation in winter. (Condensation is reduced primarily by the installation of a vapor barrier, see 197.) In addition, winter ventilation is necessary in cold climates to prevent escaping heat from melting snow that can refreeze and cause structural or moisture damage.

The best way to ventilate a roof or attic is with both low (intake) and high (exhaust) vents, which together create convection currents. Codes recognize this by allowing the ventilation area to be cut in half if vents are placed both high and low. Most codes allow the net free-ventilating area to be reduced from $\frac{1}{150}$ to $\frac{1}{300}$ of the area vented if half of the vents are 3 ft. above the eave line, with the other half located at the eave line.

Passive ventilation using convection will suffice for almost every winter venting need, but active ventilation is preferred in some areas for the warm season. Electric-powered fan ventilators improve summer cooling by moving more air through the attic space to remove the heat that has entered the attic space through the roof. The use of fans should be carefully coordinated with the intake and exhaust venting discussed in this section so that the flow of air through the attic is maximized.

Some roofing materials (e.g., shakes, shingles, and tile) are self-venting if applied over open sheathing. These roof assemblies can provide significant ventilation directly through voids in the roof itself. Check with local building officials to verify the acceptance of this type of ventilation.

A special roof, called a cold roof (see 204A), is designed to ventilate vaulted ceilings in extremely cold climates. The cold roof prevents the formation of ice dams—formed when snow thawed by escaping heat refreezes at the eave. When an ice dam forms, thawed snow can pond behind it and eventually find its way into the structure. The cold roof prevents ice dams by using ventilation to isolate the snow from the heated space.

Ⓐ **ROOF & ATTIC VENTING**

FASCIA INTAKE VENT
SEE 203B

CONTINUOUS RIDGE
EXHAUST VENT
SEE 203C & D

GABLE-END
EXHAUST VENT

THROUGH-ROOF
EXHAUST VENT

SOFFIT INTAKE
VENT SEE 202A
& C, 203A

FRIEZE-BLOCK
INTAKE VENT
SEE 202A

Intake vents—Intake vents are commonly located either in a frieze block or in a soffit or fascia. They are usually screened to keep out birds and insects. The screening itself impedes the flow of air, so the vent area should be increased to allow for the screen (by a factor of 1.25 for $\frac{1}{8}$-in. mesh screen, 2.0 for $\frac{1}{16}$-in. screen). The net venting area of all intake vents together should equal about half of the total area of vents.

Vent channels may be applied to the underside of the roof sheathing in locations where the free flow of air from intake vents may be restricted by insulation. The vent channels provide an air space by holding the insulation away from the sheathing. These channels should be used only for short distances, such as at the edge of an insulated ceiling. For alternative solutions to this problem, see 198 & 199.

Exhaust vents—If appropriately sized and balanced with intake vents, exhaust vents should remove excess moisture in winter. There are three types of exhaust vents: the continuous ridge vent, the gable-end vent, and the through-roof exhaust vent.

The continuous ridge vent is best for preventing summer heat buildup because it is located highest on the roof and theoretically draws ventilation air evenly across the entire underside of the roof surface. Ridge vents can be awkward looking, but they can also be fairly unobtrusive if detailed carefully (see 203C & D). (Another type of ridge vent, the cupola, is also an effective ventilator, but is difficult to waterproof against wind-driven rain.)

The gable-end vent is a reasonably economical exhaust vent. Gable-end vents should be located across the attic space from one another. They are readily available in metal, vinyl, or wood, and in round, rectangular or triangular shapes. Because the shape of gable-end vents can be visually dominant, they may be emphasized as a design feature of the building.

The through-roof exhaust vent is available as the "cake pan" type illustrated above or the larger rotating turbine type, available in many sizes. Through-roof vents are usually shingled into the roof and are useful for areas difficult to vent with a continuous ridge vent or a gable-end vent.

VENT CHANNEL
COMPRESSES INSULATION
FOR SHORT DISTANCE TO
ALLOW FREE PASSAGE
OF VENTILATION AIR.

THICK CEILING
INSULATION

ROOF SHEATHING

RAFTER

(A) **INTAKE & EXHAUST ROOF VENTS**

NOTCH TOP OF FRIEZE BLOCK.

FOLD SCREEN & STAPLE TO BACK OF FRIEZE BLOCK.

Notched Frieze Block

RIP FRIEZE BLOCK TO ALLOW CONTINUOUS VENT AT TOP.

FOLD SCREEN, PRESS UP TO SHEATHING & STAPLE TO BACK OF FRIEZE BLOCK.

Ripped Frieze Block

BORE ROUND VENT HOLE(S) NEAR TOP OF FRIEZE BLOCK.

STAPLE SCREEN TO BACK OF FRIEZE BLOCK.

Drilled Frieze Block

A **FRIEZE-BLOCK INTAKE VENTS**
Three Types

FASCIA

RAFTER TAIL OR TOP CHORD OF TRUSS

SOFFIT JOIST

SOFFIT

SOFFIT NAILING LEDGER

CONTINUOUS SCREENED VENT IN CONTINUOUS SLOT IN SOFFIT

SCREEN TRIM

B **SOFFIT INTAKE VENT**
Screened

FASCIA

RAFTER TAIL OR TOP CHORD OF TRUSS

SOFFIT JOIST

SOFFIT NAILING LEDGER

SOFFIT

SAMPED METAL OR VINYL VENT STRIP SUPPORTED BY SOFFIT

C **SOFFIT INTAKE VENT**
Stamped

CONTINUOUS BACKING
FOR FASCIA

RAFTER RTAIL OR TOP
CHORD OF TRUSS

AIR PASSAGE SPACE
EQUAL TO WIDTH OF
STRIP VENT (MIN.)

SOFFITED
(SHOWN) OR
BOXED-IN
OR ABBREVIATED
EAVE
SEE 142D & 143A

CONTINUOUS BACKING
FOR VENT & SOFFIT

CONTINUOUS
CORRUGATED PLASTIC
STRIP VENT

FASCIA

Ⓐ SOFFIT INAKE VENT
Corrugated Strip

ROOF SHEATHING HELD
ABOVE END OF RAFTER

SPACE BETWEEN FASCIA
& SHEATHING PROVIDES
PASSAGE FOR VENT AIR.

RAFTER TAIL OR TOP
CHORD OF TRUSS

SOFIT

LOUVERED METAL VENT
ALSO SERVES AS EAVE
FLASHING.

FASCIA

Ⓑ FASCIA INTAKE VENT
Starter

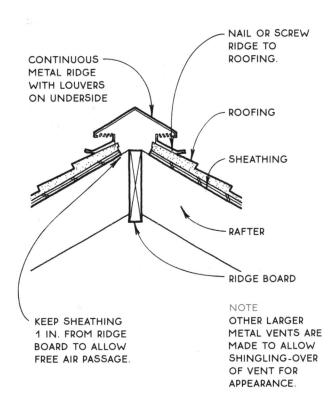

CONTINUOUS
METAL RIDGE
WITH LOUVERS
ON UNDERSIDE

NAIL OR SCREW
RIDGE TO
ROOFING.

ROOFING

SHEATHING

RAFTER

RIDGE BOARD

KEEP SHEATHING
1 IN. FROM RIDGE
BOARD TO ALLOW
FREE AIR PASSAGE.

NOTE
OTHER LARGER
METAL VENTS ARE
MADE TO ALLOW
SHINGLING-OVER
OF VENT FOR
APPEARANCE.

Ⓒ RIDGE EXHAUST VENT
Metal

CORRUGATED-PLASTIC
RIDGE VENT FOLDS
OVER RIDGE,
CONFORMING TO
SLOPE OF ROOF.

RIDGE CAP OF
SAME MATERIAL AS
ROOFING NAILED TO
SHEATHING THROUGH
PLASTIC VENT.

ROOFING

SHEATHING

RAFTER

RIDGE BOARD

KEEP SHEATHING
1 IN. TO 1½ IN.
FROM RIDGE BOARD
TO ALLOW FREE
AIR PASSAGE.

Ⓓ RIDGE EXHAUST VENT
Corrugated Plastic

AIR CHANNEL CONTINUOUS TO VENT(S) AT TOP OF ROOF. VENTS MUST HAVE AREA EQUAL TO SOFFIT VENTS AND NOT BE SUSCEPTIBLE TO CLOGGING BY SNOW.

ROOFING

2X4 SLEEPERS ALIGNED WITH RAFTERS PROVIDE CONTINUOUS AIR CHANNEL FOR VENTILATION.

3½-IN. CONTINUOUS SCREENED SOFFIT VENT

CONTINUOUS SHEATHING COVERED WITH 30-LB. FELT

INSULATION BETWEEN RAFTERS WITH VAPOR BARRIER ON WARM SIDE BELOW

NOTE
INSULATION CAN BE BATTS W/VENTED AIR SPACE OR RIGID INSULATION THAT FILLS CAVITY.

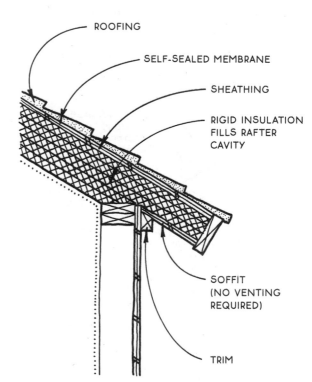

ROOFING

SELF-SEALED MEMBRANE

SHEATHING

RIGID INSULATION FILLS RAFTER CAVITY

SOFFIT (NO VENTING REQUIRED)

TRIM

The cold roof is a way to protect vaulted ceilings in cold climates from the formation of ice dams. A cold roof is a double-layer roof with the upper layer vented and the lower layer insulated. The vented layer promotes continuous unrestricted air flow from eave to ridge across the entire area of the roof. This flow of cold air removes any heat that escapes through the insulated layer below. The entire outer roof surface is thus maintained at the temperature of the ambient air, thereby preventing the freeze-thaw cycle caused by heat escaping through the insulation of conventional roofs.

The typical cold roof is built with sleepers aligned over rafters and with continuous eave vents and complementary ridge or gable vents. A 3½-in. air space has been found to provide adequate ventilation, but a 1½-in. air space does not. The sleepers must be held away from obstructions such as skylights, vents, hips, and valleys to allow air to flow continuously around them.

A modified cold roof with extra-deep rafters to provide deeper than normal ventilation space but without the double-layer ventilation system can also work.

The warm roof also protects vaulted ceilings in cold climates from the formation of ice dams. Instead of isolating the snow from the insulation like a cold roof, however, the warm roof prevents escaping heat from melting the snow by increasing insulation thickness. When the ceiling R-value is sufficient (approximately R-50 is recommended), the temperature on the surface of the roof can be maintained at the temperature of the snow. The snow will therefore not melt while the ambient temperature remains below freezing.

By using rigid insulation, the warm roof eliminates the ventilation space because there are no voids within which condensation can form, so there is no need to ventilate between the insulation and the roof surface. With snow effectively adjacent to the insulation, the insulative value of the snow itself will contribute to the insulation of the building. In this respect, the warm roof is superior to the cold roof because the cold roof exposes the outer surface of the insulation to ambient air (which can be significantly colder than snow).

When compared to the cold roof, the warm roof is less complicated to build and will insulate better. It is made with expensive materials, however, so may have a higher first cost—especially for owner-builders.

(A) COLD ROOF

(B) WARM ROOF

Flat roofs, like sloped roofs, require ventilation to prevent heat buildup and to minimize condensation. The principles of ventilation are the same for flat roofs as for sloped roofs, but flat roofs have some particular ventilation requirements due to their shape. On a flat roof, a low intake vent can rarely be balanced by a high exhaust vent (3 ft. min. above the intake vent). The net free-ventilating area therefore cannot usually be reduced from 1/150 of the area of the roof.

Flat-roof ventilators are commonly of the continuous strip type, located at a soffit, or a series of small vents scattered across the roof. Parapet walls can also provide effective ventilation for flat roofs (see 205B).

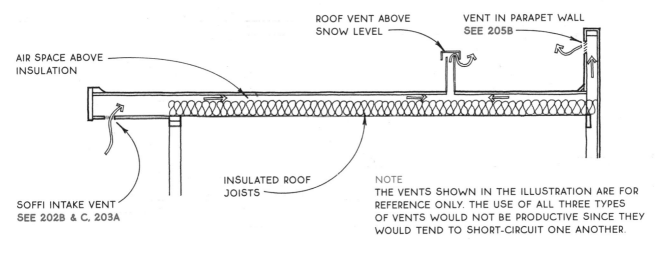

ROOF VENT ABOVE
SNOW LEVEL

VENT IN PARAPET WALL
SEE 205B

AIR SPACE ABOVE
INSULATION

INSULATED ROOF
JOISTS

SOFFI INTAKE VENT
SEE 202B & C, 203A

NOTE
THE VENTS SHOWN IN THE ILLUSTRATION ARE FOR REFERENCE ONLY. THE USE OF ALL THREE TYPES OF VENTS WOULD NOT BE PRODUCTIVE SINCE THEY WOULD TEND TO SHORT-CIRCUIT ONE ANOTHER.

(A) FLAT-ROOF VENTING

CAP FLASHING

WALL VENTS AS REQUIRED

PARAPET WALL

BLOCKING ALLOWS
SPACE FOR AIR PASSAGE

CANT STRIP

ROOF SURFACE

1-IN. AIR SPACE REQUIRED

INSULATED ROOF

HEATED SPACE

NOTE
IT MAY BE USEFUL TO BE ABLE TO VENT AN INSULATED ROOF (OR DECK) THROUGH A PARAPET WALL IN ORDER TO GET CROSS VENTILATION.

(B) VENTED PARAPET WALL
2x4 or 2x6 Wall

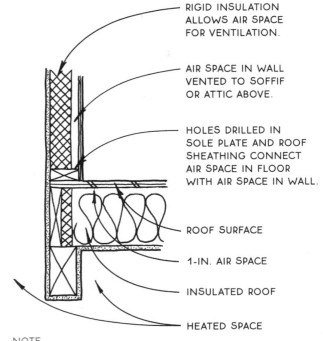

RIGID INSULATION
ALLOWS AIR SPACE
FOR VENTILATION.

AIR SPACE IN WALL
VENTED TO SOFFI
OR ATTIC ABOVE.

HOLES DRILLED IN
SOLE PLATE AND ROOF
SHEATHING CONNECT
AIR SPACE IN FLOOR
WITH AIR SPACE IN WALL.

ROOF SURFACE

1-IN. AIR SPACE

INSULATED ROOF

HEATED SPACE

NOTE
SEAL CAREFULLY BETWEEN FRAMING MEMBERS AND RIGID INSULATION TO PREVENT AIR INFILTRATION.

(C) INSULATED WALL AS VENT
2x4 or 2x6 Wall

chapter 5

STAIRS

Stairs do not really support or protect a building in the same way as foundations, floors, walls, and roofs, but this book would be incomplete without them. Stairs are the vertical connectors of the parts of the building. Most buildings require a few steps just to enter the main floor, and stairs connect any internal levels. A well-designed and well-built staircase can contribute immeasurably to the function and beauty of a building.

STAIR DIMENSIONS

More than most other parts of a building, stairs need to be proportioned to the human body for safety. The height (rise) and depth (run) of the individual step must be in a comfortable relationship for the average person and must be manageable for people who are infirm or disabled. Building codes prescribe a range of dimensions for rise and run, a minimum width for stairways, the location of handrails, and minimum head clearance over stairs. The numbers vary depending on the location of the stair, the building type, and the specific code; the typical requirements are outlined as follows:

Rise and run—Rise and run of stairs are governed by building codes, which may vary. Minimum unit rise is typically 4 in. and maximum is 7 in., except for residential stairs, which can have a unit rise of 7¾ in. For residential stairs, however, a comfortable rise is about 7 in. Minimum unit run is 11 in., except for residential stairs, which can have 10-in. treads.

Generally, deeper treads have shallower risers. Here are two useful rules of thumb for the rise/run relationship:

rise + run = 17 in. to 18 in.

run + twice the rise = 24 in. to 26 in.

Both for safety and for code compliance, it is important to make each riser of a stair the same height. Most codes allow only ⅜-in. variance between the tallest and shortest riser in a flight of stairs. The maximum total rise between floors or landings is typically 12 ft. Landings must be as deep as the width of the stairway but need not exceed 44 in. if the stair has a straight run.

Stair width—The width of stairways is also defined by building codes. Minimum width is usually 36 in. for residential stairs. Minimum widths are measured inside finished stairwells, so rough openings must allow for finished wall surfaces.

HEADROOM IS MEASURED VERTICALLY FROM AN IMAGINARY LINE CONNECTING THE NOSING OF ALL TREADS; MINIMUM HEADROOM REQUIRED BY CODE IS TYPICALLY 6 FT. 8 IN. ALTHOUGH 7 FT. IS MORE COMFORTABLE.

HANDRAIL 30 IN. TO 34 IN. ABOVE NOSING IS REQUIRED ON AT LEAST ONE SIDE OF STAIRS WITH 4 OR MORE RISERS; FOR HANDRAIL CONFIGURATION, SEE 221.

UNIT RUN
SEE LEFT

NOSING
(1 IN. TO 1½ IN.)

UNIT RISE
SEE LEFT

RISER

TREAD

Typical Stair Dimensions

STAIR CONFIGURATION

The shape or configuration of a stairway is determined primarily by the circulation patterns of a building and by available space. Virtually any configuration of stairway may be constructed using the standard details of this chapter by merely breaking the stairway into smaller pieces and reassembling them. Several typical configurations that are worthy of note are shown in the drawings that follow; for clarity, these drawings do not show railings.

Straight-run stair—The straight-run stair is the most economical standard stairway from the standpoint of efficiency of floor space taken up by the stairway itself. The straight-run stair works best in two-story buildings.

The bottom and top steps are separated horizontally from each other by the entire length of the stairway, so that a multistory building with stacked stairways requires circulation space on each floor to get from the top step of one flight to the bottom step of the next.

U-shaped stair— The U-shaped stair, also called a switchback stair, has a landing about half a flight up, and the flights run in opposite directions. The area of the stairway is increased over a straight-run stair by the area of the landing (less one step), but the top step of one flight is adjacent to the bottom step of the next. This arrangement saves circulation space at each floor level and makes this stair more efficient overall for multistory buildings than the straight-run stair.

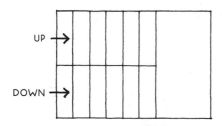

L-shaped stair—The L-shaped stair is not so common as the straight or U-shaped stair because it lacks the simplicity of the straight-run stair and the efficiency of the U-shaped stair. It can, however, be useful in tight spots, as it takes up less floor space than a U-shaped stair and requires less length than a straight-run stair. The framing of the opening in the floor for this stairway can be atypical because of its L-shape. A framed wall under one side of the floor projecting into the L or a column under the floor at the bend in the L is the most common way to support this floor.

Winder stairs at the bend in the L (or at the bend in a U-shaped stair) are common, but for reasons of safety, should not be allowed to be less than 6 in. deep at the narrow end (verify with local codes).

6 IN. (MIN.) RUN AT NARROWEST POINT OF TREAD

Spiral stair—A spiral stair saves space. It is most appropriate for accessing mezzanines and lofts where furniture and other large items may actually be hoisted from floor to floor by means other than the stairway. Spiral stairs usually have special code requirements that are somewhat less restrictive than standard stairs. They are usually prefabricated, often of metal or wood kits. Their details are idiosyncratic and not included in this book.

STRUCTURE

Stairs may be classified into two basic structural types: continuously supported and freespanning.

Continuously supported stairs—Continuously supported stairs are commonly used as interior stairs. Both sides of the stairway are supported by wall framing, so calculations of spanning capacities are not necessary. These stairs are site-built in some regions, but are predominantly prefabricated in others.

Freespanning Stair
(Shown with Open Risers)

Continuously Supported Stair
(Shown with Closed Risers)

Prefabricated Custom Stair
(May be Freespanning or
Continuously Supported)

Freespanning stairs—Freespanning stairs have the structural capacity to span from the bottom stair to the top stair without intermediate support. The freespanning stair is commonly used as an exterior stair between floors or landing levels or in conjunction with porches and decks. It is often also seen as an access stair to basements and attics. The strength of a freespanning stair is usually in the carriages (stringers) that support the treads, although the handrail may also contribute to the strength of the stair. Freespanning stairs, like continuously supported stairs, may be site-built or prefabricated. Some freespanning stairs have only a single central support.

INTERIOR AND EXTERIOR STAIRS

The basic structure of the stair depends primarily on whether the stairway is to be located inside or outside and whether it is to be protected from the weather or not. The wood-stair details discussed in this chapter can be employed for either interior or exterior stairways, although the location will suggest basic detailing differences due to the fact that one is protected from the weather and the other isn't.

Interior stairs—Interior stairs are usually more refined than exterior stairs. Interior stairways may be the showcase of a building and so are often located near the entry and used as a major circulation route. They may also provide the opportunity to connect more than one floor with natural light.

Exterior stairs—Exterior stairs (see 222) have the same minimum proportional requirements as interior stairs, but they are generally built less steep. The treads need to be deeper and risers shallower outdoors to make the stairs safer when wet or covered with snow or ice. Materials on exterior stairs must also be chosen with the weather in mind. Weather-resistant materials such as concrete, masonry, and metal are sound choices for stairs exposed to the elements. Heavy timber or pressure-treated wood is often chosen for a wood stair out of doors. Special attention should be paid to non-skid surfaces for treads exposed to the weather.

Some exterior stairs are supported directly on the ground, in which case they are usually called steps (see 223–225). Ground-supported steps follow the contours of sloping sites to provide easy access to porches or entrances or as connections between terraces and other landscape elements.

SITE-BUILT VERSUS PREFABRICATED STAIRS

Most stairs are site-built because it is economical and because the process provides a temporary stair for construction. But in some cases, stairs prefabricated in a shop are more practical. Prefabricated stairs (see 213C), whether simple or complex, can be made more solidly and precisely than site-built stairs because they are made in the controlled environment of a shop.

ADDITIONAL DECISIONS

There are several other design decisions to make regarding both interior and exterior stairs. The primary decisions concern whether the risers are open (see 214A) or closed (see 216) and the design of the balustrade (see 218–220) and the handrail (see 221).

FRAMING OF ROUGH OPENING
IN FLOOR SEE 38B

DOUBLE HEADER ABOVE BASE OF
STAIR; POSITION DETERMINED
BY HEAD CLEARANCE.
SEE 207

DOUBLE 2X HEADER AT TOP
OF STAIR (DASHED); POSITION
DETERMINED BY METHOD OF
CARRIAGE CONNECTION.
SEE 212

THIS HEADER CAN
SLOPE IN TIGHT
SITUATIONS.

JOIST

NOTE
WIDTH OF ROUGH OPENING DEPENDS ON
WIDTH OF STAIR; FOR STAIR WIDTH, SEE 207.
CODE REQUIREMENTS FOR WIDTH ARE FOR
CLEAR OPENINGS, SO ALLOW FOR THICKNESS
OF WALL FINISH WHEN DIMENSIONING
A ROUGH OPENING.

Ⓐ STAIR ROUGH OPENING

LEDGER

CARRIAGE

FLOOR OR LANDING JOIST

INTERMEDIATE
CARRIAGE FOR STAIR
OVER 30 IN. WIDE,
DEPENDING ON TREAD
& RISER MATERIAL &
THICKNESS.

HEADER AT END
OF STAIR ROUGH
OPENING
SEE 211A & 212

TOP OF CARRIAGE/
FLOOR
SEE 212A, B & C

FOR FREESPANNING
STAIR FRAMING,
SEE 213A & B.
FOR CARRIAGE FRAMING
AT OPEN BALUSTRADE,
SEE 219

BOTTOM OF
CARRIAGE/FLOOR
SEE 213A & B

CARRIAGE FRAMING/
SIDE WALL SEE 212D

THRUST BLOCK

NOTE
TOP OF BASE OF STAIR MAY TERMINATE AT A FLOOR
LEVEL OR A LANDING. THE STAIR FRAMING CAN
BE THE SAME IN EITHER CASE.

NOTE
THE TERM CARRIAGE IS
INTERCHANGEABLE WITH
STRINGER IN SOME REGIONS.

Ⓑ CARRIAGE FRAMING
Continuously Supported Stair

BLOCKING BETWEEN CARRIAGES SUPPORTS SUBFLOOR.

FINISH FLOOR

SUBFLOOR SEE 48-51

NOSING OF FINISH FLOOR SAME DEPTH AS NOSING ON STAIR TREADS

RISE FROM FINISH TREAD TO FINISH FLOOR SHOULD EQUAL TYPICAL RISE

TYPICAL RISE

HEADER AT END OF STAIR ROUGH OPENING

LEDGER, BLOCKING, JOIST HANGERS ATTACH EACH STAIR CARRIAGE TO HEADER; SEE 211B FOR LEDGER.

NOTE
SIDE CARRIERS ARE SUPPORTED CONTINUOUSLY ON WALL FRAMING. SEE 212D

(A) TOP OF CARRIAGE/FLOOR
Floor Supports Top of Stair

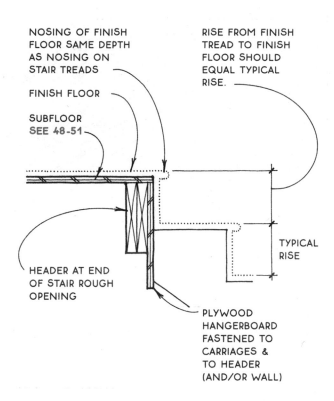

NOSING OF FINISH FLOOR SAME DEPTH AS NOSING ON STAIR TREADS

FINISH FLOOR

SUBFLOOR SEE 48-51

RISE FROM FINISH TREAD TO FINISH FLOOR SHOULD EQUAL TYPICAL RISE.

TYPICAL RISE

HEADER AT END OF STAIR ROUGH OPENING

PLYWOOD HANGERBOARD FASTENED TO CARRIAGES & TO HEADER (AND/OR WALL)

(B) TOP OF CARRIAGE/FLOOR
Hangerboard Supports Top of Stair

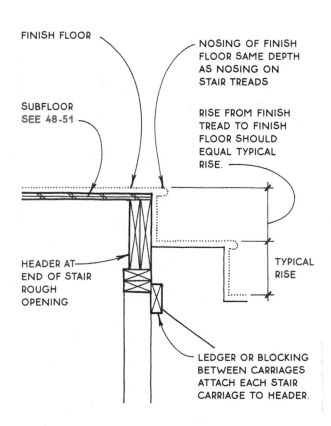

FINISH FLOOR

SUBFLOOR SEE 48-51

NOSING OF FINISH FLOOR SAME DEPTH AS NOSING ON STAIR TREADS

RISE FROM FINISH TREAD TO FINISH FLOOR SHOULD EQUAL TYPICAL RISE.

TYPICAL RISE

HEADER AT END OF STAIR ROUGH OPENING

LEDGER OR BLOCKING BETWEEN CARRIAGES ATTACH EACH STAIR CARRIAGE TO HEADER.

(C) TOP OF CARRIAGE/FLOOR
Wall Supports Top of Stair

STUD OF SUPPORTING WALL

GYPSUM WALLBOARD OR OTHER FINISH WALL

1X FINISH STRINGER

FINISH RISER TRIMS TO STRINGER.

FINISH TREAD TRIMS TO STRINGER.

BLOCKING BEHIND WALL FINISH

2X SPACER NAILED TO STUDS

CARRIAGE NAILED TO SPACER

(D) CARRIAGE FRAMING/SIDE WALL
Continuously Supported Stair

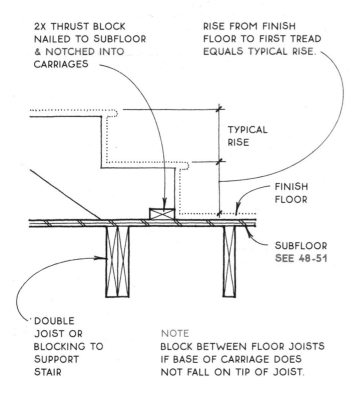

2X THRUST BLOCK NAILED TO SUBFLOOR & NOTCHED INTO CARRIAGES

RISE FROM FINISH FLOOR TO FIRST TREAD EQUALS TYPICAL RISE.

TYPICAL RISE

FINISH FLOOR

SUBFLOOR
SEE 48-51

DOUBLE JOIST OR BLOCKING TO SUPPORT STAIR

NOTE
BLOCK BETWEEN FLOOR JOISTS IF BASE OF CARRIAGE DOES NOT FALL ON TIP OF JOIST.

(A) BOTTOM OF CARRIAGE/FLOOR
Single Flight

NOTE
SIDE CARRIAGE MAY BE HUNG FROM HEADER OR ATTACHED TO WALL FRAMING.

RISE FROM FINISH FLOOR TO FIRST TREAD EQUALS TYPICAL RISE.

TYPICAL RISE

FINISH FLOOR

SUBFLOOR
SEE 48-51

HEADER AT END OF STAIR ROUGH OPENING FOR MULTIPLE FLIGHTS OF STAIRS

JOIST HANGER SUPPORTS CENTRAL CARRIAGE.

LOCATE FLOOR HEADER TO INTERSECT WITH BOTTOM OF CARRIAGES.

(B) BOTTOM OF CARRIAGE/FLOOR
Intermediate Flight

EXTEND HOUSED STRINGER SEE 217B, TO MEET BASE MOLDING.

TOP NOSING OF PREFABRICATED STAIR TYPICALLY HAS RABBET ON UNDERSIDE TO ADJUST THICKNESS TO THAT OF FINISH FLOOR.

FINISH FLOOR

SUBFLOOR

HEADER AT TOP OF STAIR ROUGH OPENING

Section at
Top of Stair

NOTES
ALIGN TOP NOSING FLUSH WITH FINISH FLOOR OR ALIGN TOP NOSING FLUSH WITH SUBFLOOR FOR WALL-TO-WALL CARPETING; BOTTOM RISER BEARS ON SUBFLOOR.

INTERIOR FINISH WALL

HOUSED STRINGER OF PREFABRICATED STAIR

$5/8$-IN. TO 1-IN. SHIM ACCOMMODATES THICKNESS OF FINISH WALL

ATTACH STRINGER WITH 16D NAILS THROUGH SHIMS INTO FRAMING

WALL FRAMING

Section at
Side Wall

(C) PREFABRICATED STAIR

NOTE
TREADS FOR OPEN-RISER STAIRS MUST BE ABLE TO SPAN FULL WIDTH OF STAIRWAY.

ATTACHMENT OF TREADS TO CARRIAGE MAY BE WITH:

WOODEN CLEAT

METAL BRACKET

TREAD MORTISED INTO CARRIAGE

WOODEN CLEATS SCREWED TO STRUCTURAL CARRIAGE;

OR

METAL BRACKET LET INTO END OF TREAD SO THAT BRACKET IS CONCEALED FROM ABOVE (AND DOES NOT PROJECT BELOW);

OR

MORTISED TREAD, WHICH PROVIDES CONCEALED CONNECTION FOR APPEARANCE; SCREW TREADS THROUGH CARRIAGE OR GLUE & TOENAIL FROM UNDERSIDE INTO CARRIAGE.

Elevation

Ⓐ TREADS WITH OPEN RISERS

FINISH FLOOR

SUBFLOOR

HEADER AT END OF STAIR ROUGH OPENING

NAIL OR SCREW FREESPANNING CARRIAGE THROUGH FLOOR FRAMING.

RISE FROM TREAD TO FINISH FLOOR SHOULD EQUAL TYPICAL RISE.

TYPICAL RISE

TREAD ATTACHED TO FREESPANNING CARRIAGE SEE 214A

NOTE
A FREESTANDING CARRIAGE LEFT EXPOSED REQUIRES A CONCEALED OR CLEAN BOLTED CONNECTION TO THE FLOOR (OR LANDING) AT THE TOP & BOTTOM OF THE CARRIAGE.

TREAD ATTACHED TO FREESPANNING CARRIAGE SEE 214A

FREESPANNING WOODEN STAIR CARRIAGE

TYPICAL RISE

RISE FROM FINISH FLOOR TO FIRST TREAD SHOULD EQUAL TYPICAL RISE.

FINISH FLOOR OR SLAB; FOR ATTACHMENT TO SLAB SEE 222B

SUBFLOOR

JOIST OR BLOCKING UNDER CARRIAGE

NAIL OR SCREW FREESPANNING CARRIAGE THROUGH FLOOR FRAMING.

Ⓑ TOP OF CARRIAGE/FLOOR
Freespanning Stair

Ⓒ BOTTOM OF CARRIAGE/FLOOR
Freespanning Stair

Finish landings must be at least as deep as the stairway is wide (automatic in the case of an L-shaped stair). Set the landing height so that the finish-floor level corresponds to the rise of the stair.

NOTE
UPPER FLIGHT OF STAIR IS SUPPORT ON LANDING SUBFLOOR (SUBFLOOR NOT SHOWN).

EXTEND LANDING UNDER CARRIAGE OF UPPER FLIGHT OF STAIRS.

ATTACH CARRIAGE OF LOWER FLIGHT OF STAIRS TO SIDE OF LANDING.
SEE 212A, B & C

FRAME LANDING AS A FLOOR SEE 32

SUPPORT LANDING ON STUD WALLS.

 STAIR LANDING

STAIRS

NEWEL POST (OR 4X4 POST AT BASE OF CLOSED RAILING)

LAG OR BOLT NEWEL TO STAIR CARRIAGE. PLACE BOLT AS HIGH AS PRACTICAL.

FINISH FLOOR

LAG OR BOLT NEWEL TO FLOOR FRAMING. PLACE ONE BOLT AS LOW AS POSSIBLE.

FLOOR FRAMING

The newel post must be firmly anchored to resist the force of a person swinging around it. The most effective way to anchor the newel (or the framing of a closed rail) is to pass it through the subfloor and bolt or lag it to the floor framing.

LOCATE BOLTS AT OPPOSITE CORNERS

Plan

1-IN. DIAMETER DRILLED ACCESS HOLE

1/4-IN.=DIA. RAIL BOLT

ADHESIVE

FINISH FLOOR

SUBFLOORING

FLOOR JOIST OR BLOCKING

1³/4 IN. MIN.

Section

With solid flooring and/or subflooring, it is possible to firmly anchor the newel post to the surface of the floor by using rail bolts. The bolts are lagged into the floor surface, slipped into predrilled holes in the newel, and tightened with a special fitting through an access hole in the side of the newel. The access hole must be plugged to make a smooth finish surface on the newel.

 NEWEL POST

NEWEL POST
Surface Anchored

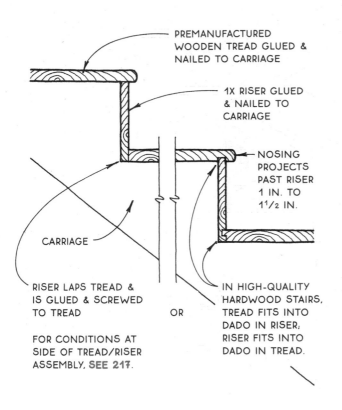

PREMANUFACTURED WOODEN TREAD GLUED & NAILED TO CARRIAGE

1X RISER GLUED & NAILED TO CARRIAGE

NOSING PROJECTS PAST RISER 1 IN. TO 1¹/₂ IN.

CARRIAGE

RISER LAPS TREAD & IS GLUED & SCREWED TO TREAD

OR

FOR CONDITIONS AT SIDE OF TREAD/RISER ASSEMBLY, SEE 217.

IN HIGH-QUALITY HARDWOOD STAIRS, TREAD FITS INTO DADO IN RISER; RISER FITS INTO DADO IN TREAD.

(A) EXPOSED FINISH TREAD & RISER
2 Alternatives with No Sub-Tread

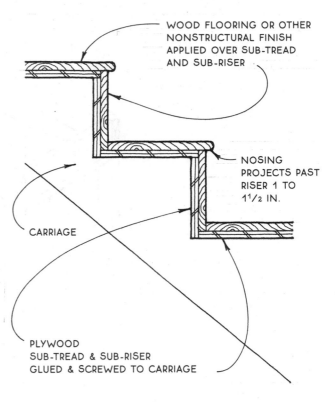

WOOD FLOORING OR OTHER NONSTRUCTURAL FINISH APPLIED OVER SUB-TREAD AND SUB-RISER

NOSING PROJECTS PAST RISER 1 TO 1¹/₂ IN.

CARRIAGE

PLYWOOD SUB-TREAD & SUB-RISER GLUED & SCREWED TO CARRIAGE

(B) EXPOSED FINISH TREAD & RISER
With Sub-Tread

CHAMFERED EDGE OF TREAD ALLOWS CARPET TO WRAP NOSING NEATLY.

RISER ANGLED 1 IN. TO 1¹/₂ IN. FROM TOP TO BOTTOM PROVIDES NOSING.

BLOCKING GLUED TO RISER STRENGTHENS JOINT.

CARRIAGE

PLYWOOD SUB-TREAD & SUB-RISER GLUED & SCREWED TO CARRIAGE

(C) CARPETED TREAD & RISER

CHAMFERED EDGE OF TREAD ALLOWS CARPET TO WRAP NOSING.

CARRIAGE CUT FOR VERTICAL RISER; CARPET WRAPS OVER NOSING TO BOTTOM OR RISER.

OR

CARPET WRAPS OVER NOSING & RETURNS TO TOP OF RISER.

CARRIAGE

PLYWOOD SUB-TREAD & SUB-RISER GLUED & SCREWED TO CARRIAGE

(D) CARPETED TREAD & RISER
2 Alternatives

FINISH TREADS & RISERS BUTT AGAINST THE SKIRT & ARE GLUED & NAILED TO CARRIAGE ON WHICH THEY ARE SUPPORTED. FOR TREAD & RISER SECTIONS, SEE 216.

STUD OF SUPPORTING WALL

GYPSUM WALLBOARD OR OTHER FINISH WALL

FINISH STRINGER FITS BEHIND CARRIAGE & IS APPLIED DIRECTLY TO FINISH WALL.

CARRIAGE NAILED TO SPACER

SPACER NAILED TO STUDS

The advantage of the skirt over the housed stringer (see 217B) is the ease of construction. A disadvantage is the potential for minor opening of butt joints at the ends of treads and risers due to minor movement of the structure. A more involved hybrid strategy that limits this disadvantage is to install the risers first from wall to wall, cut out the stringers to fit to the risers, and finally install the treads tightly between the stringers.

(A) FINISH STRINGER (SKIRT) AT FINISH WALL

HOUSED STRINGER IS ATTACHED DIRECTLY TO FINISH WALL & PROVIDES SUPPORT FOR THE STAIRWAY.

FINISH TREADS & RISERS ARE LOCKED IN PLACE WITH GLUED SHIMS INSTALLED FROM BELOW.

DEPTH OF DADO IN RISER MAY NOT EXCEED THE THICKNESS OF THE SHIM BEHIND IT. FOR TREAD & RISER SECTIONS, SEE 216.

TAPERED MORTISES ROUTED INTO CONTINUOUS HOUSED STRINGER RECEIVE ENDS OF TREADS & RISERS.

The housed stringer is a more refined and complicated way than the skirt (see 217A) to provide a finish stringer at the side of a continuously supported stairway. The advantage of the housed stringer is that joints between treads, risers, and finish stringer will not open up with shrinkage or other minor movement of the structure. Disadvantages include the extra labor to build the housed stringer and the fact that it does not provide the framing for a temporary construction stair. Good-quality prefabricated stairs (see 213C) are also made with housed stringers.

(B) HOUSED STRINGER AT FINISH WALL

CURB CAP MORTISED FOR BALUSTERS OR MADE OF SEVERAL PIECES AROUND BALUSTERS.

TRIM

GYPSUM WALLBOARD OR OTHER FINISH WALL

BALUSTER CENTERED UNDER HANDRAIL

SKIRT

FINISH TREAD TRIMS TO SKIRT.

CARRIAGE NAILED TO SPACER

SPACER NAILED TO FRAMED WALL

FRAMED-WALL DIMENSION DEPENDS ON WIDTH OF CURB.

Section

HANDRAIL SEE 221

BALUSTER SEE SECTION ABOVE

CURB SEE SECTION ABOVE

MAX. CLEAR SPACE BETWEEN BALUSTERS 4 IN. OR 6 IN. (VERIFY WITH LOCAL CODES)

NEWEL POST SEE 215B & C

RISER

TREAD

FINISH STRINGER OR HOUSED STRINGER

BASEBOARD

In an open balustrade with a curb, the treads and risers are constructed on carriages and finished on both sides with a skirt, just as if the stairway were constructed between two walls. The skirt on the open side of the stairway forms one side of the curb. This simple construction has a similar aesthetic effect as the more technically difficult open balustrade without a curb (see 219).

Ⓐ **OPEN BALUSTRADE**
With Curb

RISERS TYPICALLY MITERED TO A FINISH SKIRT BOARD.

BALUSTERS DOVETAILED INTO END OF TREAD

NOSING RETURN NAILED & GLUED TO END OF TREAD

BALUSTER CENTERED UNDER HANDRAIL

FINISH TREAD LAPS SKIRT.

FINISH SKIRT BOARD

GYPSUM WALLBOARD OR OTHER FINISH WALL

PLYWOOD SPACER SAME THICKNESS AS WALL FINISH

CARRIAGE

FRAMED WALL SUPPORTS CARRIAGE.

Section

BALUSTER

HANDRAIL SEE 221

NEWEL POST SEE 215B & C

RISER

TREAD

FINISH OR HOUSED STRINGER

BASEBOARD

NOTE STAIR FRAMING AT EXPOSED RAIL, SEE SECTION THROUGH CARRIAGE (ABOVE RIGHT).

FINISH SKIRT MITERED TO FINISH RISER

EXPOSED END OF TREAD, SEE DETAIL AT TOP LEFT & TEXT BELOW.

MAX. CLEAR SPACE 4 IN. TO 6 IN. (VERIFY WITH LOCAL CODES)

NOTE THE SIMPLIFIED BALUSTER, HANDRAIL & NEWEL COMPONENTS SHOWN IN THESE DRAWINGS ARE AVAILABLE IN FANCY TURNED & TRADITIONAL SHAPES.

In this traditional treatment of the open balustrade, the balusters rest on the treads, and the ends of the treads are exposed and finished. The balusters may be attached to the treads in four ways: toenailing, doweling, mortising, or sliding dovetail (see the detail at top left). The exposed ends of the treads may be finished in one of the following two ways. The treads may be cantilevered and rounded or chamfered like the nose of the tread (this will expose end grain). Alternatively, the treads may be capped with a finish piece called a nosing return, which is mitered at the corner and matches the profile of the nosing (see the detail at top left). This is the most refined finish treatment and is usually used in conjunction with mortised or sliding dovetail balusters.

(A) OPEN BALUSTRADE
Without Curb

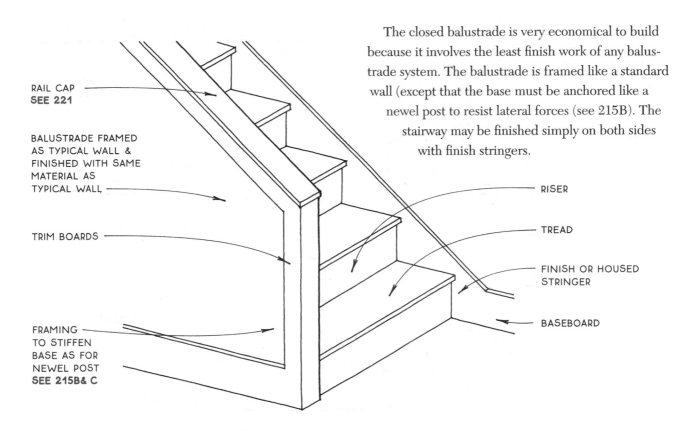

The closed balustrade is very economical to build because it involves the least finish work of any balustrade system. The balustrade is framed like a standard wall (except that the base must be anchored like a newel post to resist lateral forces (see 215B). The stairway may be finished simply on both sides with finish stringers.

RAIL CAP
SEE 221

BALUSTRADE FRAMED
AS TYPICAL WALL &
FINISHED WITH SAME
MATERIAL AS
TYPICAL WALL

TRIM BOARDS

FRAMING
TO STIFFEN
BASE AS FOR
NEWEL POST
SEE 215B& C

RISER

TREAD

FINISH OR HOUSED
STRINGER

BASEBOARD

(A) **CLOSED BALUSTRADE**

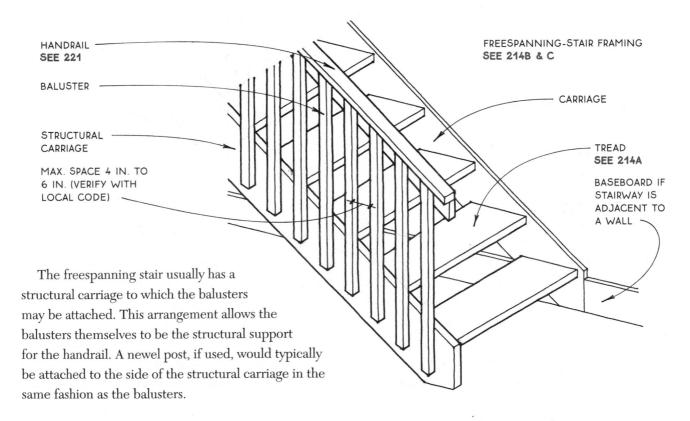

HANDRAIL
SEE 221

BALUSTER

STRUCTURAL
CARRIAGE

MAX. SPACE 4 IN. TO
6 IN. (VERIFY WITH
LOCAL CODE)

FREESPANNING-STAIR FRAMING
SEE 214B & C

CARRIAGE

TREAD
SEE 214A

BASEBOARD IF
STAIRWAY IS
ADJACENT TO
A WALL

The freespanning stair usually has a structural carriage to which the balusters may be attached. This arrangement allows the balusters themselves to be the structural support for the handrail. A newel post, if used, would typically be attached to the side of the structural carriage in the same fashion as the balusters.

(B) **FREESPANNING-STAIR BALUSTRADE**

Handrails provide stability and security for the young, the old, the blind, and the infirm. In addition, handrails are a safety feature for anyone who uses a stairway—one of the most likely and dangerous places for people to trip and fall.

In terms of safety, the most important design feature of a handrail is its ability to be grasped, especially in an emergency. The 1½-in. to 2-in. round rail is the most effective in this regard, as it allows the thumb and fingers to curl around and under the rail. Other shapes are allowable by code, but are less graspable.

The height of the handrail is usually specified by code. Most codes fall within the range of 29 in. to 36 in. above the nosing of the stairs. If the handrail is against a wall, a 1½-in. space is required between the handrail and the wall.

The tops and bottoms of handrails should be designed so as to avoid snagging clothing. For this reason, many codes require returning handrails to the wall at both top and bottom.

Handrail Screwed to Wall through Spacer

Handrail Attached to Wall with Metal Brackets

Handrail on Open Balustrade

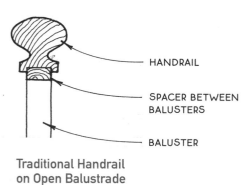

Traditional Handrail on Open Balustrade

Handrail on Closed Balustrade

 HANDRAILS

Exterior stairs made of wood should be built of weather-resistant species such as cedar or redwood or of pressure-treated lumber. Simple connections that minimize joints between boards are less likely to retain moisture. Where joints must occur, it is best to minimize the area of contact between pieces so that moisture will drain and the lumber can breathe.

Most exterior wood stairs are freespanning. For long runs of stairs, the continuous unnotched carriage is usually required for strength (see 222B & D). Short runs of freespanning stairs may be strong enough with a notched carriage (see 222C). The notched carriage is, of course, also suitable for wood stairs built between two parallel concrete or masonry walls.

Open risers are often employed in exterior wood stairs, but solid risers, common on traditional porches, are useful to stiffen the treads. For wood porches, and decks, see 52–60.

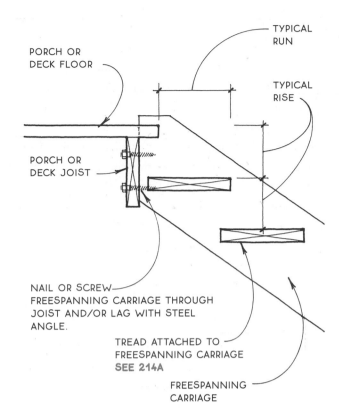

PORCH OR DECK FLOOR

PORCH OR DECK JOIST

TYPICAL RUN

TYPICAL RISE

NAIL OR SCREW FREESPANNING CARRIAGE THROUGH JOIST AND/OR LAG WITH STEEL ANGLE.

TREAD ATTACHED TO FREESPANNING CARRIAGE **SEE 214A**

FREESPANNING CARRIAGE

(A) **EXTERIOR WOOD STAIRS**
Introduction

(B) **EXTERIOR WOOD STAIRS**
Unnotched Carriage/Wood Porch

PORCH OR DECK FLOOR

DOUBLE 2X6 TREAD ALLOWS 11½-IN. RUN; DOUBLE TREAD MINIMIZES EFFECT OF CUPPING.

2X8 RISER ALLOWS 7½-IN. RISE.

VERTICAL SUPPORT AT EDGE OF PORCH OR DECK

RIM JOIST OF PORCH

HEADER JOIST AT TOP OF STAIR CARRIAGE

2 X 12 NOTCHED CARRIAGE ALLOWS ADEQUATE STRUCTURE ONLY FOR SHORT AND MEDIUM FREESPANNING STAIR RUNS.

TOP OF CARRIAGE ATTACHED WITH JOIST HANGERS OR NAILED TO HEADER JOIST AND/OR BLOCKING (NOT SHOWN)

FREESPANNING CARRIAGE

TYPICAL RISE

STEEL ANGLE LAGGED TO CONCRETE & TO STAIR CARRIAGE

CONCRETE SLAB OR WALK OR FOOTING SUPPORTS BASE OF STAIR CARRIAGE.

MAINTAIN AIR GAP BETWEEN CARRIAGE & SURFACE OF CONCRETE.

(C) **EXTERIOR WOOD STAIRS**
Notched Carriage/Wood Porch

(D) **EXTERIOR WOOD STAIRS**
Freespanning Carriage at Ground

Dry-set brick steps are supported on a bed of compacted gravel and sand on the ground and are laid dry without concrete or mortar. The bricks must be contained at the edges or they will separate. A 2x decay-resistant header used as a riser will contain the bricks at each step.

BRICK (OR CONCRETE PAGERS)

2X PRESSURE-TREATED OR DECAY-RESISTANT HEADER RIPPED TO RISER HEIGHT & ATTACHED AT ENDS TO WALLS OR HEADER

1 IN. (MAX.) SAND SETTING BED

COMPACTED ROCK BASE OR SELF-COMPACTING PEA GRAVEL

The sides of the steps may be contained with 2x headers the same height as the riser, as shown below. These side headers may be staked to the ground so that they contain the step at the sides on their own.

HEADER AT SIDE OF STEP STAKED TO GROUND

RISER

BRICK STEP

RABBETED CORNER JOINT SEE DETAIL AT TOP RIGHT

The rabbeted riser/side-header joint is nailed from two directions to lock the joint together.

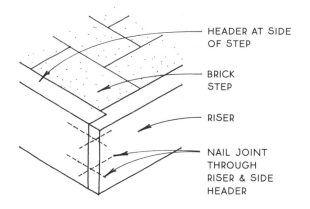

HEADER AT SIDE OF STEP

BRICK STEP

RISER

NAIL JOINT THROUGH RISER & SIDE HEADER

The sides of the brick steps may also be contained between two masonry or concrete walls.

USE SIDE HEADERS (SHOWN) OR ATTACH RISERS TO WALLS WITH METAL ANGLES.

A third alternative is to contain the sides of the steps with decay-resistant stringers at the slope of the steps. The risers may be attached directly to the stringers.

(A) DRY-SET EXTERIOR STEPS
Brick

Dry-set concrete paver steps, like dry-set brick steps, are supported on a bed of compacted gravel on the ground and are laid dry without concrete or mortar. Because of their size, large pavers like the ones shown here are more stable than bricks. For this reason, paver stairs may be constructed without containment at the riser; some paver stairs are even constructed without containment at the sides.

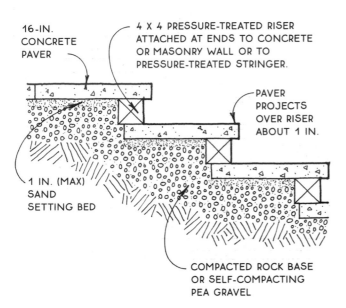

16-IN. CONCRETE PAVER

4 X 4 PRESSURE-TREATED RISER ATTACHED AT ENDS TO CONCRETE OR MASONRY WALL OR TO PRESSURE-TREATED STRINGER.

PAVER PROJECTS OVER RISER ABOUT 1 IN.

1 IN. (MAX) SAND SETTING BED

COMPACTED ROCK BASE OR SELF-COMPACTING PEA GRAVEL

Most paver stairs are contained at the sides with walls or stringers, as shown below.

CONCRETE OR MASONRY WALL

PRESSURE-TREATED OR DECAY-RESISTANT WOOD STRINGER

STAIR WIDTH IS MODULE OF PAVER WIDTH.

Paver stairs may also be contained at all edges like brick stairs with 2x risers and side headers (see 223).

Concrete steps are durable and can be reasonably inexpensive, especially if they are built along with other concrete work. They should be adequately supported on a foundation and should be reinforced. Handrails or handrail supports may be cast into the steps or into the walks, porches, or terraces adjacent to them. The steps may be covered with a masonry or other veneer.

The main problem with concrete steps is that they are difficult to repair if anything should go wrong with them. The usual problem is settling due to the extreme weight of the steps themselves and to the fact that they are often constructed on fill. The safest way to avoid settling is to provide for the porch and steps a footing that is below the frost line, with a foundation wall above. This footing and foundation wall system may be an integral part of the foundation of the main structure (see the detail below), or it may be independent of the main structure with an expansion joint adjacent to the main structure that will allow the porch to move slightly without cracking (see 225A & B). Alternatively, concrete steps may be built independent of the main structure and adjacent to a wood porch (see 225C). All methods are expensive but will avoid costly maintenance in the long run.

For areas where building on backfill cannot be avoided, a wood porch with a lightweight wood stair that can be easily releveled is the most practical (see 222).

FOOTING CONTINUOUS THROUGH STEPS

FOUNDATION WALL OF MAIN STRUCTURE

PORCH FOOTING & FOUNDATION WALL

FINISHED STEPS SEE 225

Ⓐ DRY-SET EXTERIOR STEPS
Concrete Pavers

Ⓑ CONCRETE STEPS

NOTE
ELEMENTS OF THE DETAILS ON THIS PAGE MAY BE COMBINED
IN VARIOUS WAYS TO MEET THE NEEDS OF SPECIFIC
SITUATIONS.

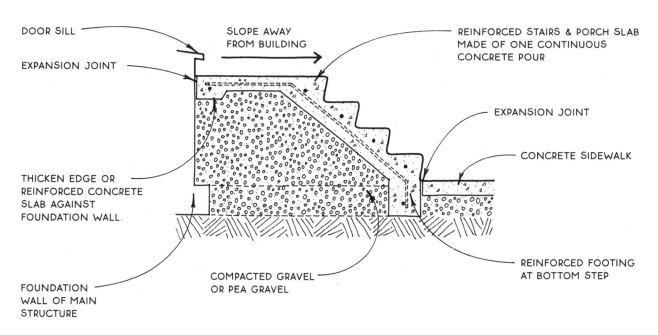

DOOR SILL

EXPANSION JOINT

SLOPE AWAY
FROM BUILDING

REINFORCED STAIRS & PORCH SLAB
MADE OF ONE CONTINUOUS
CONCRETE POUR

EXPANSION JOINT

CONCRETE SIDEWALK

THICKEN EDGE OR
REINFORCED CONCRETE
SLAB AGAINST
FOUNDATION WALL.

REINFORCED FOOTING
AT BOTTOM STEP

FOUNDATION
WALL OF MAIN
STRUCTURE

COMPACTED GRAVEL
OR PEA GRAVEL

Ⓐ CONCRETE STEPS ON GRAVEL
At Concrete Porch

REINFORCED CONCRETE PORCH
SPANS FROM STEP FOUNDATION
TO BUILDING FOUNDATION.

EXPANSION
JOINT

CONCRETE STEPS
FORMED & PLACED ON
BLOCK FOUNDATION

CONCRETE
SIDEWALK

EXPANSION
JOINT

FOUNDATION
WALL OF MAIN
STRUCTURE

STACKED BLOCK FOUNDATION
SOLID THROUGHOUT OR
FILLED WITH GRAVEL

WOOD PORCH
SEE 52-60

REINFORCED
CONCRETE STEPS

STEM WALL
INCLUDING
SIDES IF
REQUIRED

CONCRETE
SIDEWALK

REINFORCED
FOOTING BELOW
FROST LINE

COMPACTED
GRAVEL OR PEA
GRAVEL

EXPANSION JOINT

NOTE
COORDINATE WOOD
PORCH SKIRT WITH EDGE
OF CONCRETE STAIR.

Ⓑ CONCRETE STEPS ON BLOCK
At Concrete Porch

Ⓒ CONCRETE STEPS AT WOOD PORCH
On Block or Gravel

legend

CONCRETE

CONTINUOUS STRUCTURAL
FRAMING MEMBER

GRAVEL FILL

BLOCKING (NOT
CONTINUOUS)

UNDISTURBED SOIL

WOOD FINISH
MATERIAL

SAND FILL

PLYWOOD OR OTHER
STRUCTURAL PANEL

RIGID INSULATION

STUCCO OR GYPSUM
WALL BOARD (G.W.B.)

BATT INSULATION

MATERIAL BURIED IN
ANOTHER MATERIAL,
E.G., REBAR IN CONCRETE

MASONRY-BRICK OR
CONCRETE BLOCK

FUTURE
CONSTRUCTION

list of abbreviations

&	AND		LB.	POUNDS
FT	FOOT/FEET		PSF	POUNDS PER SQUARE FOOT
F.F.L.	FINISH FLOOR LEVEL		PSI	POUNDS PER SQUARE INCH
H	HEIGHT		PSL	PARALLEL-STRAND LUMBER
IN.	INCH(ES)		P.T.	PRESSURE TREATED
LSL	LAMINATED-STRAND LUMBER		REBAR	REINFORCING STEEL
LVL	LAMINATED-VENEER LUMBER		SQ.FT.	SQUARE FOOT/FEET
MAX.	MAXIMUM		T & G	TOUNGE AND GROOVE
MIN.	MINIMUM		TYP.	TYPICAL
#	NUMBER		W	WIDTH
O.C.	ON CENTER		WWM	WELDED WIRE MESH

resources

TRADE AND PROFESSIONAL ASSOCIATIONS

American Concrete Institute, ACI International
P.O. Box 9094
Farmington Hills, MI 48333-9094
248-848-3700
www.concrete.org

American Forest & Paper Association
1111 19th Street NW
Washington, DC 20036
202-463-2700
www.afandpa.org

American Institute of Architects
1735 New York Avenue NW
Washington, DC 20006-5292
202-626-7300
www.aia.org

American Society of Heating, Refrigerating
& Air-Conditioning Engineers
1791 Tullie Circle NE
Atlanta, GA 30329
800-527-4723
www.ashrae.org

APA—The Engineered Wood Association
7011 South 19th
Tacoma, WA 98466
253-565-6600
www.apawood.org

Brick Industry Association
11490 Commerce Park Drive, Suite 301
Reston, VA 20191
703-620-0010
www.bia.org

Building Research Council
One East St. Mary's Road
Champaign, IL 61820
217-333-1801
www.arch.uiuc.edu

Canadian Wood Council
99 Bank Street, Suite 400
Ottawa, Ontario, Canada KIP 689
800-463-5091
www.cwc.ca

Energy Efficient Building Association
6520 Evendale Boulevard, Suite 112
Eden Prairie, MN 55346
952-881-1098
www.eeba.org

Environmental Building News–Building Green, Inc.
122 Birge Street, Suite 30
Brattleboro, VT 05301
www.buildinggreen.com

Forest Products Society
2801 Marshall Court
Madison, WI 53705-2295
608-231-1361
www.forestprod.org

Forest Stewardship Council
11100 Wildlife Center Drive, Suite 100
Reston, VA 20190
703-438-6401
www.fscus.org

National Association of Home Builders
1201 15th Street NW
Washington, DC 20005
800-368-5242
www.nahb.org

National Concrete Masonry Association
13750 Sunrise Valley Drive
Herndon, VA 20171-4662
703-713-1900
www.ncma.org

National Roofing Contractors Association
10255 W. Higgins Road, Suite 600
Rosemont, IL 60018-5607
847-299-9070
www.nrca.net

Northeastern Lumber Manufacturers' Association
272 Tuttle Road
Cumberland, ME 04021
207-829-6901
www.nelma.org

Sheet Metal and Air Conditioning Contractors
National Association
4201 Lafayette Center Drive
Chantilly, VA 20151-1209
703-803-2980
www.smacna.org

Southern Forest Products Association
2900 Indiana Avenue
Kenner, LA 70065
504-443-4464
www.sfpa.org

U.S. Green Building Council
1800 Massachusetts Avenue NW, Suite 300
Washington, DC 20036
800-795-1747
www.usgbc.org

Western Wood Products Association
522 SW Fifth Avenue, Suite 500
Portland, OR 97204-2122
503-224-3930
www.wwpa.org

FURTHER READING

Allen, Edward. *Fundamentals of Building Construction: Materials and Methods.* 4th ed. New York: John Wiley & Sons, 2004.

Allen, Edward and Thallon, Rob. *Fundamentals of Residential Construction.* 2nd ed. New York: John Wiley & Sons, 2006.

American Institute of Architects. *Architectural Graphic Standards.* 11th ed. New York: John Wiley & Sons, 2007.

American Institute of Architects. *Architectural Graphic Standards for Residential Construction.* New York: John Wiley & Sons, 2003.

Fine Homebuilding. Bimonthly magazine. The Taunton Press, Inc. (P.O. Box 5506, 63 South Main Street, Newtown, CT 06470-5506).

Journal of Light Construction. Monthly magazine. Builderburg Partners Ltd. (1025 Vermont Avenue NW, Washington, DC 20005).

Riechers, A. F. J. *The Full Length Roof Framer.* Palo Alto, CA: Buccaneer Books, 1995.

glossary

This glossary is designed to clarify the concepts presented in the book. Words are included based on the frequency of their use and their absence from common language. Many of the words have other meanings not defined here for reasons of space.

A

Air-infiltration barrier A continuous layer at the insulated envelope of a building to prevent the entry of air.

Anchor bolt A metal bolt connecting the wood parts of a building to its foundation.

Apron Trim below a window sill or stool.

B

Backband Trim surrounding window or door casing, usually for the purpose of increasing depth.

Backer block Small plywood or OSB patch added to the web of I-joists where hangers are attached.

Backer rod An expansive material used to fill wide gaps behind caulk or sealant.

Backing Framing added for the purpose of providing a nailing surface where none exists.

Back-up clip A small metal or plastic flange attached to framing for the purpose of supporting gypsum wallboard.

Balloon framing The nearly archaic method of building with studs continuous from foundation to roof.

Baluster A single vertical component of a balustrade.

Balustrade A protective railing at a stairway, porch, or balcony made of numerous vertical elements.

Barge rafter The rafter at the edge of an overhanging gable roof; called fly rafter on the East Coast.

Batt insulation Fluffy insulation resembling cotton candy; usually made of fiberglass, either with a facing or unfaced.

Beam A large horizontal structural member spanning between two supports.

Bearing capacity The ability of soil to support the load of a building, measured in psf.

Bearing wall A wall that carries structural loads from above (as opposed to a partition wall which does not).

Bird's mouth A notch near the bottom end of a rafter made to form a level attachment with the top of a wall.

Bituminous Containing asphalt or tar.

Blocking Framing made of small pieces running perpendicular to or at an angle to studs, joists, or rafters. Blocking may support panel edges, prevent rotation of framing members, and retard the spread of fire.

Brick mold A deep exterior casing traditionally used with brick.

Bridging Bracing at the midspan of long joists or rafters to prevent their rotation.

Butt joint A joint in which the ends of two square-cut boards meet.

Buttress A compression brace of a masonry or concrete wall.

C

Cantilever The portion of a structural member that projects beyond its support.

Carriage The structure supporting a site-built stair; also called a jack or a stringer.

Casing The trim at head and jamb of a window or door.

Caulk Pliable viscous material used to fill gaps between materials. See also sealant.

Chamfer A bevel on the edge of a board or timber.

Chord The top or bottom component of a truss or I-joist where stresses are greatest; also, part of the structural perimeter of a diaphragm or shear wall.

Clad Covered for protection from the weather.

Cleat A concealed or exposed clip used to fasten flashing that does not penetrate the flashing itself.

Closed cell A type of rigid insulation that cannot be saturated by moisture.

Cold roof An insulated vaulted ceiling with a ventilation space above to isolate snow and prevent its melting.

Collar tie A horizontal tie between opposing rafters in order to prevent their spreading.

Concrete-rated The ability to be placed adjacent to concrete without deterioration due to chemical reaction.

Control joint A score line in a concrete slab, creating a weak point where cracking will likely concentrate.

Cornerboard Trim boards at exterior corners for shingle or horizontal board siding.

Counterflashing Flashing that laps over another flashing.

Counterfort A buried tension brace of a masonry or concrete retaining wall.

Crawl space A usually unheated and uninhabitable space between the first floor and the ground.

Crib wall A short framed wall within a crawl space providing support for the first-floor structure.

Cricket A roof flashing above a chimney or other medium-sized object to divert water around it.

Cross-grain shrinkage Shrinkage of wood perpendicular to its length due to moisture loss.

Curb A built-up edge such as to mount a skylight or to provide a base for a balustrade.

D

Dado A rectangular groove cut into a board.

Dead load The weight of the structure itself.

Decking Parallel boards providing the structural surface of a floor or roof.

Diagonal bracing Wood or metal structural member providing triangulation to brace a wall (or roof).

Diaphragm A structural plane acting like a beam between braced walls to resist lateral forces.

Dimension lumber Milled lumber cut to standard sizes.

Diverter A short flashing integrated with roofing to divert rainwater where a gutter is not practical.

Dormer A small building element that contains a window emerging from a roof.

Dovetail A locking finish joint shaped like the spread feathers of a bird's tail.

Downspout The pipe that conducts rainwater down from the gutter; also known as downpipe or leader.

Drag strut A structural tie connecting a portion of a diaphragm to braced walls that are not directly under it.

Drainage plane The space between siding and moisture barrier in a rain screen wall.

Drip A thin edge of material designed to direct the dripping of water away from the surface of a building.

Dry-set Masonry laid without mortar.

Dry well A hole in the ground filled with rocks, designed to collect and distribute storm water.

Duckboard A thin decking laid over a waterproof deck for the purpose of protecting the deck from abrasion.

Dummy A roof element such as an eave or rake that is discontinuous from the principal roof structure.

E

Eave The horizontal lower edge of a roof.

Edge nailing Nailing at the perimeter of a structural panel or larger structural element.

End-matched Boards having tongue and grooves at their ends.

Engineered lumber Structural lumber made of small pieces of wood glued together.

Envelope The exterior insulated skin of a building.

Expansion joint A flexible joint inserted into rigid materials such as concrete or brick to accommodate thermal expansion and contraction.

Exposure rating Rating that indicates the ability of composite panels such as plywood to withstand exposure to the weather.

F

Fascia Trim board at the eave of a roof.

Felt A heavy tar-impregnated paper used as a moisture barrier.

Filter fabric An underground textile that separates rock from soil and allows the passage of water.

Finish stringer The finish trim at the side of a stair.

Fireblock A block installed in a wood frame for the purpose of inhibiting the passage of fire from one section of the frame to another.

Firestopping See Fireblock.

Flashing A thin metal layer designed to divert water at the surface of a building.

Flat-grain A board with the annual growth rings oriented across its width.

Footing The spread portion at the base of a foundation.

Framing anchor A metal clip designed to add strength at the connection of framing members.

Frieze block Blocking between rafters at the eave of a roof.

Frost line The depth to which the ground freezes in a given locality.

Furring Strips of wood applied to a framed structure to adjust the plane of the finish surface.

G

Gable The triangular end wall of a building that has two equally pitched roofs opposed to each other.

Girder A structural member similar to a beam but larger.

Glue-laminated beam A composite beam made of 2x lumber stacked on one another and glued.

Grade beam A concrete beam at ground level that supports structure above.

Grout A mix of cement, sand, small aggregate, and water used to fill the cells of concrete block, locking reinforcing steel into the system.

Gusset A thin wooden plate attached to the surface, used to join two or more pieces of wood.

Gutter A horizontal trough used to collect rainwater at the eave of a building; also called an eave trough.

Gypsum board A panel made of gypsum plaster coated with heavy paper or fiberglass. Also known as drywall.

H

Handrail A safety device designed to be grasped by the hand while using a stair.

Head The zone at the top of a window or door.

Header A structural member over a window or door opening.

Header joist A joist that supports common joists at the edge of an opening in a floor or roof.

Hemmed edge A turned-over edge of a flashing.

Hip The outside intersection of two planes of a roof.

Hold-down A large steel connector used to anchor the base of sheer walls against overturning.

Housed stringer The side of a premanufactured stair, notched to receive the ends of treads and risers.

Hydrostatic pressure Water pressure in the ground.

I

Ice dam A buildup of ice, usually at the eave, caused when snow is melted by heat that escapes through the ceiling then refreezes when it reaches the cold eave.

I-joist A composite joist shaped like a steel beam to place most material where the stresses are greatest.

Insulating concrete form (ICF) A system in which the formwork for concrete walls is made of rigid insulation that stays in place to provide thermal protection.

Interlayment A loose overlapping underlayment used with shake roofs.

J

Jamb The zone at the sides of a window or door, or the frame around a window or door.

Jamb extender An extension of a window or door frame to make it flush with the interior finish surface.

Joint reinforcement A method of placing horizontal reinforcement of masonry within the mortar joints.

Joist A relatively small repetitive horizontal structural member set on edge and spaced evenly.

Joist hanger A metal support used at the end of joists.

K

Kerf A shallow sawcut in wood.

Kiln-dried Wood dried in a large oven or kiln to 19% or 15% moisture content.

L

Lag bolt A relatively large screw used to make strong connections in wood; also known as lag screw.

Laminated strand lumber (LSL) A composite structural member used primarily for rim joists and headers.

Laminated veneer lumber (LVL) Composite structural member used primarily for beams and headers.

Landing A wide level platform partway up a stairway, used as a turning point or resting place.

Lap joint A joint in which the ends of two boards are lapped, one over the other.

Lateral bracing The stabilizing of a building to resist horizontal forces.

Lateral force Any force such as a wind or earthquake that acts horizontally on a building.

Lateral load See Lateral force.

Ledger A horizontal member attached to a wall for the purpose of supporting other structural members such as joists or rafters.

Let-in Notching of one or more members so that another member such as a brace or ledger may be added flush with the original member(s).

Lintel A structural member over a window or door opening in masonry construction.

Live load The weight or force imposed on a structure by things other than the structure itself, such as furniture, occupants, snow, wind, or earthquake.

Load bearing Supporting a weight or force.

Lookout A cantilevered structural support of a rake.

M

Miter A butt joint made by bisecting the (usually right) angle between two intersecting pieces.

Moisture barrier A membrane designed to prevent the passage of water into a structure or space. On walls, also called a water-resistant barrier.

Moisture content The percent of the weight of wood that is water as compared to its bone-dry weight.

Mortise A rectangular cut into wood; the female receptor of a tenon in a mortise-and-tenon joint.

Mudsill The first wooden member bolted to a foundation forming the base of a wood frame.

N

Nailer A framing member added to a structure for the purpose of providing nailing for other members.

Nailing fin A continuous metal or plastic flange around the edge of a modern window or door to allow attachment to the wall and to seal the rough opening.

Nailing plate A nailer attached to a hard surface such as metal so other members may be nailed to it.

Neoprene A synthetic rubber.

Newel post A post at the top or bottom of a stair rail.

Nonbearing Not supporting any loads other than its own weight.

Nosing A rounded cantilevered edge of a stair tread.

O

Oriented strand board (OSB) A composite structural panel made of flakes of wood oriented for strength.

P

Parallel strand lumber (PSL) A composite structural member used primarily for beams and headers.

Parapet The part of an exterior wall that projects above a roof.

Particle board A nonstructural composite panel made of small particles of wood.

Partition wall A nonbearing wall that does not support anything but its own weight.

Pea gravel A self-compacting fill material composed of pea-size rocks.

Perimeter insulation Insulation at the edges of a floor where the floor contacts the exterior environment.

Permanent wood foundation (PWF) A foundation system that is made almost entirely of preservative treated wood.

Permeability The ability of a material to allow water vapor to pass through it.

Pilaster A vertical wall stiffener in masonry construction.

Pitch Roof slope expressed as a ratio, as in 4:12.

Plate A horizontal element that holds studs in place at the top and bottom of a framed wall.

Platform framing The common method of building with stud height limited to one floor.

Plumb Vertical.

Point load A concentrated load such as at a column.

Pony wall A framed wall at the perimeter of a building between the foundation and the first floor.

Portal frame A rigid frame consisting of two columns and a beam of similar dimensions.

Preformed metal Roofing metal manufactured to fit together in the field without special tools.

Prehung A door manufactured with hinges in a frame.

Pressure-treated Wood injected under pressure with chemicals that retard deterioration.

Protection board A cushion or shield that protects a moisture barrier from abrasion during backfill.

Purlin A horizontal structural element in a roof.

R

R-value The measure of resistance of a material to the passage of heat.

Rabbet A groove along the edge of a piece of wood.

Radon A radioactive odorless gas that emerges from the ground and is present at very low concentrations in all air.

Rafter The principal structural component in a sloped roof, including many types such as common, hip, valley, jack, barge, and verge.

Rain screen A siding system that provides a space for drainage between siding and moisture barrier.

Raised-heel truss A truss that is tall at the building edge to accommodate thick ceiling insulation.

Rake The sloped end portion of a roof.

Rat slab A thin concrete layer applied over the ground in crawl spaces.

Ridge beam A structural support at the top of rafters.

Ridge board A nonstructural board to which rafters are nailed.

Rigid insulation Any of a variety of insulative panels that retains its form through its own strength.

Rim joist A joist at the perimeter of a floor to which the common joists are attached; also known as band joist.

Rise The vertical distance between treads in a stair.

Riser A board that forms the vertical surface between treads in a stair.

Roof jack A roof flashing to allow plumbing vents to penetrate the roof surface.

Roof joist The principal structural element in a flat roof.

Rough opening An opening in framing made to fit a manufactured unit such as a door or window.

Run The horizontal distance between risers in a stair.

S

Sash A frame that holds glass in a window unit.

Scab A piece of wood on a surface of another piece.

Screed A straightedge used to level concrete.

Scupper A metal collector of rainwater at the edge of a flat roof to channel the water through a parapet.

Sealant A grade of caulk designed to prevent the passage of water, air, or other substance.

Setting block A small chunk of neoprene at the lower edge of glass that supports the weight of the glass.

Shake A wood shingle that is split from a bolt.

Shear wall A structural wall engineered to resist extreme lateral forces.

Sheathing The structural skin applied to the loadbearing surface of a wall, floor, or roof.

Shingle A thin, overlapping piece of material that will shed water; used for roofing or siding.

Sill The zone at the bottom edge of a door or window, or the sloped exterior base of a door or window.

Sill gasket A compressible material between mudsill and foundation or slab to inhibit air infiltration into heated spaces.

Sill pan A metal or plastic water barrier to protect framing at the base of a window or door.

Single-wall A type of construction where the sheathing acts as the finish wall.

Slab-on-grade A concrete slab supported by the ground.

Sleeper A framing member laid flat across a series of joists or rafters to support other framing members.

Slope See Pitch.

Snow guard A small protrusion integrated with roofing to hold snow on the roof.

Soffit A horizontal surface at the eave, extending between fascia and wall.

Sole plate The bottom plate in a stud-wall assembly.

Solid sawn lumber Milled lumber cut to standard sizes.

Spacing The distance between repetitive structural elements such as studs, joists, or rafters.

Span The horizontal distance between the two supports of a structural member such as a beam, joist, or rafter.

Splash block A concrete block designed to distribute rainwater at the base of a downspout.

Splash pan A metal flashing on a roof surface at the base of a downspout to direct rainwater over the roof.

Spray-foam insulation Liquid foam that expands and solidifies to provide insulation, an air-barrier, and vapor control.

Squash block A short block with grain oriented vertically, used where heavy loads could crush I-joists.

Stick-frame A colloquialism describing light wood frame.

Stool A horizontal shelflike trim at the interior base of a window.

Stop A protrusion around a window or door jamb that stops the hinged sash or door at the plane of the wall.

Storm drain A drain that carries rainwater runoff.

Storm sash A glazed unit applied to the exterior of a window as protection against storms and heat loss.

Storm sewer A large municipal drain for rainwater.

Strap A long piece of wood or metal used to tie one structural piece to another.

Strapping A layer of boards applied to the interior of framing to smooth the surface or to increase insulation.

Stringer See Carriage.

Strut Part of the structural perimeter of a diaphragm or shear wall.

Stud The principal vertical structural component in a framed wall, including many specialized types such as king, trimmer, and cripple studs.

Sub-fascia A structural fascia beneath a finish fascia.

Subfloor The structural plane supporting the finish floor.

Subflooring See Subfloor.

Superinsulation Insulation that significantly exceeds code minimums.

T

Tenon A rectangular extension of the end of a piece of wood, sized to fit a mortise in a mortise-and-tenon joint.

Termite shield A metal barrier to prevent termites from entering a wooden building.

Thermal bridge A component within an insulated assembly such as a wall or roof that conducts heat well and spans or bridges between the interior and exterior surfaces of the envelope, allowing heat to escape.

Threshold The weatherstripped transition between finish floor and sill at the base of a door.

Thrust block A block that is firmly attached to the floor at the base of a stair to prevent its horizontal movement.

Toenail A method of nailing diagonally through the end of one piece of lumber into another.

Tongue-and-groove An interlocking edge detail running the length of boards.

Top plate The longitudinal uppermost member of a stud wall, usually doubled.

Tread The level plane that forms the steps of a stairway.

Trimmer joist An extra structural joist parallel to common joists at the edge of an opening in a floor or roof.

Truss An arrangement of structural members forming triangles that works efficiently to span long distances.

Turned-down slab A concrete slab with a thickened edge that acts as a footing to support a structure above.

Twist strap A metal strap with a 90-degree twist allowing surfaces perpendicular to one another to be tied.

U

Underlayment A moisture barrier located between roofing and roof sheathing.

Uniform load A load that is evenly distributed over a given area or length.

V

Valley The sloped channel formed when two planes of a roof meet at an interior corner.

Vapor retarder A membrane or other building element that retards the transmission of water vapor.

Vaulted ceiling A sloped ceiling following the roof pitch.

Vent channel A device that compresses insulation at the eave to allow ventilation of the roof assembly; also called a baffle.

Verge rafter A rafter attached to the building at the gable end; interchangeable with the term barge rafter.

Vertical grain A board with the annual growth rings oriented perpendicular to its width.

W

Waferboard A composite panel made of flakes of wood.

Warm roof A vaulted ceiling superinsulated with rigid insulation and with no ventilation space.

Weatherstripping A seal around doors and windows to reduce air infiltration.

Web The structural part of a truss or composite joist that holds the chords in position relative to one another.

Web stiffener An extra layer of plywood or OSB laminated to the web of an I-joist for stiffness.

Weep hole A small opening at the base of masonry construction to allow moisture to escape.

index